THEODORE ROOSEVELT
The Making of a Conservationist

THEODORE ROOSEVELT

The Making of
a Conservationist

PAUL RUSSELL CUTRIGHT

UNIVERSITY OF ILLINOIS PRESS

Urbana and Chicago

This book is printed on acid-free paper.

Library of Congress Cataloging in Publication Data

Cutright, Paul Russell, 1897–
  Theodore Roosevelt, the making of a conservationist.

  Bibliography: p.
  Includes index.
  1. Roosevelt, Theodore, 1858–1919—Views on natural
history. 2. Roosevelt, Theodore, 1858–1919—Books and
reading. 3. Natural history. 4. Presidents—United
States—Biography. 5. Naturalists—United States—
Biography. I. Title.
E757.C985 1985   973.91'1'0924   84–16205
ISBN 0-252-01190-2 (alk. paper)

*I take unmeasured pride in dedicating
this book
to my four beloved great-grandchildren:*

RANDALL JACOB LARRIMORE
and
JOHN ALEXANDER LARRIMORE
and
PAUL BROOKS CUTRIGHT, JR.
and
MOLLY TEARE CUTRIGHT

Contents

Acknowledgments

I AM INDEBTED to the following individuals and to the several institutions they represent: Josephine Charles, head of Reader Services and reference librarian, and Marion Green, Reader Services assistant, Beaver College, Glenside, Pennsylvania; Wallace Finley Dailey, curator of the Theodore Roosevelt Collection, and Clark A. Elliott, associate curator of the Harvard University Archives, Harvard University Library, Cambridge, Massachusetts; John W. Ryan, Jr., museum technician, National Park Service, New York City; Donald W. Gray, vice-president, National Wildlife Refuge Association, Winona, Minnesota; George T. Jones, curator of the Oberlin College Herbarium, Oberlin College, Oberlin, Ohio; Alton A. Lindsey, professor emeritus of biological sciences, Purdue University, West Lafayette, Indiana; Gary G. Roth, museum curator, and Mary Burhans, museum assistant, Sagamore Hill Historic Site, Oyster Bay, New York; William A. Deiss, acting archivist, and Bonnie Farmer, museum technician of the Division of Birds, Smithsonian Institution/National Museum of Natural History, Washington, D.C.; John A. Gable, executive director, Theodore Roosevelt Association, Oyster Bay, New York; Michael J. Brodhead, professor of history, University of Nevada, Reno; George Miksch Sutton, late professor emeritus of zoology, University of Oklahoma, Norman; Earl L. Core, professor emeritus of botany, and Maurice G. Brooks, professor emeritus of wildlife management, West Virginia University, Morgantown; and William H. Smith, acting dean of the School of Forestry, Yale University, New Haven, Connecticut.

I also express my gratitude to: Harold A. Billian, H. B. Billian Company, Paoli, Pennsylvania; W. A. Fletcher, postmaster, Paul Smiths, New York; Colonel C. A. Peairs, Jr., Massachusetts Bar, Westboro, Massachusetts; P. James Roosevelt, P. J. James Roosevelt,

Inc., Oyster Bay, New York, and Harper & Row, Publishers, 10 East 53d Street, New York City, for permission to use specified material from the Harper & Brothers 1956 publication, *Theodore Roosevelt, the Naturalist,* by Paul Russell Cutright.

Three individuals have read the manuscript of this study, and to them I am especially beholden: Marjorie Darling, dean emeritus of admissions, Beaver College, Glenside, Pennsylvania, for generous, skilled editorial assistance, Dean Amadon, Lamont curator emeritus of ornithology, the American Museum of Natural History, New York City, for setting my course aright in those instances where I had strayed ornithologically, and to Wilmoth P. Hammersley, my gifted niece, for her contributions as a computer expert in fashioning the index.

Introduction

ONE MAY ASSUME that a concern for the conservation of wildlife and other natural resources does not depend on professional training in natural history or any related science; this is, at least today, a part of our common conscience in America as elsewhere in the world. A consciousness of the necessity for conservation; an awareness of the threats to which conservation is the reply, and of the gravity of these threats; and a concern for the preservation of those elements of our natural environment whose value is not immediately obvious imply a prior acquaintance with and interest in that environment beyond the everyday awareness derived from farm or backyard.

It is the thesis of this book that the pioneering conservation measures taken and promoted by Theodore Roosevelt had more than a coincidental basis in the natural history interest and studies of his youth. The catalogue of Roosevelt's boyhood activities as a naturalist is impressive. In a less active life, one feels, they would have left little room for the domestic, political, military, and social lives that this energetic man also lived. It is difficult, in considering the catalogue of his youthful activities, to avoid the impression that natural history—the application of a scientific bent of thought to a not uncommon taste for hunting and collecting—was the dominant interest of his boyhood.

Theodore Roosevelt's youthful technical background consisted of the following components, all tied together by an unfaltering interest in animals:

Reading—As soon as Roosevelt was old enough to know one word from another, he showed a marked preference for reading material about animals.

Letters—Roosevelt's childhood letters, whether to family or friends, invariably contained news about birds or other animals.

Diaries—In 1868, aged nine, Roosevelt began his first diary, and his initial entry was a yarn about a bear. Succeeding entries, spanning several years, abounded with zoological experiences and observations.

Museum—It was in that same year (1868) that Roosevelt founded his own museum, calling it the Roosevelt Museum of Natural History. Before he discontinued this museum, it housed specimens numbering in the hundreds.

Collecting—In order to insure the growth of his museum and, at the same time, to increase his knowledge of animals, Roosevelt collected extensively, not only in American locales such as Long Island, the Adirondacks, and Maine, but also in foreign lands, including Egypt, Palestine, and Syria.

Essays—During his youth, Roosevelt wrote several essays about animals, the first bearing the title "The Foregoing Ant." Additional ones described his experiences with such other animals as a shorttailed shrew, a jackal, and a cow heron.

College Studies—Roosevelt entered Harvard University in 1876 and graduated in 1880. As a Harvard student, he received formal instruction in such natural history courses as zoology, botany, comparative anatomy, physiology, and geology. He had entered Harvard with the firm resolve of becoming, as he later wrote, "a scientific man of the Audubon, or Wilson, or Baird, or Coues type."[1]

Publications—In his sophomore year at Harvard Roosevelt published (jointly with Henry Minot, a classmate) *The Summer Birds of the Adirondacks in Franklin County, N. Y.*, this being Roosevelt's first published contribution to science. The following year, and on his own, he published *Notes on Some of the Birds of Oyster Bay*.

Natural History Notebooks—Spanning the decade 1869–79, Roosevelt wrote a baker's dozen of boyhood natural history notebooks: "Notes on Natural History"; "Remarks on Birds [of Europe, Syria, and Egypt]"; "Ornithological Observations Made in Europe, Syria and Egypt"; "Catalogue of Birds [of Europe, Syria, and Egypt]"; "Ornithological Record [of the Birds of Europe, Syria, and Egypt]"; "Zoological Record [of Mammals and Other Animals of Europe, Syria, and Egypt]"; "Remarks on the Zoology of Oyster Bay"; "Journal of Natural History"; "Journal of a Trip to the Adirondacks, 1874"; "Journal of a Trip in Adirondack Mts., August 1875"; "St.

Regis Lake, Adirondack Mts., 1875"; "Notes on the Fauna of the Adirondack Mts."; and "Field Book of Zoology, 1876, 1877, 1878, 1879."

The quantity of zoological information in these several notebooks is nothing short of astounding and all, of course, in Roosevelt's youthful handwriting. When typed double-spaced (the form in which I have this material), the pages exceed 300. But the quality impresses more than the quantity, the pages being filled with examples of his observational competence. Indeed, the sum of information in them, primarily about birds—their songs, flight, habitat, migration, behavior, food habits, and other attributes—is so bounteous that it tends to transcend in importance all of the other components of his boyhood faunal industry.

To be sure, Roosevelt's youthful background in natural history was later supplemented by knowledge gained in the Dakota Badlands and other parts of the West, by lessons learned as a member (and first president) of the Boone and Crockett Club, and by experience acquired as the governor of New York State, but without the earlier natural history basics, so vital and durable, it is most unlikely that, on assuming the office of president of the United States, Theodore Roosevelt, in a few short years, would have become widely acclaimed as the foremost exponent of conservation in our nation.

Note

1. Theodore Roosevelt, *An Autobiography* (New York: Charles Scribner's Sons, 1913), 23.

THEODORE ROOSEVELT

The Making of a Conservationist

1

"Have Gained Their Habbits from Ofservation"

ONE WINTER DAY early in the year 1867, a blue-eyed, fair-haired, eight-year-old boy, frail and thin-shanked, trotted down the steps of his brownstone home on East 20th Street, New York City, and headed toward Broadway, a stone's throw away. He turned onto Broadway, then, as now, an important Manhattan street, where horse-drawn carriages and drays slowly rumbled over uneven cobblestones.

The boy soon found himself in front of a store where he had often been sent on other days to buy strawberries and other fruits. He was about to pass by when his eyes perceived a large, elongate body stretched out on a slab of wood at the entrance to the store. Going nearer, he recognized the body as that of a seal and learned on inquiry that it had recently been killed in the harbor of the city. In some manner the owner of the market had obtained the animal and had placed it on display in front of his place to attract customers.

The small boy did not know just what kind of seal it was; he did not care, although it may well have been a harbor seal (*Phoca vitulina*), a small species attaining a length of five or six feet, which inhabits waters of the western Atlantic Ocean. What mattered to him was that it was a real seal, whiskers, flippers, and all, and, though dead, it brought home to him forcefully the sensations of excitement, adventure, and romance so easily stirred in a youthful, questioning mind. Had it been a fabled griffin or a seven-headed monster such as Hercules had slain in the Peloponnesian marshes, the boy could hardly have been more excited. For several minutes he

1

paced back and forth, first on one side of the seal and then on the other, before he could tear himself away.

The next day the boy reappeared in front of the market and was delighted to find that the seal had not been removed during his absence. This time he carried with him a folding foot-rule, a pencil, and a notebook. Immediately he fell to work measuring the length of the seal, then its width, and, finally, as best he could with a folding foot-rule, its circumference. He next took stock of the general shape of the animal, its color, and other features of its external anatomy, dutifully recording these measurements and observations in his notebook.

The seal remained for several wintry days in front of the market, and the boy came back again and again. During these visits an idea gradually took shape: Why not try to persuade the merchant to give him the seal? Though soon disappointed in this ambition—perhaps because of parental objections—the boy did eventually succeed in obtaining the seal's skull.[1]

The boy shortly made two decisions, each of which would importantly shape his future. He determined, first, that he would become a naturalist and, next, that he would found his own museum, using the seal skull as a nucleus about which to congregate other natural history specimens.

The boy was Theodore Roosevelt. He called his museum The Roosevelt Museum of Natural History, and, in time, as everyone knows, he became the twenty-sixth president of the United States.

2

Theodore Roosevelt was the son, and second child, of Theodore Roosevelt, Sr., and Martha Bulloch Roosevelt. He was born on October 27, 1858, at 28 East 20th Street, New York City. Four children in all were born of this union: Anna, the oldest, and, after Theodore, Elliott and Corinne.

The family, closely knit, inclined to nicknames. Even before marriage, Theodore, Sr., responded to "Thee" and Martha to "Mittie." After the children arrived, Anna, at least *en famille*, was called "Bamie," Theodore "Teedie," Elliott "Ellie," and Corinne "Conie." In the later years of his life Theodore's many admirers abbreviated Theodore to "Teddy."

Theodore's father was, by profession, a glass merchant, and a rich one. He was rich, too, in generosity, kindness, sympathy, concern for the poor, and love of family. He demonstrated these virtues in various ways. He helped to form a Newsboys' Lodging Home and practically every Sunday evening left his own home to spend time with the newsboys. He was also a founder of New York's Children's Aid Society and the Society for the Prevention of Cruelty to Animals. In another direction, and of certain impact on his son Theodore, he played key roles in the founding of the American Museum of Natural History and of the Metropolitan Museum of Art.

In spite of his many obligations as a merchant and philanthropist, Theodore, Sr., never neglected his family. He always found time to romp with his children, to comfort them when they were ill, and to encourage their worthwhile interests. According to Theodore, Jr.: "My father was the best man I ever knew. He combined strength and courage with gentleness, tenderness and great unselfishness. He would not tolerate in us children selfishness or cruelty, idleness, cowardice, or untruthfulness. . . . With great love and patience, and the most understanding sympathy and consideration, he combined insistence on discipline."[2] These virtues of his father were later conspicuous in the son Theodore—some of them to an even more marked degree—and may be regarded as motivating factors behind many of the actions that made him famous.

The Roosevelts were Dutch in origin, with the first of that name arriving in New York City early in the seventeenth century soon after another Dutchman, Peter Minuit, had bought Manhattan Island from the Canarsee Indians for the sum of 60 guilders (about $24).

Theodore's mother, Martha Bulloch, had been born in Roswell, Georgia, just a few miles north of Atlanta. She was a woman of exquisite coloring and beauty, with lovely jet-black hair. About the middle of the seventeenth century her forebears had emigrated to the United States from Scotland. Her great-grandfather had been the first Revolutionary "president" of Georgia. It was in a typically southern white-columned mansion in Roswell that Martha had spent her childhood years, and it was in that same mansion that Theodore, Sr., first met her. After their marriage, on December 22, 1853, they made their home at 28 East 20th Street, New York City, and in that home their four children were born.

3

During the hours immediately preceding young Theodore's birth, those of the family in attendance experienced considerable anxiety, especially Mrs. Bulloch, Martha's mother, for, as her daughter's birth pains became increasingly acute, Mrs. Bulloch was first upset on being informed that the family doctor was ill. Her distress mounted when she was unable to obtain a second, and then a third, doctor. When finally successful on a fourth attempt, Mrs. Bulloch "never felt more relieved" in her life.[3]

Writing next day to a daughter in Philadelphia,[4] Mrs. Bulloch, after first describing the day before, went on to say: "Mittie had a safe but severe time. She is this morning as well as one could wish her to be. It is as sweet and pretty a young baby as I have ever seen; weighed eight pounds and a half before it was dressed. No chloroform or any such thing was used, no instruments were necessary, consequently the dear little thing has no cuts or bruises about it. . . . Mittie says I must tell you she thinks the baby is hideous. She says it is a cross between a terrapin and Dr. Young."[5] Obviously Mittie was a prime contributor to her son Theodore's later well-developed sense of humor.

Family letters reveal that in months and years ahead Theodore was a sickly child, and a continuing concern to his parents. More often than other children of his age he was subject to the common childhood complaints: colds, coughs, fevers, and stomachaches. Far more worrisome, he suffered from asthma, with attacks occurring often, and sometimes distressingly prolonged. On all too many occasions, he found breathing at night difficult unless he was in a sitting position. As a grown man Theodore recalled: "One of my memories is of my father walking up and down with me in his arms at night when I was a very small person, and of sitting up in bed gasping, with my father and mother trying to help me."[6]

Although Theodore's parents knew nothing of the causes of asthma—even the doctors of that day were generally at a loss—they were ceaseless in their search for a remedy. They chose various environments, among them that of Madison, New Jersey, and those of Spuyten Duyvil and Tarrytown up the Hudson. In the summer of 1868 they vacationed in the Catskills. Here Theodore began a diary, and his first entry stated, "I had an attack of the Asmer."[7]

As a result of his several frequent ailments Theodore, as a small boy, was not only sickly but also underweight and unable to take part in the more strenuous games and other activities enjoyed by youngsters of his age. It is certain that his parents at times thought he might not live. Years later, when visiting the Bull Run battle-fields, Theodore remarked to a companion: "When the Union and Confederate troops were fighting over these fields I was a little bit of a chap, and nobody seemed to think I would live."[8]

3.

Young Theodore's interest in natural history had begun before the incident of the seal. Being an especially bright boy he started to read early, and one of the first books to attract his attention was David Livingstone's *Missionary Travels and Researches in South Africa*. This book had been published in 1857, the year before Theodore's birth, and had become an almost instant bestseller. No doubt Theodore's parents were among the first of New York City's residents to obtain a copy, being eager to read of Livingstone's dramatic experiences with dangerous African animals and of his acclaimed discovery of Victoria Falls and other previously unknown geographical features of Africa.

It is said that when Theodore began reading Livingstone's book he had trouble, because of his size, carrying it from one room to another.[9] He expressed delight with the explorer's accounts of adventures with giraffes, zebras, antelopes, rhinos, and other African animals, and also with the illustrations, one depicting a buffalo cow defending her young from a lion, another showing an elephant attacked by natives, and still another portraying Livingstone's near escape from a charging lion.

Young Theodore enjoyed, too, the books of Captain Mayne Reid, among them *The Boy Hunters, Afloat in the Forest,* and *Wild Life, or Adventures on the Frontier,* even though the scientific information was sometimes inaccurate. All the Roosevelt children read *Our Young Folks*, a magazine with a high percentage of articles on natural history topics. To Theodore, it was "the very best magazine in the world."[10] When he read the *Swiss Family Robinson,* he already knew enough zoology to condemn it "because of the wholly impossible collection of animals met by that worthy family as they ambled inland from the wreck."[11] The first and generally more popular part of *Robinson Crusoe* he liked less than the second part, this containing Crusoe's experiences with wolves in the Pyrenees.[12]

After it had become plain to Theodore's parents that his interest in natural history was much more than a passing fancy, his father bought books for him on that subject, one of the first being *Homes without Hands,* by the then popular naturalist J. G. Wood.[13] Theodore so cherished this book that he read it again and again, becoming intimately familiar with its content. It was in *Homes without Hands* that Theodore, according to one source, read certain passages about ants and their habits. On one page he came to a paragraph beginning, "The foregoing ant. . . ." There then followed much information about this insect, information that Theodore found so entertaining that he put aside the book and at once, with the material fresh in mind, wrote an essay of undetermined length called "The Foregoing Ant." When he had completed this composition, he read it aloud to his family. Aside from the fact that it was received with "tender amusement," and that its author was then just seven years old, we know nothing further about it.[14]

Theodore's early decision to become a naturalist—a prelude to his becoming also a conservationist—was influenced in part by the family summer outings away from the city. Each year he looked forward with undisguised eagerness to the summer vacations in the country and, as they neared an end, was unhappy at the thought of returning to the city. Life in the country was full of strange and exciting experiences. It was there that he first discovered happiness in the presence of wild animals, in unexpected encounters with lizards, snakes, and turtles, in watching the movements of minnows and salamanders in clear-running streams, in listening for the first time to songs of thrushes, sparrows, bobolinks, and other birds, and in chancing upon other larger animals, such as rabbits, skunks, and foxes. It was during one of his earlier visits to the country that, as he wrote, he first "hunted frogs successfully and woodchucks unsuccessfully."[15]

By contrast, life for Theodore at home on 20th Street was generally dull. However, there were incidents to enliven his days. Some of these were due to the fact that one of his uncles, Robert Barnhill Roosevelt, lived next door and, at one time or another, kept such intriguing pets as a parrot, a peacock, a pheasant, and a monkey.

Another stimulus to Theodore's growing interest in animals

was provided by his mother's sister, Anna Bulloch—Theodore's Aunt Anna—who had come north from Georgia at the outset of the Civil War. She was Theodore's first tutor and the source of numerous stories about exciting events that had taken place at Roswell during her youth. There was the tale, for example, of the black bear that had almost scalped one of the slaves at Roswell and others about deer, raccoons, and wildcats.[16] Aunt Anna, too, could be counted on for a select lot of "Br'er Rabbit" stories, familiar to her long before they were published and made popular by Joel Chandler Harris.[17]

In later life Theodore was once asked how he came by his love of birds and other animals. He replied: "I can no more explain why I like natural history than why I like California canned peaches."[18] Theodore's family, of course, were not totally indifferent to birds, flowers, and other living creatures. Each of his parents possessed an eye for the beauty of plants and an ear for the music of birds; and his father gave expression to these feelings in practical ways, notably his helping to found the American Museum of Natural History.

Then there was Theodore's Uncle Robert. Throughout much of his life, Robert Barnhill Roosevelt exhibited an interest in wildlife, following a pattern similar to that later pursued by Theodore himself. He foresaw the eventual decrease, and possible extinction, of many game animals, unless conservation measures were promptly adopted to protect them. He expressed his concern in books, among them *Game Fish of the Northern States of America and British Provinces* and *Game Birds of the North*, both of which were published in the 1860s while Theodore was a child.

Because Uncle Robert lived next door to Theodore, the two, we can assume, often saw each other. Uncle Robert, too, must have been among the first to know of Theodore's pronounced interest in natural history and, because of his own interest, should have been eager to lend encouragement. If so, however, Theodore seems never to have acknowledged it. Nowhere, in any of his writings, have we found mention of his Uncle Robert's furthering his nephew's decision to become a naturalist. Everything indicates that, in this matter, Theodore made his own decision, uninfluenced, at least to any conspicuous degree, by any other person. Having made the decision, his zest for the study steadily increased, as he read many books on nature, listened closely to stories of wilderness creatures told to him by his elders, and observed at every chance the animals of woods, stream, and field. Even at the age of seven, according to his sister Corinne, his knowledge of natural history "was strangely accurate."[19]

4

It seems clear that Theodore had definite ideas on how to establish his own museum. The location of the Roosevelt Museum of Natural History at first was his own room, but not for long. The family maid soon lodged understandable complaints, with the result that Theodore was shortly ordered to move it to a case in the upstairs hallway. Here the cranium of the seal, which had served as the motive to the formation of the museum, was soon surrounded by nests and eggs of birds, and by shells, insects, minerals, and other objects.

Little more than this would be known of the origin and growth of the Roosevelt Museum if it were not for a hand-written document called "Record of the Roosevelt Museum." This record consists of only a few pages of ordinary lined paper on which is written, on both sides, the early history of the museum. Reading the first paragraph gives one a sense of the importance of the museum to Theodore. "At the commencement of the year 1867 Mr. T. Roosevelt, Jr., started the Museum with 12 specimens, at the close of the same year Mr. J. W. Roosevelt [West Roosevelt, a first cousin][20] joined him but each one kept his own specimens, these amounting to hardly 100. During 1868 they accumulated 150 specimens, making a total of 250 specimens."

From this brief account it may be seen that The Roosevelt Museum of Natural History had a modest beginning. It is evident, too, that Theodore was not only the founder of the museum but also its curator and general custodian. Soon after West Roosevelt had joined, another first cousin, Emlen Roosevelt,[21] gained admittance. Emlen became the permanent secretary of the museum and, from notes supplied by Theodore, wrote the above and succeeding minutes.

Theodore took the founding of his museum seriously. He wanted to see it grow and flourish, and he seems to have overlooked few opportunities to add specimens. Evidence of his resolve is found in letters he wrote in the spring of 1868 to his parents, who, with Conie and the family nurse, had gone south to visit Georgia relatives. In these letters he makes it clear that he expects them to contribute generously of their time in collecting "curiosities" to be brought back to him. To his mother, on April 28, 1868, he wrote: "I have just received your letter. . . . My mouth opened wide with astonishment when 'I heard how many flowers were sent into you. I could revel in the buggie ones. I jumped with delight when I found you had heard a mockingbird. Get some of the feathers if you can. . . . I am sorry the trees have been cut down. . . . In the letters you write to me tell me how many curiosities and living things you have got for me. I miss Conie very much. I wish I were with you . . . for I could hunt for myself."[22]

Two days later Theodore followed the above with requests to his father, these bordering on the extraordinary:

I received your letter yesterday. Your letter was more exciting than mother's. I have a request to make of you, will you do it? I hope you will. If you will it will figure greatly in my museum. You know what supple jacks are, do you not? Please get two for Ellie and one for me. Ask your friend to let you cut off the tiger-cat's tail, and get some long moos and have it mated together. One of the supple jacks (I am talking of mine now) must be about as thick as your thumb and finger. The other must be as thick as your thumb. The one which is as thick as your finger and thumb must be four feet long and the other must be three feet long. One of my mice got crushed. It was the mouse I liked best though it was a common mouse. Its name was Brownie. Nothing particular has happened since you went away for I cannot go out in the country like you can. The trees and the vine on our piazza are buding and the grass is green as can be, and no one would dream that it was winter so short a time ago.

It would be most helpful if Theodore had kept a record of the specimens he acquired, one which would have provided the names, dates obtained, and other pertinent facts. If he had, and if it were available, we might then learn if his parents had brought back with them the supple jacks, the "long moos," and the tiger-cat's tail and, more particularly, their identity. The supple jacks were probably plants of that name: woody climbers (*Berchemia scandens*) growing commonly in low woods from Virginia to Florida. Their stems were then sometimes a source for canes, and Theodore's insistence on specific width and length suggests that he wanted supple jack canes as yet additional "curiosities" for his museum. The "long moos" he requested must have been Spanish moss (*Tillandsia usneoides*), which, as is commonly known, grows abundantly on trees, chiefly in swamps, in southern states. As to the tiger-cat's tail, it may have been that Theodore, Sr's. friend had killed a bobcat (*Lynx rufus*), and Theodore thought it would be an act of true scientific merit to lop off the cat's tail, which he might then place on exhibit in his museum.

Just how responsive Theodore's parents were to his requests cannot be said, but on receipt of his letters, so appealingly worded, they would have been less than human if they had ignored them entirely. On the contrary, being affectionate parents, they probably returned with many additions for the Roosevelt museum. And, in all likelihood, so did the family nurse, Dora Watkins, for Theodore had written to her: "I have one request to make of you. Press plenty of plants, and leaves and get a good many seeds for me, and some beetles and butterflies, get feathers and wood too. Get as many live things as you can."[23] As a candidate for collecting animals and plants, Theodore apparently rated Dora's capabilities highly indeed.

5

Except when immobilized by asthma or other complaint, Theodore seems to have enjoyed a fairly active and happy childhood. Thus, while his parents and Conie were in the South, we may deduce from the tone of his letters that he was quite content. To Conie, in a letter of April 1868, he supplied one reason for his peace of mind. "I have got four mice, the white skined, red eyed velvety creatures, very tame for I let them run all over me, they trie to get down the back of my neck and under my vest, and two brown skined, black eyed, soft as the others but wilder. Lordy and Rosa are the names of the white mice, which are male and female. I keep them in different cages."

At the bottom of this letter, for Conie's enlightenment, Theodore drew sketches of the two mouse cages, perhaps the first of numerous drawings with which he later illustrated letters. Indeed, in his next letter to his father, he included three animal sketches, with this explanation: "The chaffinch is for you. The wren for mama. The cat for Conie."

During the summer of 1868 the Roosevelt family vacationed up the Hudson at Barrytown, then a small rural village. It was here that

Theodore, on August 10, began his first diary, an abbreviated one ending on September 5 and containing just fifteen entries. Not surprisingly, it included a number of references to animals, the first being about a bear that had endangered the life of a Catskill man. According to Theodore, this individual had been "a good deal scared."

In another entry Theodore wrote of visiting a brook in which he saw a number of aquatic animals, among them crayfish, eels, salamanders, and water spiders, and in yet another entry he reported finding nests of a swallow, a robin, and a catbird. His entry of September 4 revealed a highlight of the summer: "I was called in from breakfast to a room. When I went in there what was my surprise to see on wall, curtains and floor fourty [sic] swallows. All the morning long in every room of the house (even in the kitchen) were swallows. They were flying south. Several hundred were outside and about 75 in the house. . . . One flew on my pants where he stayed till I took him off."[24]

How else did Theodore spend his days that summer in Barrytown? In his entry of August 20 we find: "Had a ride of six miles before breakfast. I will always have a ride of six miles before breakfast now." These "Mornings on Horseback" were on a pony named Grant. He also wrote occasional letters, a particular one being to Dora Watkins's husband: "I know where six birds nests are. I wish you were out here. There are plenty of squirrels out here. There are three kinds of them. There names are chipmuck and the rat-tailed and gray squirrels. There is plenty of animals here."

Whatever the length of the Roosevelts' stay that summer in Barrytown, it was all too short for Theodore. Back in the city there would be no six-mile pony rides before breakfast and, as he knew full well, no "plenty of animals."

6

His museum having become a reality, Theodore seems to have considered that he should next establish himself as an author. Accordingly, he soon completed an essay about insects and fish. So far as is known, it was his first *serious* attempt to make a contribution to science. For his purpose he obtained a small four-by-six notebook, wherein he penciled altogether some forty pages of information. On

11

the cover one can still read the title, name of author, and date: "About Insects and Fishes, Natural History, by Theodore Roosevelt, 1869."

Quite professionally, Theodore began his essay with a preface, starting: "All these insects are native of North America. Most of the insects are not in other books. I will write about ants first." The information that Theodore then proceeded to reveal was, for the most part, decidedly entertaining, misspelled words regardless:

Ants are difided into three sorts for every species. These kinds are officer, solider and work. There are about one officer to ten soilders and one solider to two workers.

The brown path ant is common. The house is half under ground and half above. There are several rooms in each house. The entrance is generally at the top. The ant hills differ in size and shape very much. The ants eat caterpillars, worms, etc. These ants are very swift.

The shiny ant is pure black except the officer who is striped with yellow. It is pretty common. It eats flies, misquetoes etc. They sometimes have fights with spiders. They are slow except the workers. They are strong. The houses are the same as the brown ants.

The double ant is made differently from the rest, half of it being red. it builds its nests on the branches of shrubs. It eats flies, caterpillars, etc.

Having thus summarily disposed of the ants, Theodore turned to other insects—with equal enthusiasm and observational competence:

The tumble tard lives in holes in the ground. It eats cowdung. This beetle lays its young in a round ball of cowdung and then pushes it (with its hind feet) into a hole. It is black. It can fly. Two or three of them generally work at the same ball of cowdung. It is rather rare.

The firefly does not give as much light as the glowworm, but it can fly. It is not nocturnal as is generally thought but gives forth the light in the daytime as well as the night, but in the day the sun is out and so you cannot see them. It is very common. It gives out its light at intervals.

The darning needle has brown transparent wings through which you can read writing. Its color is blueish green. There is a foolish superstition about its sewing up peoples cheeks which I scarcely add is not true.

In this essay, Theodore wrote similarly about other insects, among them the "johnny crook horse" and the "double feathered butterfly," and also about a number of fish; limits of space disallow additional descriptions. We cannot, however, exclude an especially pertinent statement, with which he concluded his descriptions of insects: "All the insects that I write about in this book inhabbit North America. Now and then a friend has told me something about them but mostly I have gained their habbits from ofservation." [25]

So, even at this early age, Theodore Roosevelt, Jr., had made purposeful strides pursuing his curiosity into a world then vaguely known to him. The evidence is adequate to prove that he was well on his way to becoming a full-fledged naturalist. There should be no difficulty in recalling the extent of his industry and enthusiasm when founding his museum, his eager intensity when describing the eccentricities of the double ant and the tumble tard, and his elation on learning that his mother, in Georgia, had heard a mockingbird sing.

Notes

1. Roosevelt, *Autobiography* 14.

2. Ibid., 7–8.

3. Carleton Putman, *Theodore Roosevelt, the Formative Years, 1858–1886,* 1 (New York: Charles Scribner's Sons, 1958), 22.

4. Susan Bulloch West, wife of Dr. Hilborne West, and both living in Philadelphia.

5. Putnam, *Theodore Roosevelt,* 1:23.

6. Roosevelt, *Autobiography,* 13.

7. Theodore Roosevelt, *Diaries of Boyhood and Youth* (New York: Charles Scribner's Sons, 1928), 3.

8. *New York World,* Nov. 16, 1902.

9. Hermann Hagedorn, *The Boys' Life of Theodore Roosevelt* (New York: Harper & Brothers, 1918), 22.

10. Roosevelt, *Autobiography,* 15.

11. Ibid., 16.

12. Ibid.

13. John George Wood (1827–89), English curate and naturalist. Wood was born in London and educated at Merton College, Oxford. *The Illustrated Natural History,* in three volumes, was perhaps Wood's most important scientific work. One of these volumes, on "Birds," was in the Roosevelt library at Sagamore Hill as recently as 1982.

14. Corinne Roosevelt Robinson, *My Brother, Theodore Roosevelt* (New York: Charles Scribner's Sons, 1921), 2.

15. Roosevelt, *Autobiography,* 7.

16. Anna Roosevelt Cowles in letter/memoirs to her son Sheffield Cowles. For this document, see Theodore Roosevelt Collection, Harvard College Library, Cambridge, Mass.; hereafter cited as TRCHL.

17. Joel Chandler Harris (1848–1908), American author, was born in Eatonton, Ga. His *Uncle Remus,* in which the Br'er Rabbit stories first appeared, was an outstanding literary event of 1880. Roosevelt, while president, honored Harris by having him as an overnight guest at the White House.

18. *The Works of Theodore Roosevelt, Memorial Edition,* 24 vols., ed. Hermann Hagedorn (New York: Charles Scribner's Sons, 1923), 6:443; hereafter cited as Roosevelt, *Works, Mem. Ed.*

19. Robinson, *My Brother,* 1–2.

20. James West Roosevelt (1858–96) was a son of Theodore's Uncle Silas Weir Roosevelt. He studied medicine and, at the time of his death, was chief resident physician at the Roosevelt Hospital, New York City. It may be noted that West Roosevelt, on Sept. 12, 1887, at Sagamore Hill, officiated at the birth of Theodore Roosevelt, Jr., first child born to Theodore and Edith Roosevelt.

21. Emlen Roosevelt (1857–1930) was the son of Theodore's Uncle James Alfred Roosevelt. As a comparatively young man he became the senior partner of Roosevelt & Son, Wall Street. It was Emlen Roosevelt and his wife who, at Oyster Bay in 1923, founded the Theodore Roosevelt Sanctuary, a wildlife preserve and educational center.

22. All letters of Theodore Roosevelt used in this study, unless otherwise stated, are from the Theodore Roosevelt Collection, Harvard College Library (TRCHL).

23. "Dora Watkins' Letters," *New York Times,* Oct. 8, 1933.

24. Roosevelt, *Diaries of Boyhood,* 3.

25. Throughout his life Roosevelt had trouble with his spelling. As a youthful diarist and letterwriter he not only misspelled but also erred in punctuation and capitalization. I have not edited his writings, except in those rare instances where his words would have been unintelligible to the reader.

2

"Having A Verry Dull Time"

EARLY IN 1869 Theodore Roosevelt's parents decided that a year abroad, touring European countries, would be of great educational value to all members of the family, and to the children in particular. From the start Theodore opposed the idea. The study of natural history was foremost in his mind, and a year away from his museum and favorite outdoor haunts, spent walking unfamiliar streets, viewing celebrated paintings, visiting medieval castles, and surveying mountain scenery, held little appeal. He felt that somehow science would be cheated if he were away for such an extended period. Even when his father explained to him that the change in climate might benefit his health and that he would surely have the opportunity of collecting foreign specimens for his museum, he still had no appetite for the trip.

It was on this trip that Theodore kept his first sustained diary. Reading it today we gain an intimate, if not an entirely complete, picture of his day-to-day travels, with their mixed highlights of homesickness, adventure, joy, and frequent unhappiness. He penned his initial entry on May 12, 1869, the day the family sailed from New York: "We go to Europe today. We sail in the English Steamship, Scotia. It was very hard parting from our friends. Old Grand Papa [Cornelius V. S. Roosevelt] came up to us. While going to the docks I cried a great deal."[1]

For a boy of ten (he would be eleven during the course of the trip), Theodore's diary impresses us as a worthy product of purposeful industry. Not once from the time he left New York until he embarked from England to return—a period of twelve long, difficult months—did he fail to make his daily entry. Also, in penning the whole, he used more than 40,000 words, an average in excess of 100 a day.

15

The transatlantic crossing, from New York to Liverpool, took ten days. In that time Theodore was alternately miserable and happy. On Sunday, May 16, he wrote: "As it was a little rough and I a little sick and being down I could not go to service. While lieing in bed with nothing to do I got so, so, homesick."[2] However, on other days, as he sighted animals of the sea, his spirits rose appreciably. On the third day out, for instance, he told of seeing "a shoal of Porpoises," on the fourth day some dolphins, and on the eighth "one shark, some fish, several gulls and a boatswain."[3] Theodore then carefully explained that the boatswain was a sea bird and so named "because its tail feathers are supposed to resemble the warlike spike with which a boatswain (man) is usually represented."[4]

Theodore's spirits rose after meeting a fellow passenger by the name of St. John. He first mentioned him in his entry of May 18: "I made the acquaintance today of Mr. St. John, a most interesting gentleman from the West Indies. We had a long talk in the cabin after supper."[5] Except for a letter that Theodore's mother wrote to a sister we would know nothing more about this man. She wrote that he was "a quaint little well of knowledge, very fond of natural history and fills Teedie's heart with delight. Teedie brought him up and introduced him to me, his eyes dancing with delight and he constantly asks me, 'Mama, have you really conversed with Mr. St. John?'"[6]

Thus during the crossing, for a brief period at least, Theodore had the good fortune to spend time with a man who not only made his hours pass more pleasantly but who also responded to Theodore's obvious enthusiasm for birds and other animals. It seems likely, too, that it was Mr. St. John who identified the boatswain for Teddy and provided the information about its tail feathers. As soon as the *Scotia* docked in Liverpool, however, the man and the boy went separate ways.

After leaving Liverpool, the Roosevelts spent the better part of two months in England and Scotland, visiting Edinburgh, Glasgow, York, Oxford, and, of course, London. Highlights for Theodore of the stay in London included two visits to the zoological gardens. On the first of these, according to his diary entry of June 22, he saw "a great many animals, zebras, lions, camels, Elephants, monkeys, bears, etc. etc. all common to other menageries but we also saw various kinds of wild asses etc. not common. I was a little disappointed."[7]

Even so, Theodore revisited the London Zoo on the next day, and this time, as he reported, he saw "more kinds of animals not common to most menageries," among them "ixhrinumens,[8] little earth dog queer wolves and foxes, badgers and raccoons and rattels[9] with the queer antics." More than that, he watched "two she bears and a wildcat and a caracal fight."[10] Obviously Theodore enjoyed this second visit to the London Zoo more than he did the first.

2

In mid-July the Roosevelts crossed the English Channel to the mainland, where, during the next ten months, they traveled from one country to another (Belgium, Holland, Germany, Switzerland, Italy, Austria, and France) and visited many cities, the more important being Antwerp, Amsterdam, Cologne, Munich, Berlin, Heidelberg, Strasbourg, Lucerne, Zurich, Rome, Naples, Florence, Venice, Trieste, Vienna, and Paris. Having both time and means at their command, they moved deliberately.

At times during the year, Theodore's parents possibly regretted a trip of such length and wished that they had agreed upon a shorter, less ambitious one. Their greatest concern, as the year developed, was Theodore's health. A recurring entry in Theodore's diary was, "I was sick last night." While on the continent, he recorded some forty similar entries, these averaging out to an illness about every nine days. His major health problem was, of course, bronchial asthma, though occasionally the illness was something else, as in Munich on October 8, 1869, when he had "collerer morbos[11] a sickness which is not at all dangerous," and in Chamonix, on August 9, 1869, where he reported, "I have got a pain in the stomach."[12]

Theodore's asthmatic attacks, minor at first, worsened with the approach of winter. In late September while in Venice he wrote, "I was sick with asthma and did not sleep at all after quarter past two." Two days later, while crossing the Adriatic to Trieste: "I was sick of the asthma last night. I sat up for 4 consecutive hours and Papa made me smoke a cigar." Three weeks later, his asthma flaring again, another procedure was tried. Reported Theodore: "I was rubed so hard on the chest this morning that the blood came out."[13]

For Theodore and other victims of asthma there were a few life-sparing features. In general the attacks were transient, limited to hours of the night, and, no matter the frequency or severity of the attacks, the lungs did not suffer. Also, once the attack had ended, the victim experienced euphoria, a feeling of being able to undertake most any physical activity, large or small. Thus Theodore, following the night in which he had smoked a cigar, spiritedly walked the streets of Trieste, visiting an old fortress, "the piazza d'Ammi," the custom house, and a fruit and vegetable market.[14]

In addition to these physical health problems, Theodore periodically had to contend with the depression resulting from homesickness. In Switzerland, on August 15, he revealed: "I walked the hall and thought of each happy time home, counting nuts by the kitchen fire, picking nuts in the morning wind, playing at animals in the nursery or traping animals in play or learning natural history from nature."[15] At no time, however, it would appear, was he more homesick than on November 22 in Paris after his mother had showed him a picture of Edith Carow,[16] for "her face stirred up in me homesickness and longings for the past which will come again never, alack never."[17]

Was Theodore as unhappy throughout the trip as some of his diary entries suggest? Surely not. One day he and the other children, "dressed up in towels, wrappers, went about the house attacking all the chambermaids." On many days he dispelled nostalgia and ennui reading books. With four months of the tour completed, he reported: "I suppose we have read 50 [books] since we left America." Theodore also enjoyed walking, and, whether on city streets or mountain slopes, he was often exercising his legs—and very strong legs they must have been. One day in Switzerland, according to his diary, "Papa walked 22 miles, I 19," and ten days later, "I walked 20 and Papa 22 miles."[18] Very good going for a ten-year-old—if completely accurate.

3

In reading Theodore's day-to-day account of the Roosevelts' travels through European countries, one senses little of the depth of his innate enthusiasm for natural history. From beginning to end, his diary contains no more than a score of entries—out of a total of nearly 400—relating explicitly to animals, and these, for the most part, are brief and restrained. His first was written in France, en route to Mt. Blanc: "We saw a live tame chamois[19] and I bought an Ibex horn." Two days later, after the ascent of Mt. Blanc, "I have bought several things for the museum." Then, on a rainy day that followed, he wrote that he had stayed inside all day drawing birds.[20]

More than a month then elapsed before Theodore, in his diary, again referred to animals. By then the family was in Italy and on their way to Lugano: "I evenced a curiosity in the lizards (chamolens) that thronged the way [and] our driver caught 2 for me one of which fought like fury."[21]

With few exceptions, Theodore's further zoological entries resulted from visits to museums and zoos. The animals in the Vienna museum at once caught his attention because two of them were old friends: the Baltimore (northern) oriole and the "waxen chaterer" (cedar waxwing). He found the museum of Dresden of greater interest to him: "All alone I went to the Natural History Museum. It has 101 animals in all of it but has a good collection of reptiles and fish but birds are the chief thing and it has the best collection of nests I have ever seen. I have two of the reptiles and 1 nest and 3 birds in my museum at home and I have seen several birds and nests wild at home."[22]

From the above passage it is clearly evident that Theodore's interest in wildlife was still vitally alive, and he supplied further evidence one week later. After a visit to the Berlin museum, he proudly wrote of recognizing four birds and four other animals. He then added, as a reflection of his continuing homesickness: "Perhaps when I'm 14 I'll go to Minnesota, hip, hip, hurrah'hhh!"[23]

The next day—being as far from Minnesota as ever—he went instead to the Berlin aquarium. The displays here stirred him to uncommon literary heights: "all of us went to the aquarium whose walls and ceilings are artificial rocks, and in places looking down from above it looked like a dark beetleing precipice with dark water beneath and in the dark crannies of the rocks flew and perched ravens, gulls and others, while cornaments and rare wild ducks swam below diving after fishes in the dark water while gaudey birds of the tropics at the sunny top contrasted with the seabirds below in the darkness. We saw birds in there nests on trees and anemonese and snakes and lizards. We had a walk [afterward] and played chamois and after goats which I a grizzly bear tried to eat."[24]

During the remaining months on the continent, Theodore alluded infrequently to animals, and then in few words. In France (on September 10) he reported buying some shells. In Rome (on February 14) he heard a nightingale singing, and in Florence (on March 2) he wrote of visiting the zoo, where he saw "the bears fed and drew one of them."[25]

In Florence, on March 1, Theodore had written "Us two boys went to Mr. Elliotts [sic] where we saw a beautiful book of birds written by him."[26] The "Mr. Elliott" alluded to was Daniel Giraud Elliot (1835–1915), a prominent American ornithologist and an excellent artist. Also, like Theodore's father, he had been active in the founding of the American Museum of Natural History and was no stranger to Theodore. The "beautiful book of birds," about which Theodore had exclaimed, was probably an 1869 Elliot monograph, *The New and Heretofore Unfigured Species of the Birds of North America.*[27]

Years later, as a grown man, Theodore Roosevelt summed up his recollections of the 1869–70 trip to Europe: "I do not think I gained anything from this particular year abroad."[28] In respect to his growth as a naturalist, his opinion was doubtless true. A number of reasons, most of them obvious, may be cited. A primary one was the difficulty of collecting animal specimens in an environment composed largely of hotels, railway coaches, and paved city streets. Others were Theodore's expressed dislike for the trip, his occasional bouts with homesickness, his frequent illnesses, and his tendency of one so young to think only of events of the day when exposed to such a rapidly changing series of happenings and experiences.

4

Because Theodore kept a diary, it has been possible to gain a sizable body of information about his asthma. His journal reveals the frequency of his attacks, dates on which they occurred, something of their severity, examples of treatment, and expressions of gratitude to his parents for their concern and thoughtful care, as evidenced by their fear-stricken consultations with physicians: in London (June 26, 1869), in Vienna (October 4, 1869), and in Paris (January 23 and 25, 1870).

Manifestly the doctors attending Theodore, at home as well as abroad, made every effort to determine the cause of his asthma, paying special attention to foods, plant pollens, household dusts, particles from cat and dog scurf, odors, air, and climate. Indeed, in making the decision to spend a year in Europe, Theodore's parents were motivated, in part at least, by a desire to discover a more salutary climate for Theodore.

No one until recently has proposed a theory attempting to explain plausibly the cause of Theodore's attacks of bronchial asthma. This theory is to be found in David McCullough's *Mornings on Horseback*, a distinguished and sensitively written biography of Roosevelt, which devotes a full chapter to the history of asthma (past and present) and, in particular, to the pulmonary attacks experienced by the youthful Theodore.

In explaining his theory, the author begins by retelling an incident of Theodore's childhood (first told, we believe, in Hermann Hagedorn's *The Boys' Life of Theodore Roosevelt*). One day, as the story went, Theodore chanced to be playing near the Presbyterian church that stood on one side of Madison Square. Here he encountered the church sexton, who asked if he should like to come inside. But Theodore stubbornly refused, and for an understandable reason. To Theodore, the church housed a "zeal," a fearsome beast that might devour him. The answer to Theodore's haunting fear, of both beast and church, did not surface until Theodore's mother unearthed a biblical passage, which her son presumably had heard in some earlier church service. The passage read: *"The zeal of thine house* hath eaten me up."[29] To young Theodore this incident was no joke, and, according to McCullough, it "should not be discounted"; he had "experienced a peculiar and memorable fear of church."[30]

Aware that physicians regarded many asthmatic attacks as psychosomatic in origin, and entertaining the notion that those of Theodore—because of the "zeal" incident—might also be so regarded, McCullough sought confirmation in Theodore's 1869–70 diary. Turning the pages, he ultimately found "a distinct pattern" emerging, that of Theodore's asthma striking "on weekends, usually Saturday nights or what was actually early Sunday morning." After citing a number of such instances, and implying that each had been self-induced by Theodore to prevent his going to church, McCullough declared: "The pattern is too pronounced to be coincidental."[31]

McCullough's theory may be right, of course, but we think not.

In our opinion the entries in Theodore's European diary refute it. First, more of Theodore's asthmatic attacks struck on weekdays rather than on weekends:

Monday—Berlin, Germany (October 25, 1869). "I was sick."

Tuesday—Strasbourg, France (July 27, 1869). "I was verry sick in the morning."
Stresa, Italy (September 14, 1869). "I was dreadfully sick."
Munich, Germany (October 12, 1869). "I had a miserable night."
Berlin, Germany (October 26, 1869). "I was sick."

Wednesday—Vienna, Austria (September 29, 1869). "I was sick."
Paris, France (November 24, 1869). "I got worse and worse."
Naples, Italy (January 5, 1870). "I was sick in the night."

Thursday—Rome, Italy (January 20, 1870). "Bad night."
Paris, France (March 10, 1870). "I was sick."

Friday—Dresden, Germany (October 15, 1869). "I was rubed . . . on the skin."
Paris, France (January 21, 1870). "I had a verry bad night."

McCullough informs that Theodore, because of illness, missed Sunday services as follows: Lucerne (August 29, 1869), Lake Como (September 12, 1869), en route to Trieste (September 26, 1869), Vienna (October 3, 1869), Munich (October 10, 1869), Paris (November 14 and 21, 1869), Rome (January 8, 1870), and Florence (February 27, 1870). These add up to a total of less than a dozen.

The Roosevelts spent fifty-two Sundays altogether in Europe, and if one reads Theodore's diary carefully, he will learn that Theodore attended church on twenty-seven of these Sundays. More than that, Theodore's entries for these twenty-seven Sundays contain not even a hint of protest or discontent and definitely no mention of a cough, a wheeze, or other possible pulmonary complaint. Indeed, a number of his entries provide evidence that he actually enjoyed occasional Sunday services, among them three successive services in Rome: "[January 30, 1870], we all went to church and there heard the most interesting sermon." "[February 6], Ellie and I went to church all alone and heard a most interesting sermon." And "[February 13], we all went to church and at prayers all of a sudden a donkey brayed!! quite discordent."[32]

The larger cities of Europe, among them London, Paris, Strasbourg, Rome, Venice, Florence, and Vienna, have architecturally celebrated cathedrals. After visiting the famed cathedral in Strasbourg, Theodore wrote: "We saw the cathedral where there was a remarkable clock where death struck and a cock crew."[33] At one time or another the entire family entered most of these edifices, including Westminster Abbey, though again with no expressed remonstrance from Theodore.

The question may now fairly be asked: if it was the fear of churches that triggered Theodore's weekend asthmatic attacks, what sparked his attacks on weekdays, and what inhibited them on so many weekends—twenty-seven of fifty-two—when he did attend Sunday church services?

5

Antiasthmatic remedies prescribed by physicians in the 1860s and 1870s were many and varied. Though Theodore became acquainted with only a few, such as tobacco, ipecac, and coffee, the average person today is so unfamiliar with them that they need explanation and definition.

En route to Trieste, on September 26, 1869, Theodore's father made his son smoke a cigar. This act was hardly another instance of "man's inhumanity to man." At that date the practice of using tobacco, in one form or another, to ease the labored breathing of asthmatics, was widely regarded as therapeutic and continued to be so regarded. Writing as late as 1899, William Osler, professor of medicine at Johns Hopkins University, said: "The sedative antispasmodics, such as belladonna, henbane, stramonium, and lobelia, may be given [to asthma patients] in solution or used in the form of cigarettes. . . . Excellent [medicinal] cigarettes are now manufactured and asthmatics try various sorts. . . . I have known several patients to whom tobacco smoke inhaled was quite as potent as the prepared cigarettes."[34]

In Naples, on January 5, 1870, Theodore was given a dose of ipecac, with "dreadfull effects." Ipecac is, of course, an emetic, a drug used to produce vomiting. Since Theodore, after taking it, experienced horrid results, it may be taken for granted that he had vomited copiously. But more was expected of ipecac in this instance

23

than emptying the stomach; there was the additional expectation that vigorous retching would also loosen and release accumulated mucus from the bronchioles.

Two weeks later, in Rome, Theodore announced: "I had a verry bad night. I was awake for 2 or 3 hours. I had some coffy to drink (much to my horror, and good)."[35] In the nineteenth century, and on into the twentieth, caffeine (an alkaloid) was judged by some physicians to be an effective remedy in treating asthmatics. Osler thought it to be "a more suitable drink than tea."[36] Apparently it often eased Theodore's respitory malaise, for his mother in a letter to her sister said that Theodore's father "had warded off one or two attacks with this coffee, but likes to keep it for our trump card."[37]

In years ahead Theodore Roosevelt outgrew his predisposition to asthma and seemingly was none the worse for his childhood phthisicky miseries. It appears extraordinary that, at no time or place, did Theodore, following an attack of asthma, use words suggestive of mental impotence or of being sorry for himself. He appears to have mastered each seizure, just as in future he mastered other problems, some even more painful and intolerable.

Notes

1. Roosevelt, *Diaries of Boyhood*, 13.
2. Ibid., 14.
3. The boatswain is one of a number of common names for the white-tailed tropic-bird (*Phaëton lepturus*), characterized by two central tail feathers sweeping out behind for a distance of a foot and a half. It ranges north in the western Atlantic to latitude 40° N, and south to the West Indies.
4. Ibid.
5. Ibid.
6. Robinson, *My Brother*, 42.
7. Roosevelt, *Diaries of Boyhood*, 24.
8. Theodore was probably referring to the mongoose or ichneumon (*Herpestes ichneumon*).
9. Probably the African ratel (*Mellivora ratel*), a mammal which is badgerlike in size, form, and habit.
10. Ibid. The caracal (*Lynx caracal*), a member of the cat family, inhabits parts of northern Africa and southwestern Asia.
11. Cholera morbus is a term, now rarely used, for an inflammation of the gastrointestinal tract often marked by cramps, diarrhea, and vomiting—such as small boys sometimes experience from eating too many green apples.

12. Ibid., 74, 40.

13. Ibid., 66, 67, 77.

14. Ibid., 67–68.

15. Ibid., 42.

16. Edith Carow, a childhood playmate of Theodore Roosevelt. She later became his second wife.

17. Ibid., 103.

18. Ibid., 45, 63, 40, 44.

19. The chamois (*Rupricapra rupricapra*) is the well-known hoofed mammal of mountainous regions of Europe and the source of "chamois skin."

20. Ibid., 38, 39, 40.

21. Ibid., 60.

22. Ibid., 70, 79.

23. Ibid., 84–85.

24. Ibid., 85.

25. Ibid., 99, 101–2, 191.

26. Ibid., 190. Elliot on occasion engaged one or another European artist to illustrate his works, one of them being Josef Wolf.

27. In later years Elliot became a member (active and honorary) of the Boone and Crockett Club, perhaps through the persuasion of Roosevelt. Still later, he was a co-author, with T. S. Van Dyke and A. J. Stone, of Roosevelt's *The Deer Family* (New York: Macmillan, 1902).

28. Roosevelt, *Autobiography*, 13.

29. John 2:17.

30. David McCullough, *Mornings on Horseback* (New York: Simon and Schuster, 1981), 103.

31. Ibid., 101.

32. Roosevelt, *Diaries of Boyhood*, 172, 178, 180–81.

33. Ibid., 35.

34. William Osler, *The Principles and Practice of Medicine* (New York: D. Appleton and Co., 1899), 632.

35. Roosevelt, *Diaries of Boyhood*, 166.

36. Osler, *Practice of Medicine*, 632.

37. McCullough, *Mornings on Horseback*, 91.

3

"I Saw a Bald-headed Eagle"

THEODORE ROOSEVELT, JR., was jubilant at being home again: "This morning May 25 [1870] we saw land of America and swiftly coming on passed Sandey Hook and went into the Bay. New York!! Hip! Hurrah!"[1] After a year abroad Theodore found the familiar sights and sounds of Lower Manhattan a most refreshing balm to his mutable spirit. East 20th Street, though lamp-lit, cobble-stoned, and otherwise primitive, like many other streets of the nineteenth-century city, was not only home to him, but also the site of his natural history museum.

Almost at once Theodore began giving thought to his museum. He was delighted, therefore, when on June 1—just one week after his homecoming—he found himself again in the country, at a small place up the Hudson called Spuyten Duyvil.[2] Here, with purposeful and determined energy, he promptly threw himself into the task of again collecting native specimens.

Fortunately Theodore continued his diary. As a result we learn that, on June 3, he "found 6 nests three with birds the others old. The last I took." And three days later, "We . . . found a birds nest with 3 eggs (but we did not take them)."[3] By this date, as is evident, Theodore had learned an important lesson: when collecting bird nests take only the empty ones. To do otherwise would be an act of cruelty to the birds.

It was sometime during this stay at Spuyten Duyvil that Theodore decided on a broader approach to his collecting, one that would enlist neighborhood boys in his behalf. Accordingly, he spread the news that he wanted field mice and that he would pay the handsome sum of ten cents for each individual mouse and thirty-five cents for families. The response exceeded expectations, as a small army of youngsters, spurred on by the prospect of sudden riches, scoured the nearby woods and fields. In short order the Roosevelt summer home was almost flooded with field mice and other animals—for the word soon circulated that Theodore was interested in obtaining most any creature that could swim, fly, run, or crawl. Theodore's joy knew no bounds. Others of the family were somewhat taken aback, especially on occasions when Theodore absented himself for a day or two and the care of his specimens fell to them. Even the family laundress became upset, threatening to leave after she had found three turtles moored to her wash tub.[4] This incident may have occurred on June 28, 1870, for on the 29th Theodore confided to his diary, "Made a turtle pen."[5]

About this same time, but of more importance, was Theodore's decision to record his observations on animal life. For this purpose he bought a small, inexpensive notebook and therein regularly recorded the numerous faunal events and observations that had most forcibly impressed themselves on his youthful mind. Theodore's "Notes on Natural History," as he called this boyhood document, spanned roughly the years 1870–72 and included information gained in several places, not only in Spuyten Duyvil, but also in such other places on the Hudson as Riverdale, Dobbs Ferry, and Tarrytown (not to be confused with the frequented Barrytown, farther up the Hudson).

Theodore began "Notes on Natural History" with a personal observation: "The vesper finch [sparrow] was observed on or shortly after the first of April. . . . On the fifteenth of the month they became common." Subsequent entries were both short and long, with several only a sentence in length: The nest of the white-footed mouse "is five to six inches in diameter, and is usually placed under or near a log or board, but often in the open field." The mole "swims fairly, but if turned on its back drowns." Young cottontail rabbits "are very stupid, and fall an easy prey to almost any assailant." The hog-nosed snake, when alarmed, "often puffs out the skin of its head and neck."

It is regrettable that Theodore did not become better acquainted with the hog-nosed snake. He had been close enough to watch it inflate its cobralike head, but, if he had gone closer, particularly in a threatening manner, the reptile would have played dead by rolling onto its back and remaining motionless. But the hog-nosed snake overplays its part, for, at this point, if Theodore should have turned the snake over on its belly, it would have at once turned again onto its back, obviously of a mind that that is the only suitable position for a dead snake. How Theodore would have revelled in this performance.

Friends and relatives, knowing the extent of Theodore's interest in animals, often related their experiences to him. The ones with greatest appeal found their way into his "Notes on Natural History." There were the tale told to him by his grandfather of a goshawk that swooped down on a rooster; the account told to him by the family gardener of a crow attacking a robin's nest; and the story, attributed to "a lady friend of mine," about a chipmunk adopted and raised by a motherless cat.

Obviously Theodore liked to write, especially when recording his own personal adventures. At Tarrytown red squirrels were so common that "they literally inhabited the house" and became "somewhat troublesome, their chattering and romping awaking us early in the morning." But, as Theodore said, they "never molested" any of them. At Riverdale Theodore found a nest of the blue-gray gnatcatcher that "was composed of soft vegatabale substance and was covered with lichen on the outside so that it looked like a mere excresence on the branch." On another day, Theodore captured and took into the house a tree frog. "At night it offered the entire family much amusement, being then let out, and put on the table, by the lamp, where it proved a remarkable flycatcher, leaping at any insect that was attracted near the light." And in Barrytown Theodore witnessed "a great assembly of the barn swallow, for the purpose of migration." These, like the red squirrels, invaded the house, though none was hurt except one that fell "a victim to a cat."

An experience during late summer in 1872 at Dobbs Ferry proved to be the highlight of that year for Theodore and is best told in his own words:

A nest of the gray squirrel . . . was situated in a chestnut tree, at the junction of a large branch with the trunk. . . . It was composed of leaves and twigs, and lined with shreds of pine bark. . . . The nest contained three young, whose eyes were not yet open, and whom I took home and reared. I at first endeavored to persuade them to lap up some milk but they were too young to do so, so I purchased a syringe and tried them with that, squeezing a few drops of milk into each ones throat. One (a male) seized the syringe and sucked it on the second trial. I let him have as much as he wanted, and when he had finished, I felt how heavy he was and then pumped milk into the other two untill they had attained his weight. In a day or two, they all took to the syringe, and after that I had no more difficulty with them, giving each squirrel as much food as he wanted, three times a day. Their home was in an old box, at the bottom of which I had arranged a lot of hay which was changed once a day. One squirrel died soon, but the others lived happily on, and in about a week opened their eyes. We now gave them sugar and bread soaked in milk, and sometimes nuts. I and my sister took turns feeding them, and they soon learned to recognize us, and whenever they got loose would run towards us, continually uttering their "chuck, chuck, chuck, chuck." We now let them out for several hours daily, either in a large room or else on the lawn. They were very happy when loose but always objected to being put back in the box, scolding loudly and even occasionally trying to bite,—for which they were punished by having their noses tapped with a small stick. When we had had them a little over a month they grew to be so large and lively that we thought it would be cruel to keep them in a box and con-cluded to let them go. We first accustomed them to their natural diet by giving them open hickory nuts and chestnuts, then cracked ones, and finally whole ones. I then placed the box in a large oak tree and let them out. They enjoyed their freedom intensely, and kept perpetually racing up and down the trees, but they never went very far from our house, and were very tame, coming down from the trees to receive nuts from our hands, so that they added greatly to the beauty of the place. At first they slept in the box we had placed in the tree for them, but afterwards went off to somewhere else. Two or three months afterwards one wandered off, or was killed, but the other is still living.

Those were exciting days for Theodore—and perhaps for the en-tire Roosevelt family—when he was mothering the infant gray squirrels. Unquestionably he never forgot the experience. We cannot help wondering, however, if he remembered ever afterward with equal zest another incident of that year, of which he wrote briefly in "Notes on Natural History." Some of the choicer things in life, like this one, often come in small packages: "*Meph[i]tis chinga* [skunk]. Common. One fell in our sistern, where it remained three weeks, to the decided detriment of the water."

2

It now seems important to reconsult the "Record of the Roosevelt Museum." By so doing, one learns of museum problems solved and of continued progress:

In the spring of 1869 Mr. T. Roosevelt, Jr. went to Europe where he collected several hundred specimens.[6] In the spring of 1870 he returned and in the fall they had 1000 specimens. They then passed a resolution making everything common property. A bank was then started with ten dollars; Mr. I. Elliott[7] was procured as agent; about this time two rival museums were started by Messrs. F. and E. Roosevelt;[8] the first of these was entirely and the second partly bought out before the end of the winter. In the beginning of the year 1871 Mr. W. E[mlen] Roosevelt was admitted, a Museum Library was established, in the fall the bank had $27. A constitution was also adopted and Mr. F. Roosevelt became an agent. One of the provisions of the constitution was that a secretary should be elected yearly to keep a record of the doings of the Museum, in fulfillment of this duty Mr. W. E. Roosevelt first secretary has written this history of the commencement of the Museum from notes furnished by Mr. T. Roosevelt, Jr.

Obviously the founder of the museum had not been sitting on his hands; looking to the future, he had successfully engineered the founding of a bank, the establishment of a library, the passage of a constitution, and the beginning of a history. But more was in the offing. At an ensuing meeting, held on November 11, 1871, Theodore made sure that several specific resolutions were passed:

Resolved that Mr. J. W. Roosevelt be appointed geologist, antiquary and anatomist.

Resolved that Mr. W. E. Roosevelt be appointed Conchologist, taxidermist and Entomologist.

Resolved that Mr. T. Roosevelt, Jr. be appointed naturalist.

Resolved that as Mr. J. W. Roosevelt is about to travel in Europe four dollars be deposited with Mr. J. W. Roosevelt to be used for the Museum at the discretion of Mr. J. W. Roosevelt.

This display of knowledge by Theodore, in the use of such terms as conchologist and entomologist, has a ready explanation. His father, while active in the founding of the American Museum of Natural History, had undoubtedly discussed at home many of the steps necessary to the successful formation of a museum. Theodore had listened attentively and thus learned that all great institutions of this kind sooner or later elected specialists, one of whom might be versed in shells (a conchologist) and another in insects (an entomologist). But Theodore's decision to become a "naturalist" in his own museum was not from anything his father had said. He alone made that decision—and the reason seems obvious. He associated the word with men like Alexander Wilson and John James Audubon, both great and wondrous naturalists, who had spent their lives filled with all manner of strange birds and beasts.

3

During 1870–72 a number of events occurred that enhanced Theodore's zest for natural history. First, he discovered a previously unsuspected handicap. He became aware of it one day when he found that he could not read the lettering on a nearby billboard. His father lost no time in taking Theodore to an eye doctor, who, determining that Theodore was extremely nearsighted, fitted him with glasses. Before he had obtained these glasses, Theodore later wrote, he had studied nature "only so far as could be compassed by a mole-like vision" and thus his only biological triumphs had been restricted to such things as trying "to tame an excessively unamiable woodchuck, and in making friends with a gentle, pretty, trustful white-footed mouse which reared her family in an empty flower pot."[9] He revealed, too, "I had no idea how beautiful the world was until I got those spectacles."[10] The immediate results of Theodore's corrected vision were not only keener eyesight and thus greatly improved observational competence but also an increase in his field studies.

Soon after getting his spectacles Theodore received his father's permission to study taxidermy. Only a boy especially endowed with a fervor to increase his knowledge of animals can fully understand Theodore's elation at this opportunity. Moreover, his teacher was to be John G. Bell,[11] a pioneer in the art of taxidermy, who had accompanied the great Audubon on a trip to the Upper Missouri in 1841. Theodore later said of him: "Mr. Bell was a very interesting man, an American of the before-the-war type. He was tall, straight as an Indian, with white hair and a smooth-shaven, clear-cut face; a dignified figure, always in a black frock coat. He had no scientific knowledge of birds or mammals; his interest lay merely in collecting and preparing them."[12]

Bell's laboratory, well known to sportsmen of his day, was situated in a building at the northwest corner of Broadway and Worth Street, New York City. While studying under Bell, Theodore visited this building regularly, and there learned not only how to stuff and mount birds but also how to prepare the conventional museum birdskin.[13] Bell may possibly have increased Theodore's knowledge of animals, for, though formally untrained as a zoologist, he had during his travels learned much about them. On one occasion he told Theodore a story that quickly found its way into "Notebook on Natural History." The story was about a fight Bell had watched in his garden between a rooster and a field mouse. "The field mouse fought long and valiantly," Theodore wrote, "but at last was overcome, although not until after a protracted battle."

During these same years Theodore also advanced his natural history education by visiting established museums, one in Philadelphia. In a letter to his father from that city, he wrote: "I think I will stay till Saturday as I am having a splendid time. I go to the Academy of Natural Sciences of Philadelphia every spare moment and am allowed to have the run of all the 38,000 books in the library. They have got quite a number of specimens, also. I have not time to write more." The Academy of Natural Sciences of Philadelphia, founded in 1812, was, by the early 1870s, the most important scientific museum in the United States, just as the city of Philadelphia was then the acknowledged scientific center. That Theodore proposed to stay longer in Philadelphia and that he spent "every spare moment" in the Academy strongly suggest that he respected the high position then held by the Academy.

On his visits to Philadelphia, Theodore stayed at the home of his uncle, Dr. Hilborne West, who had married Susan Elliott, a half-sister of Theodore's mother. Uncle Hill was well versed in the sciences and may well have accompanied Theodore on some of his visits to the Academy.

Just as soon as the American Museum of Natural History opened its doors to the public, Theodore was among the first to frequent the offices and laboratories of that fledgling institution. Many years later Theodore wrote to Henry Fairfield Osborn,[14] then president of the American Museum: "As a boy I worked in the [American] Museum and specifically remember skinning some rather reddish white-footed mice which I thought were golden mice and was much disappointed to find that they were not. . . . I remember very well once being allowed to look over a large number of South American mice in the Museum . . . and appealing to Dr. Bickmore[15] to know how I could get at the relationship of the South American with the northern mice of the same family."[16]

It may have been on one of these early visits to the American Museum that Theodore first met Frederick Osborn, a younger brother of Henry Fairfield Osborn. The two, of about the same age, became fast friends and in weeks and months ahead were often together scouring the woods and fields of the Hudson River highlands in search of specimens. Frederick was mainly interested in birds, while, as we know, Theodore's faunal tastes were varied. In his "Notes on Natural History," Theodore included a sample of Frederick's observations: "Mr. F. Osborn informs me that he has known a large flock of English [house] sparrows to attack a yellow-bellied woodpecker which had strayed into New York City and, by continually striking it with their beaks, worry it to death. The woodpecker defended itself furiously and killed one of its assailants by striking it in the eye, the bill penetrating to the brain." In this same notebook Theodore had an observation of his own—a timely one—about the house sparrow: "Very abundant in New York, Boston and Philadelphia, and rapidly becoming common in all neighboring towns." In due course, as we shall learn, Theodore will become a participant in what became known as "The Sparrow War."

Getting back to the friendship of Theodore and Frederick, on one of their field trips they experienced a moment of embarrassment. Their day had been successful, with the result that all available pocket space had been filled with specimens. As they started home, Theodore spotted a frog that he thought might possibly be a new species and, with pockets already bulging, he slipped it under his hat. Soon afterward, on the road they were taking, they met a carriage in which were riding the Honorable Hamilton Fish, then U.S. secretary of state, and Mrs. Fish. These distinguished figures were known to Theodore, and civil courtesy demanded that he doff his hat. For a brief moment the frog remained perched on Theodore's head, fully exposed to public view, before it leaped into the air and plopped to the ground. Though doubtless red-faced, Theodore hurriedly retrieved the frog, its capture being of greater importance to him than whatever the secretary and his lady may have said or done.[17] Presumably the frog did not prove to be new to science, and we hear nothing further about it.

Even more regrettable, the close friendship between these two enthusiastic, youthful naturalists lasted only briefly. In 1875 it ended tragically, when Frederick drowned.

4

Perhaps the greatest boon in this period to Theodore's growth as a naturalist was a trip in the summer of 1871 to the Adirondacks and the White Mountains. It lasted all of August and included Theodore's immediate family as well as a few relatives, among them West Roosevelt and Uncle Hill.

In the months preceding this trip, Theodore had acquired a number of advanced scientific books, among them William M. Bailey's *Our Own Birds*, a gift from his father on Christmas Day, 1870; Thomas Nuttall's *A Manual of the Ornithology of the United States and Canada*, previously the property of his parental grandfather; and Volume 1 of John D. Godman's *Natural History*. Also recently acquired, and of greater worth to Theodore, were Spencer F. Baird's publications on birds and mammals. Baird's *Birds*, published in 1859, marked a new epoch in American ornithology and exerted an influence equal to that earlier enjoyed by the works of Wilson and Audubon. Baird's *Mammals of North America*, also an 1859 publication, was equally influential in the field of mammalogy. On this trip to the Adirondacks and the White Mountains, Theodore seems to have taken with him Baird's books, if none of the others. He carried, too, reference works on amphibians and reptiles. As a consequence, he possibly felt that he was in a position to identify almost any land vertebrate he might encounter. The above books without exception, it should be said, had been written for adults, not one of them for twelve-year-olds (Theodore was then two months short of his thirteenth birthday).

From Manhattan the Roosevelts, en route to the Adirondacks, had traveled by train to Glens Falls, New York, and then by stagecoach to Lake George. Theodore's diary, the principal source of information about this trip, provided a day-to-day account. It furnished evidence, too, of Theodore's more serious approach to the study of animals. Witness, for example, his entry at Lake George for August 3, 1871: "After breakfast our party went off in a small steamboat but after an hour of this West, Ellie and I got tired of it and were put ashore to stay till the steamboat came back. We wandered about and I picked up a salamander (*Diemictylus iridescens*). I saw a mouse here which from its looks I should judge to be a hamster mouse (*Hesperomys myoides*). We saw a bald-headed eagle (*Hali[ae]etus leucocephalus*) sailing over the lake."[18]

As this and succeeding entries attest, Theodore by now had taken a sizable step forward as a naturalist, consistently employing the scientific names of animals as well as the common ones. In so doing, he makes it clear that he was familiar, at least to some degree, with the system of classification devised by Carolus Linnaeus[19] of giving to each described species of animal or plant a name in Latin consisting of two words, one generic and one specific. The great triumph of the Linnaean system, of course, was that it provided a universal language for the classification of living things. Before its advent there were as many names for the house sparrow, to cite a specific example, as there were languages: in German it was *haussperling*, in French *moineau domestique*, in Portuguese *pardal*, in Spanish *gorrion*, in Dutch *musch*, and so on. Today, because of Linnaeus, whatever the language, the house sparrow is *Passer domesticus*.

Theodore would soon learn, if he did not already know, other facts about classification, among them the grouping of genera into families, families into orders, orders into classes, and classes into phyla. This method of grouping may be illustrated by that of the English house sparrow: Phylum—*Chordata*; Class—*Aves*; Order—*Passeriformes*; Family—*Phocidae*; Genus—*Passer*; Species—*domesticus*.

There can be little doubt that T. Roosevelt, Jr., already knew such elementary facts about the Linnaean system. He may first have learned of the existence of the system from his Uncle Hill, who, according to one source, "talked science and medicine and natural history with Teedie, who always craves knowledge."[20] It is more likely, however, that he originally gained insight into the system from a careful study of the books by Baird[21] and others; certainly they were the source of the scientific names of the animals encountered at Lake George and elsewhere on this trip.

Leaving Lake George, the Roosevelt party traveled by way of Lake Ticonderoga and Plattsburg to Paul Smith's, at that time the leading Adirondack hotel, situated on Lower St. Regis Lake. The driver of the stagecoach bearing the Roosevelts to Paul Smith's volunteered the information, as Theodore reported: "There are wolves (*Canis occidentalis*), bears (*Ursus americanus*) and numbers of deer (*Cervus virginianus*) found here."[22]

Paul Smith's, founded in 1859 as a modest boardinghouse, was, by 1871, a well-established and well-known hotel, but no better known than its owner, Paul Smith himself. A man of large build, large appetite, and large humor, he was the most genial of hosts. He had a passion for the outdoor life and supplied from the surrounding woods the venison and other meats that his wife prepared with unfailing skill and the guests consumed with unfailing relish. Not surprisingly, in years ahead, Theodore will revisit Paul Smith's. On this first visit he and the others stayed there eight days. From Theodore's diary, which carries an entry for each day, it is evident that he found the Adirondack environment faunally congenial: August 6—"I saw here . . . several species of frog (*Rana Pipiens, fontinalis* and *palustris*)." August 7—"In passing through Spitfire lake we saw several loons (*Colymbus torquatus*)." August 8—"While in the lake St. Regis we saw other kinds of wild ducks . . . and a great blue heron (*Ardea herodias*). . . . I also saw a kingfisher (*Ceryle alcyon*) dive for a fish and a mink (*Putorius vison*) swam across the stream . . . and grouse (*Bonasa umbellus*) rose from the banks."[23]

In succeeding days Theodore identified other Adirondack animals, but always professionally, using scientific as well as vernacular names. It was on August 9 that he may well have come close to ending his life in the same way Fred Osborn would do. Theodore described the incident: "I attempted to cross the rapids, but I had miscalculated my strength for before I was half way across the force of the current had swept me into water which was over my head. . . . I struck out for [and reached] a rock . . . half walking, half swimming."[24]

The Roosevelts left Paul Smith's on August 14 for Lake Placid. From there they traveled by way of Ausable Chasm and Lake Champlain to Burlington, Vermont, where they spent ten days, mainly sightseeing, horseback riding, and climbing Mt. Lafayette and Mt. Washington. Theodore's diary of the Vermont interlude contained just two items of particular zoological interest. One referred to a tame bear he had encountered, which ate cake "like a Christian," and the other to a bird "that looked like a *Regulus calendula* [Ruby-crowned kinglet]."[25]

For Theodore, the month went by entirely too rapidly, especially the time spent in the Adirondacks. He had delighted in the beauty of forest and lakes, in the "cool, invigorating air," in the presence of heretofore unfamiliar birds and mammals, and in the majestic "deciduous trees often reaching the height of a hundred feet, and the white pines even that of a hundred and thirty."[26]

5

One of the earliest annual reports of the American Museum of Natural History, that for 1872, reveals that in 1871 Theodore Roosevelt, Jr., had enriched the museum by a gift of: "1 Bat, 12 Mice, 1 Turtle, 1 skull: Red Squirrel and 4 Birds' Eggs."[27] The reasons behind this gift of Theodore to the American Museum seem obvious. He had followed closely most of his father's several steps in founding the museum, had surely been aware of the meeting at 28 East 20th Street—in the Roosevelt's front parlor—on the evening of April 8, 1869, at which time the original charter of the American Museum had been signed,[28] and may well have heard his father's statement that if a monument were ever raised to his work on earth, to prove that he had "done something" with his life, he wanted it to be for his efforts in founding the American Museum.[29] Being thus conversant with his father's contributions to the founding of the American Museum, Theodore had been moved to make one of his own, though ever so modest. In making the gift he probably, at the same time, had been additionally motivated by the thought he would please his father, whom he seems to have loved more than any other person.

Notes

1. Roosevelt, *Diaries of Boyhood*, 227.
2. In 1870 Spuyten Duyvil was a small community on Spuyten Duyvil Creek, a narrow channel that separates Manhattan Island from the mainland (the Bronx) and connects the Hudson and Harlem rivers. Tradition has it that Spuyten Duyvil received its name after an inebriated Dutchman vowed to swim the creek at midnight, "in spite of the devil."
3. Ibid., 228–29.
4. Robinson, *My Brother*, 52.
5. Roosevelt, *Diaries of Boyhood*, 233.
6. The majority of these specimens collected in Europe were seemingly coins and minerals, certainly not animals.
7. We are uncertain of the identity of I. Elliott, though he may have been a nephew of Teddy's Aunt Elizabeth Elliott Roosevelt, wife of his Uncle Robert B. Roosevelt.

8. We have failed to identify F. Roosevelt. E. Roosevelt was certainly Elliott, Theodore's brother.

9. Roosevelt, *Works, Mem. Ed.*, 6:444.

10. Roosevelt, *Autobiography*, 18.

11. John Graham Bell (1812–79), taxidermist and naturalist, was born in Sparkill, N.Y. Ornithologists, holding Bell in high esteem, named at least three birds after him: Bell's vireo (*Veiro bellii* Audubon), Bell's sparrow (*Amphispiza belli* Cassin), and Bell's warbler (*Basileuterus belli* Giraud).

12. Roosevelt, *Works, Mem. Ed.*, 6:445.

13. A birdskin is the skin of a bird, specifically the external part prepared for study by removing most parts internal to the skin and replacing them with cotton or tow (coarse broken flax or hemp fiber prepared for spinning).

14. Henry Fairfield Osborn (1857–1935), paleontologist, anatomist, and writer, was born in Fairfield, Conn. He taught at Princeton and Columbia and later (1908–33) was president of the American Museum of Natural History. Osborn wrote voluminously on biological and geological subjects.

15. Albert Smith Bickmore (1839–1914), naturalist, was one of the founders of the American Museum and served (1869–84) as its first director.

16. Henry Fairfield Osborn, *Impressions of Great Naturalists* (New York: Charles Scribner's Sons, 1924), 188–89.

17. Ibid., 167–68.

18. Roosevelt, *Diaries of Boyhood*, 142–43.

19. Carolus Linnaeus (1707–78), eminent Swedish botanist, who, in 1735, published *Systema Naturae*. This work ran through twelve editions, the tenth of which is now recognized as the starting point for binomial nomenclature.

20. Robinson, *My brother*, 52.

21. Spencer Fullerton Baird (1823–87), outstanding American naturalist, was born in Reading, Pa., graduated from Dickinson College (1840), and was appointed assistant secretary of the Smithsonian Institution (1850). He served in that capacity until he became secretary in 1878.

22. Roosevelt, *Diaries of Boyhood*, 244.

23. Ibid., 245–47. The scientific names Theodore used were those in vogue in the 1870s. Even today, more than a century later, the majority of them remain unchanged, though some have been updated. For example, *Colymbus torquatus* (the common loon) is today *Gavia immer*.

24. Ibid., 248.

25. Ibid., 255, 258.

26. Roosevelt, *Works, Mem. Ed.*, 6:464.

27. Paul Brooks. *Speaking for Nature* (Boston: Houghton Mifflin, 1980), 105.

28. McCullough, *Mornings on Horseback*, 29.

29. Ibid., 132.

4

"Egypt, the Land of My Dreams"

EARLY IN 1872 Theodore Roosevelt's parents began giving serious thought to another year abroad. It was their opinion that "the benefits of a year on the Nile, and a summer studying German in Dresden, would outweigh the disadvantages of breaking into the regular school studies of the three children of the 20th Street nursery."[1] The trip lasted a full year, with a month in Syria sandwiched between the longer stays in Egypt and Germany.

With distinctly unpleasant memories of the previous trip abroad, Theodore at first was unenthusiastic about another one. He began to develop an interest in it only after his father had assured him that, once in Egypt, he would be allowed the use of a gun in collecting birds and other animals for his museum. This assurance put an entirely different aspect on the trip for Theodore. Accordingly, as the day of departure drew nearer, his zeal mounted appreciably. As evidence, he took stock of the implements and materials that he, as an enterprising young field collector, should take with him. He knew or soon found out that, in addition to a gun, he would need: (1) plenty of ammunition, including gunpowder, wads, and caps; (2) scalpel, forceps, scissors, and penknife (for dissecting); (3) cotton batting or tow, for stuffing the internal cavities left empty by the removal of viscera; (4) arsenic, as a preservative; (5) gypsum, corn meal, or plaster of Paris, for cleaning the plumage; (6) a collecting chest, preferably compartmentalized, to house the completed birdskins as well as tools of the trade; (7) a pocket lens, often a necessity, particularly in determining the sex of immature birds; and (8) a quantity of writing paper, for recording observations.

Because Theodore had studied taxidermy under J. G. Bell, and had undoubtedly prepared many birdskins, he may well have had already in his possession most of these implements and materials. He also wanted a supply of specimen labels. Consequently, with a design already in mind, he visited a printer. Quite a number of these labels are still extant, in one museum or another, so that it is known what they look like. Each is about one-inch wide and three-inches long and carries the words "No.," "Roosevelt Museum," and "Hab[itat]." Between these words there is ample space for the name of the species, the sex, and other information.

2

The Roosevelts sailed from New York City aboard the U.S.S. *Russia.* The date was October 6, 1872, and their immediate destination, as in 1869, was Liverpool. For Theodore, this crossing of the Atlantic was again attended by seasickness. His diary entry for October 24 stated: "A gale came on today and I was so sick that I kept to my berth all day."[2] Indeed, Theodore seems to have been sick on seven of the eleven days it took the *Russia* to cross the ocean. As a result, he had minimal opportunities to pace the deck and look for animals. On October 22, however, he reported seeing "Several gulls, terns and kittiwakes (*Larus, Sterna* and *Rissa*)" and, on October 27, "a snow bunting (*Plectrophanes nivalis*) flew on board and was captured."[3] If he saw other animals during this crossing, he failed to report them.

The snow bunting, or snow flake as it is also called, is an interesting bird. It breeds farther north than any other land bird, in high latitudes near the North Pole, and in its annual autumnal migration south invades all continents of the Northern Hemisphere. Not surprising, therefore, that in the same year Theodore reported collecting a snow bunting in the Atlantic (near Ireland), another American naturalist, Elliott Coues, announced the arrival of this same species far to the west, at Fort Randall, in what was then Dakota Territory.[4] Not so many years would pass until Theodore would find the snow bunting again, first in Maine and later in the Rockies.

The *Russia* docked in Liverpool on the morning of October 26. Theodore's diary reads: "We went to the Adelphy Hotel. Hardly were we in our rooms when Uncle Irving[5] and Aunt Ella arrived. How delighted we all were! After a while I went out to the market." Theodore had ample cause to visit a market. He had suddenly remembered that, before leaving New York, he had failed to obtain a supply of arsenic, essential to the successful preparation of a birdskin. Seemingly, its purchase could not be delayed. However, once in the store, Theodore met with an unexpected problem: the manager refusing to sell this product to him until he produced an adult witness willing to swear that he (Theodore) had no intention of committing "murder, suicide, or any such dreadful thing."[6]

With this sensitive matter resolved, probably with the aid of his father or his Uncle Irving, Theodore hurried to the Liverpool Museum. To his disappointment, the zoological specimens there were not nearly as well mounted nor as rare as those in the American Museum back home. He found fault with the city, too: "Liverpool has all the dirt of New York (and a good deal of its own besides—afterward I went and took a bath."[7]

During the next three days, still in Liverpool, Theodore reported events of more than passing importance to him: October 27th—"Today is my birthday and I am fourteen years old." October 28th—"Today in the morning we went out and . . . I bought some snipe and partridges which I proceeded to skin—and with great success." October 29th—"In the afternoon I skinned a starling and a snipe."[8]

Theodore had prepared his first birdskins while studying with Bell and, as a necessary preliminary, must have visited New York markets to obtain birds for that purpose. Whether or not he added to his museum any of the birdskins made under the supervision of Bell cannot be said, but no doubt exists as to those prepared in Liverpool of the snipe, partridge, and starling.[9] These were special to him, being the first of well over a hundred prepared by him during this year abroad.

In his diary entry of November 4, Theodore disclosed that he and Elliott had obtained parental consent to go to Bonn, Germany, where West Roosevelt was then attending school. Theodore and West enjoyed a week together, spending much of their time skinning birds, presumably bought in local German markets. Of this visit Theodore wrote: "I had not seen West (who is my partner in the museum) for over a year and I do not know which of us was the most delighted."[10]

On November 14, after a sixteen-hour train ride to Paris, Theodore and Elliott rejoined the others of the family. On five of the seven days the Roosevelts spent in the French capital, Theodore continued his practice, started in Liverpool, of preparing birdskins, presumably in his hotel room.

Theodore wrote at least one letter while in Paris, this to his Uncle Hill:

From Theodore the Philosopher to Hilborne, Elder of the Church of Philadelphia. Dated from Paris, a city of Gaul, in the 16th day of the 11th month of the 4th year of the reign of Ulysses [Grant]. Truly, O Hilborne! this is the first time in many weeks that I have been able to write you concerning our affairs. I have just come from the city of Bonn in the land of the Teuton, where I have been with our fellow labourer James of Roosevelt, surnamed the Doctor, whom I left in good health. In crossing the Sea of Atlantis I suffered much of a malady called sickness of the sea, but am now in good health, as are also all our family. I would that you should speak to the sage Leidy[11] concerning the price of his great manuscript, which I am desirous of getting. Give my regards to Susan of West, whom I hope this letter will find in health. I have procured birds of kinds new to me here, and have preserved them. This is all I have to say for the time being, so will close this short epistle.[12]

Theodore, it would appear from this letter, had reached that stage of adolescence when he fancied himself as a wit. Also, and more important, he had advanced mentally to the point where he felt he should inform himself on prehistoric animals as well as on present ones, hence his desire to obtain a copy of Joseph Leidy's manuscript, probably "Contributions to the Extinct Vertebrate Fauna of the Western Territories."[13]

Leaving Paris on November 21, the Roosevelts traveled through Turin and Bologna to Brindisi, on the Italian heel. Here they took passage for Alexandria, Egypt, where they arrived on November 28. During this Mediterranean passage, Theodore was seasick again and recorded only one faunal observation: "Some seamews [possibly mew gulls, *Larus canus*] are the only creatures we have seen."[14]

Theodore, like most poor sailors—Charles Darwin was among the most celebrated—recovered as soon as his feet touched land. Indeed, he seems to have fully recovered with his first glimpse of Egypt: "At eight oclock," he wrote on the morning of November 28, "we arrived in sight of Alexandria. How I gazed on it! It was Egypt, the land of my dreams; Egypt the most ancient of all countries; a land that was old when Rome was bright, was old when Babylon was in its glory, was old when Troy was taken! it was a sight to awaken a thousand thoughts, and it did." In 1872 Alexandria retained but few vestiges of its former splendor, principally Pompey's Pillar and Cleopatra's Needle. After viewing the former, Theodore declared, "I *felt* a great deal but *said* nothing."[15] The latter interested him less.

The contemplation of Egypt's ancient monuments and crumbling ruins was for Theodore a pleasant, at times even fascinating diversion, but only a diversion. From first to last, its animal life surpassed all other interests. For example, as soon as he had completed paying his respects to the remnants of Alexandria's former glories, he hurried to one of the city's markets in search of birds that might in future grace the interior of his Manhattan museum cabinets. Almost at once he spotted a quail, one of a species new to him. Theodore's diary best relates what then followed: "I seized the quail and said (in English) 'how much?' He [the Egyptian owner] held up eight fingers and said something in Arabic of which I only understood the word piastre. 'I'll give you two,' said I holding up that number of fingers. A shake of the head from him and he put up seven. I put up three; he put up six; I put up four and he accepted it! for exactly half of its original price." As a closing remark to his description of this bit of cold-blooded dickering, Theodore soberly declared, "Arabs always talk a great deal."[16]

The six-hour train ride through the delta of the Nile, from Alexandria to Cairo, provided Theodore with ample time and opportunity to observe the animals of the Nile valley: "numerous birds of various species arose, while herds of buffaloes and zebus grazed quietly in the marshy fields. Among the birds were snipe, plover, quail, hawks, and great black vultures."[17] Though these were Old World birds, they were sufficiently similar to those of North America to be recognizable to Theodore. Before long he will be using the scientific as well as the common names here, too.

Before leaving England, first in Liverpool and then again in London, Theodore had tried unsuccessfuly to find a book on Egyptian birds. Now, in Cairo, he found one. Writing at a much later date, he described its value to him: "I had no knowledge of the ornithology of Egypt, but I picked up in Cairo a book by an English clergyman whose name I have now forgotten, who described a trip up the Nile and in an appendix to his volume[s] gave an account of his bird collection. I wish I could remember the name of the author now, for I owe that book very much. Without it I should have been collecting entirely in the dark, whereas with its aid I could generally find out what the birds were."[18]

The author, whose name Roosevelt could not recall, was the Reverend Alfred Charles Smith, and the title of his book was *The Attractions of the Nile and Its Banks, a Journal of Travel in Egypt and Nubia* (2 vols., London: John Murray, 1868). In the appendix of this work (actually chapter 10 of the second volume), which was sixty-eight pages, the Reverend Smith had listed 108 species, each with its scientific name, and had provided brief to lengthy non-technical descriptions for most of them. He had included no illustrations, however. In spite of these shortcomings, this work was valuable to Theodore in identifying the birds of the Nile valley. Very little is known about the Reverend Smith other than that he was an enthusiastic amateur ornithologist, had previously collected in Switzerland and along the coasts of Spain and Italy, and had gained his knowledge of taxidermy from Charles Waterton (1782–1865), the English naturalist who had made a name for himself through several trips to the Guianas and his publication (1825) of *Wanderings in South America*.[19]

It had been the Roosevelts' plan to ascend the Nile, mainly to visit such celebrated ruins as those of Karnak, Thebes, and Luxor, these being situated near the first cataracts of the Nile and the city of Aswân. The trip had to be made by boat, as there was then no railroad upriver from Cairo. Theodore, Sr., rented a dahabeah, a light-draft houseboat equipped with lateen sails. The name of this particular craft was *Aboo Erdan* and, when Theodore learned that Aboo Erdan is Egyptian for ibis, he thereafter referred to their dahabeah as *The Ibis*.

While the houseboat was being manned, provisioned, and fitted out, the Roosevelts busied themselves in various ways, principally by making trips from Shepheards Hotel—then one of the world's best—to nearby places of interest, including the Sphinx and the Pyramids. At another time Theodore, seemingly by himself, visited a Cairo garden, where he "examined the habits of some birds through my spectacles. Of these there were two which were especially common, viz., the white wagtail (*Motacilla alba*) and the hooded crow (*Corvus cornix*)."[20] Two comments are in order: one, beyond doubt Theodore's spectacles were just that (not binoculars), for he later expressly mentioned the use of opera glasses; and, two, he was already using the Reverend Smith's Latin binomials.

Friday, December 13th, turned out to be an unusually happy and exciting one for Theodore. As his diary discloses he, for the first time, was permitted the use of a gun: "In the morning Father and I went out shooting and procured two small warblers and blew a chat to pieces in a walk of a hundred yards. One of those was the first bird I had ever shot and I was proportionately delighted. . . . In the afternoon I went out with the gun and shot a wagtail."[21]

If the use of a gun and the obvious glee over blowing "a chat to pieces" seem strange in a boy who was later to spend much of his life in the protection and preservation of wildlife, it must be understood that all knowledge of birds and other animals began with anatomical studies. Theodore was here, in Egypt, collecting in the same spirit that had motivated such great earlier American ornithologists as Alexander Wilson, John James Audubon, John Cassin, Spencer F. Baird, J. A. Allen, Elliott Coues, and others. Theodore shot birds as they had done, made birdskins as had been their custom, and in time placed his specimens in museums as they had done. Theodore's efforts should not be subject to criticism, any more than those of Wilson and Audubon were. The elevated position enjoyed by the science of ornithology today is largely due to the field and laboratory work of such men.

Years later Theodore Roosevelt would write that his "first real collecting as a student of natural history" began in Egypt.[22] This collecting was made possible by two fortuitous events—both occurring within the space of a few days. The first was his acquisition of the Reverend Smith's book, and the second, his father's permission to use a gun. The result was that almost overnight his interest in natural history attained new heights. Positive evidence of this upsurge is to be found in notebooks in which he recorded observations of Egyptian and Syrian animals. These notebooks, five in all, were filled with a wide-ranging assortment of natural history facts. He titled them: "Remarks on Birds"; "Ornithological Observations"; "Ornithological Record"; "Catalogue of Birds,"; and "Zoological Record."

Since much of the material of this chapter, and more particularly of the one following, is dependent on these notebooks, it seems important to describe each. "Remarks on Birds," the lengthiest of the five, is forty-eight typewritten pages[23] and describes forty-seven species of birds. "Ornithological Observations," ten pages in length, provides information, generally in few words, on sixty-one avian species. "Ornithological Record" is fifteen pages about sixty-four species. "Catalogue of Birds," nine pages, is a simple listing—by scientific name only—of sixty-two species. "Zoological Record," seven pages, is a listing of mammals, reptiles, and amphibia (mainly mammals) that Theodore collected and/or observed during the year abroad in various African, Asian, and European settings. It speaks well for Theodore's indomitable persistence that the pages of these five notebooks, when typed, number eighty-nine.

3

With crew and passengers aboard, the *Aboo Erdan* began its ascent of the Nile on the afternoon of December 20, 1872. This vessel would be home to the Roosevelts for two eventful months, and a more agreeable means of river transport could hardly have been found. It moved leisurely, made no set stops, and left at no appointed time or signal. Its motive power was the wind; when that failed, as often happened, the native crew poled and towed. On occasion the boat grounded on a sandbar long enough to permit Theodore and his father to clamber ashore in search of specimens. Theodore reported such an incident soon after the dahabeah had started upstream from Cairo: "Father and I went on shore shooting, and found ourselves in a great forest of Palms in a truly African scene. Among the Palms Hooded Crows, southern owls, Spanish sparrows, Senegal Doves and Sardinian Warblers flew and we . . . had splendid sport and returned with full gamebags. As a finishing touch to the morning sport we had a chase along shore after our Dahabeah which was passing us, but we finally overtook it. In the afternoon three flocks of Geese, Ducks and Ibises passed us and we saw a pelican fly by."[24]

The Roosevelts spent Christmas Day aboard the dahabeah. By then they were some 150 miles up the Nile from Cairo, and near the town of Beni Suef. In all likelihood Theodore never forgot that particular Christmas; his father gave him the shotgun he had been using during the previous two weeks. Of it and its eccentricities he later wrote: "My gun was a breech-loading, pin fire double-barrel, of French manufacture. It was an excellent gun for a clumsy and often absent-minded boy. There was no spring to open it, and if the mechanism became rusty it could be opened with a brick without serious damage. When the cartridges stuck they could be removed in the same fashion. If they were loaded, however, the result was not always happy, and I tattooed myself with partially unburned grains of powder more than once." [25]

It was natural that Theodore, Sr., should accompany his son on these first hunting trips, mainly to instruct him in the proper use of the double-barreled shotgun. At the same time, he seems to have enjoyed the companionship. Writing home soon after Christmas, he said: "I presented Teedie with a breech-loader at Christmas. . . . He is a most enthusiastic sportsman and has infused some of his spirit into me. Yesterday I walked through the bogs with him at the risk of sinking hopelessly and helplessly . . . *but I felt I must* keep up with Teedie." [26]

As the Egyptian craft continued its ascent of the Nile, the days passed rapidly, perhaps all too rapidly for Theodore. Corinne was an interested, if not fascinated, spectator: "Teedie and Father go out shooting every day, and so far have been very lucky. Teedie is always talking about it whenever he comes into the room,—in fact when he does come in the room you always hear the words 'bird' and 'skin.' . . . He never rests from his studies in natural history. When not walking through quivering bogs or actually shooting bird and beast, he, surrounded by the brown-faced and curious sailors, would seat himself on the deck of the dahabeah and skin and stuff the products of his sport." [27]

Once a bird had fallen to Theodore's gun, his most time-consuming job, and the one requiring the greatest skill, was the preparation of the birdskin. The steps are several, as many as twenty-five according to one ornithologist. [28] As a novice, Theodore possibly spent as much as an hour or more preparing a skin and was at times disappointed with the end product. As he became more practiced, he may have been able to complete satisfactorily a half dozen or more in the same length of time. Of course, he never came close, at any time, to matching the speed and competency of the seasoned, professional ornithologist. A long-remembered event at the Smithsonian Institution was a match arranged between Elliott Coues[29] and Henry W. Henshaw[30] to determine who was the more proficient in this art of preparing a birdskin. As an interested observer later described the match: "Accordingly, material having been prepared and supplied in the form of English Sparrows, they sat down side by side and commenced their work. Mr. Henshaw skinned his bird and prepared it for purposes of study in one minute and thirty-five seconds. Dr. Coues required one minute and forty seconds."[31]

In his diary entry of December 24, Theodore wrote: "My time today was fully occupied with skinning birds."[32] On succeeding days he was even busier, not only with skinning birds, but also with filling pages of his notebooks with observations. If Theodore's notebook pages are compared with those of the Reverend Smith's, one arrives at the conclusion that, of these two naturalists, the fourteen-year-old was the more advanced. The English clergyman, in describing each bird, supplied both common and scientific name and a few rambling, nontechnical notes. Theodore, additionally, when writing of a species, included date and place where collected, sex, anatomical detail, and stomach content. He also provided commentary of greater or lesser length on topics ranging from color and habitat to flight pattern, quality of song, and behavioral oddities. He often embellished his descriptions with technical terms, among them rictus, culmen, coverts, and gonys, terms that the Reverend Smith did not employ.

To Theodore, certain days along the Nile proved to be more exciting than others. That was particularly true of those on which he went afield on a rented donkey. The want of caution he now and then displayed, as he urged his mount to breakneck speed over the irregularities of the local terrain, amused some onlookers, but disturbed others. There was the day, for example, when a party of young men from another dahabeah hurriedly scattered as Theodore, astride his donkey, came charging up—reminiscent of the future Rough Rider—with the barrels of the breech-loader pointing menacingly in their direction.[33]

As the days went by, and Theodore encountered more and more birds unfamiliar to him, he apparently depended increasingly on the Reverend Smith's *Ornithology of Egypt* for identification—he apparently had no other source. Theodore's entry of December 29, which contains a rash of Latin binomials, is evidence: "In the morning, we passed a large flock of about sixty Egyptian geese. They were wading in the shallows, but soon came out into deep water, where they arranged themselves in an irregular long line and as we approached, divided themselves into several squads and flew off in various directions. At about 12 oclock we stopped and took a walk, during which I observed [but did not shoot, this being Sunday] no less than seven species of hawks, crows, stercho finches, and small waders in easy shot. In the afternoon we passed a large sandbar, on which I counted the following species of birds: *Charadrius crepitans Aegypticus, Ardea cenireans Nycticorax, Grus cenierea, Ciconia alba & nigra, Platella Cucondian, Anser albifrons, Phalacrocorax corbo, Anas forctas, achta creca."* [34]

Less than a week later, Theodore, in another diary entry, used additional Latin binomials, these being of sandpipers, snipe, and a plover. He then continued with information proving his growing familiarity with these species: "Both the snipe are rather rare here, although common in the Delta and are only found in the marshes. The green sand snipe and little ringed plover are tolerably common, but the common sand snipe can be seen everywhere, where there is any water." [35]

Events occurred that were entirely unrelated to natural history: some humorous, some annoying, and others exciting. According to Theodore, when the party stopped at Beni Suef, the town's American consul lent Theodore's father a horse on which he "had a splendid time, with mother accompanying him on a donkey." The next evening Theodore and his father made a courtesy call on the consul and "saw his harem." Annoying was a collision on December 27 of the *Aboo Erdan* with another dahabeah, resulting in a broken spar of the latter and a torn sail of the former. [36]

By January 2 Theodore may have felt that he was fast approaching the interior of "Darkest Africa." Evidencing excitement, he wrote, "At night we heard jackals." A few days later he reported three additional "excitements": (1) the *Aboo Erdan* broke her tiller, (2) a gust of wind snapped the mast of an accompanying boat, and (3) the entire family saw a rarely witnessed phenomenon, a mirage. [37]

As earlier stated, the principal attractions prompting the Roosevelts to undertake the long boat trip up the Nile were the ancient ruins of Karnak, Thebes, and Luxor. Those of Karnak, which they reached on January 10, are among the most magnificent on earth. They drew from Theodore some rather startling language, for a fourteen-year-old: "In the evening we visited Karnak by moonlight. It was not beautiful only, it was grand, magnificent and awe-inspiring. It seemed to take me back thousands of years, to the time of the Pharaohs and to inspire thought which can never be spoken, a glimpse of the ineffable, of the unutterable."[38]

On reaching Thebes, the family stayed there four days, in which time they visited the Colossi, the Rameseum, Medinet Habu, and Luxor. Although surrounded by the glories attributed to such ancient rulers as Amenhotop I, Thotmes I, Rameses I, and Queen Hatsheptu, Theodore's mind, if his diary is to be believed, was more on birds than on any of the temples, tombs, and ruins. Thus, on the same day he visited the great temple of Medinet Habu, he also "procured a vinous grosbeak, a sand-lark, four chats, a crested lark, a ringed plover, and a dove."[39]

In Egypt then, and for long afterward, there were no laws forbidding or restricting hunting, no closed seasons. Consequently, to the bark of the jackal and the cry of the snipe, there was also added on occasion the crack of the gun, including Theodore's. As he wandered about among fallen monoliths and broken tombs, he had no thought of their being in any way sacred or free of violation. Ornithologists had preceded him to Thebes and vicinity, among them the Reverend Smith, and others would soon follow. In one of Theodore's notebooks is to be found proof of a temporary insensibility to his august surroundings: "I shot one specimen of this chat [red-tailed chat, *Saxicola moesta*] from a column of the Ramesseum at Thebes."[40]

From Thebes, the Roosevelts moved on to Aswân. Here they remained for six days, with Theodore alternating hunts in the desert with visits to Philoe and the cataracts. On January 24 the family began the descent of the Nile. Twenty-three days later, on February 16, they were back in Cairo. On the return trip, Theodore continued collecting, there being only a few days in which he failed to obtain additional specimens for his museum. Though he converted the majority of these into birdskins, he did stuff and mount at least three: an Egyptian spur-winged lapwing (*Haplopterus spinosus*), a crocodile bird (*Pluvianus aegypticus*), and a white-tailed lapwing (*Vanellus leucurus*). All three are extant today, prized specimens of the American Museum of Natural History.

Throughout the months spent in Egypt, Theodore's store of energy seems to have been near inexhaustible, one reason being that not once did he suffer from asthma or any other ailment. The extent of his enthusiasm about the Nile events may be judged from a letter he wrote in late January to one of his aunts: "I think I have never enjoyed myself so much as in this month. There has always been something to do, for we could always fall back upon shooting when everything else failed. . . . I have had great enjoyment from the shooting here, as I have procured between one and two hundred skins. I expect to procure some more in Syria. Inform Emlen of this. As you are probably aware, Father presented me on Christmas with a double-barrelled, breech-loading shot gun, which I never move on shore without, excepting on Sundays. The largest bird I have yet killed is a crane which I shot as it rose from a lagoon near Thebes."[41]

Many years later (1909–10), as leader of the Smithsonian-Roosevelt Expedition, Theodore Roosevelt returned to Africa. After several months on the continent, mainly in British East Africa, he came out by way of Khartoum, Aswân, and Cairo. He had no difficulty in recalling birds that he had collected on his earlier visit, even though thirty-seven years had elapsed: "As we went down the Nile we kept seeing more and more of the birds which I remembered, one species after another; familiar cow-herons, crocodile plovers, noisy spurwing plover, black-and-white kingfishers, hoopoes, green bee-eaters, black-and-white chats, desert larks, and trumpeter bull-finches."[42]

Notes

1. Robinson, *My Brother*, 55.

2. Roosevelt, *Diaries of Boyhood*, 263.

3. Ibid. The genus *Plectrophanes* has since been updated to *Plectrophenax.*

4. Elliott Coues, *Birds of the Northwest* (Washington, D.C.: Government Printing Office, 1874), 118.

5. Theodore's Uncle Irving was Irvine Bulloch, his mother's brother.

6. Roosevelt, *Diaries of Boyhood*, 264.

7. Ibid.

8. Ibid., 265. The birds Theodore bought and skinned were probably the common snipe (*Gallinago coelestis*) and the gray partridge (*Perdix perdix*).

9. In 1872 the starling (*Sturnis vulgaris*) had not yet been introduced into the United States, hence Theodore's unfamiliarity with it.

10. Roosevelt, *Diaries of Boyhood*, 268–69.

11. Joseph Leidy (1823–91), eminent Philadelphia anatomist and pa-

51

leontologist. In 1853 Leidy was appointed anatomist at the University of Pennsylvania, a post he held until his death.

12. Robinson, *My Brother*, 54–55.

13. Years later Theodore wrote: "What would I not have given fifty years ago for a writer like Henry Fairfield Osborn, for some scientist who realized that intelligent laymen need a guide capable of building before their eyes the life that was, instead of merely cataloguing the fragments of the death that is." Roosevelt, *Works, Mem. Ed.*, 6:444.

14. Roosevelt, *Diaries of Boyhood*, 275.

15. Ibid., 276–77. Actually there were then two Cleopatra's Needles in Alexandria. In 1878 one of them was brought to London and, in 1880, the other to New York City.

16. Ibid., 278–79.

17. Ibid., 280.

18. Roosevelt, *Autobiography*, 19.

19. There is today, at the Sagamore Hill National Historic Site, a copy of the Reverend Smith's *Attractions of the Nile*, apparently the same copy that Theodore obtained in 1872 while in Cairo.

20. Roosevelt, *Diaries of Boyhood*, 286.

21. Ibid., 290–91.

22. Roosevelt, *Autobiography*, 19.

23. We here refer to typed copies of Theodore's original handwritten notebooks. It may be mentioned that Theodore, while on this trip, wrote at least one essay, "Ornithology of Egypt Between Cairo and Assouan."

24. Roosevelt, *Diaries of Boyhood*, 294.

25. Roosevelt, *Autobiography*, 18–19.

26. Robinson, *My Brother*, 56–57.

27. Ibid.

28. Frank M. Chapman, *Handbook of Birds of Eastern North America*, 7th ed. (New York: D. Appleton and Co., 1906), 24–27.

29. Elliott Coues (1842–99), brilliant American ornithologist, was born in Portsmouth, N.H., and educated in Columbian College (now George Washington University). For twenty years, at various posts, he served as surgeon in the U.S. Army. A prodigious writer on many topics, his most important and influential work was *Key to North American Birds*.

30. Henry Wetherbee Henshaw (1850–1930), American naturalist, was born in Cambridge, Mass. He later (1879–93) served with the U.S. Bureau of Ethnology and still later (1905–16) with the U.S. Biological Survey.

31. H. C. Yarrow, "Personal Recollections of Old Medical Officers," *Military Surgeon* 60 (1927): 588–99.

32. Roosevelt, *Diaries of Boyhood*, 296.

33. Robinson, *My Brother*, 57.

34. Roosevelt, *Diaries of Boyhood*, 298–99. It seems likely that Theodore, or whoever later transcribed his diary entries, was guilty of error. It is doubtful that *Charadrius crepitans Aegypticus* and *Ardea cenireans nycticorax* were trinomials, as they appear to be; in 1872 trinomials were rarities.

It is easier to believe that Theodore—or someone else—left out a couple of ampersands and that the name should read *Charadrius crepitans & Egypticus*, the former being, according to the Reverend Smith, the great plover and the latter the crocodile bird, and that the second should read *Ardea cinerea & Nycticorax*, namely, the common (or gray) heron and the night heron. Thereafter, *Grus cinieraa* is the common crane; *Anser albifrons*, the white-fronted goose; *Pelecanus onocrotalus*, the rosy pelican; *Phalacrocorax carbo*, the common cormorant; and *Ciconia alba & nigra*, the white and the black stork. *Anas forctas* may have been intended for *Anas boschas*, the "wild duck" of the Reverend Smith. The remaining names are still unidentifiable.

35. Ibid., 300.

36. Ibid., 296, 297.

37. Ibid., 300, 301.

38. Ibid., 304.

39. Ibid.

40. See Theodore's "Ornithological Record."

41. Robinson, *My Brother*, 60.

42. Theodore Roosevelt, *African Game Trails* (New York: Charles Scribner's Sons, 1910), 529.

5

"A Raven Was Wheeling Overhead"

AFTER A FEW DAYS in Cairo, the Roosevelts left Egypt for Syria on February 21, 1873, traveling in short time from one continent to another. Theodore, his father, and Elliott went overland to the Suez Canal and Port Said; the others of the family, preferring a less strenuous route, traveled by train to Alexandria and then by boat. Reunited in Port Said, they sailed to Jaffa, arriving on February 24.

Current maps differ conspicuously from those of 1873. The Syria that the Roosevelts visited was then a province of the Ottoman Empire (Turkey) and would remain so until World War II. Palestine (the Holy Land) in 1873 was merely a political division of Syria, and a relatively small one at that. Modern maps also include Lebanon, Israel, and Jordan, all independent countries, carved from the original Syria.

In Jaffa (now Tel Aviv–Jaffa), the Roosevelts tarried briefly, long enough to obtain horses for the trip that afternoon to Ramleh. The next morning early they left for Jerusalem. En route, Theodore reported seeing "some red partridges, ravens, bulbuls, owls, etc. but could not get any."[1] While in the Holy City, where the family stayed five days, they visited many of the more celebrated sites, among them the Church of the Holy Sepulchre, the Mount of Olives, the Mosque of Omar, the Wailing Wall, and, as Theodore wrote, "the peaceful garden of Gethsemane, where it was a delight to walk about."[2]

In Syria Theodore continued his almost daily regimen, begun along the Nile, of collecting on every possible opportunity. Not even the sanctity associated with the Holy City diverted him. On the morning of February 28, his third day in Jerusalem, he reported, "I went out hunting, with a good deal of success."[3] In his notebook,

"Remarks on Birds," Theodore identified the specimens he collected: two species, one being a great titmouse (*Parus major*) and the other a chaffinch (*Fringilla coelebs*). Thus he may well have been the first American ornithologist—if not the last—to collect and return to the United States birds from the ancient and modern capital of Israel.

On the morning of March 3, the family headed for Jericho. Theodore wrote that he saw "a good many birds" and killed some, that they stopped for lunch under "the shadow of a great rock in a thirsty land," and that after reaching Jericho, he "went out shooting immediately." He further said: "the country was rich, interspersed with streams and covered with trees and bushes, among which were birds of various species. Quails and partridges rose from the short grass, bulbuls and warblers hopped among the bushes, while doves, hawks, finches, jays and verdons flew among the trees."[4]

After a night in Jericho, the party (some thirty-five beasts of burden and twenty-five persons) visited the nearby Jordan River, and then the Dead Sea. Theodore's diary entry of March 4 reads:

The way was green and fertile until we reached the holy river, where we found a number of Pilgrims assembled. We took a delicious bath in the Jordan which is what we should call a rather small creek in America. After we left the Jordan the way was very desolate and through a sandy desert. We reached the Dead Sea (which is a singularly beautiful lake) in time for lunch. Of course we bathed in it. It was a strange bath. You could not sink. You could really sit upright in deep water. The after effects were by no means unpleasant. We then rode off to the mountains and then a perfect scene of desolation burst upon us. The mountains were bare and barren, the plants were dried up, and the only living things in sight were a huge vulture that was soaring over the valley, and a black raven that was wheeling overhead.[5]

The party spent that night near a convent, where their tents were almost blown away, and then proceeded to Bethlehem. Here they stopped long enough to view "the place of the Nativity" and then went on to Hebron, with Theodore obtaining "two very pretty little finches" along the way. On the next day they were again in Jerusalem.[6]

From Jerusalem, the Roosevelts returned to Jaffa, where on the morning of March 9 they took passage on a boat for Beirut. That evening Theodore revealed, "In the afternoon was very seasick";

that night, in a Beirut hotel—which was "middling"—"I had an attack of asthma." In Beirut Theodore, Sr., quickly arranged for a trip to the ruins of Baalbek, less than fifty miles northeast of Beirut. Traveling again by horseback, it took the party one full day and parts of two others to reach Baalbek. On the first day out, Theodore failed to get even one bird, but on the second, where the family stopped for lunch, he "procured a swallow, a bunting and some other birds." On the third day (March 14), he reported at greater length: "We had a beautiful canter from Abla to Baalbek, which we did in rather over three hours. The ruins are, with the exception of Karnak the grandest and most magnificent I have ever seen, and they gave me the same feeling as to contemplate the mighty temples of Thebes." He then went on to say that, in the afternoon, he had collected "a yellow throated finch, a lark and a gardel."[7] Beyond much doubt, Theodore had been briefed in advance about Baalbek, the ancient name of which was Heliopsis, so that he knew the city dated back to the Roman period, when it was a major city in the worship of Baal, one of the deities of ancient Semitic peoples having power over the soil's fertility and the size of crops.

The next stop on the Roosevelts' itinerary was Damascus, only about forty-five miles distant, but requiring two overnight stops. Theodore experienced ups and downs, physically, during this journey. On the morning of the first day, with fortune favoring him, he succeeded in collecting "a number of gardels, warblers, sparrows, finches and linnets." That night, however, he "had a bad attack of Asthma and Cholera Morbus."[8] On the third day, nearing Damascus and apparently completely recovered from his recent ailments, he was able to engage in a bit of sport so novel and exhilarating that he described it at length:

while riding from Baalbek to Damascus . . . I came to where two jackals had just pulled down a goat, and were devouring him, while sixty or seventy vultures waited attendance. At my approach they [the jackals] made off, and I followed one which was carrying a shoulder of the goat in its jaws, and though the ground was fearfully bad, being intersected by deep gullies and ravines, and covered by loose stones of every size and shape, yet thanks to the surefootedness and cat like activity of my Syrian horse, I pressed him so hard that he was forced to drop his booty. The chase was very exciting and I was within a few yards of him when he jumped into a ravine some twelve feet deep and clambered up the opposite side. My horse nearly went into the ravine, and after finally finding a crossing place I could see no trace of the jackal.[9]

The Roosevelts spent four days in Damascus. Theodore's diary discloses that he and the others visited the horse market, "the Bazaars," the mosque of St. John, "the famous general Abd-El-Keader," and the home of the American consul. On three of the four days in Damascus, Theodore hunted. He said that he did his hunting "round Damascus," which may—or may not—have been his way of stating that he had done his hunting beyond the city limits. On one of these days (March 19), the English consul, a Mr. Greene, "kindly took me out shooting. Procured a squirrel and a jay." On other days Theodore had better luck, obtaining a thrush, two warblers, a pipit, a blackbird, some titmice, several chaffinches, and a "Hooper," this last being perhaps a hoopoe.[10] Theodore lost no time in preparing the skins of these birds and in cleaning the skull of the squirrel. The latter, as Theodore's "Zoological Record" reveals, became skeletal specimen No. 34 of his Old World collection of mammals.

On March 22 the Roosevelts left Damascus for Beirut, where they arrived late on the same day. Theodore's diary supplies an excellent compression of the major events of the day's trip: "We were up at three in the morning and started in the Dilegence [stagecoach] at halfpast four. We changed horses ten times and arrived here in Beirut at five. . . . We passed a herd of Gazelles on the way."[11]

The travels of Theodore Roosevelt in this part of Syria ended three days later, on March 25, when he and the others of his family left Beirut on a vessel that took them to Athens. For Theodore, who was seasick again, this Mediterranean voyage produced just one highlight. He described it in his diary entry of March 27: "A number of birds flew on board today and I offered a reward for them, in consequence of which received some hawks, two ———, a chat, a cuckoo and a warbler." Immediately following this unexpected, fortuitous avian windfall, Theodore, according to his father, stuffed his prizes, "to the edification of a large audience."[12]

After a few days in Athens, the family moved on to Constantinople, where they stayed for more than a week. It was while here that Theodore, in a letter to Edith Carow, reported a personal loss. He wrote: "I think I have enjoyed myself more this winter than I ever did before. Much to add to my enjoyment Father gave me a gun at Christmas which rendered me happy and the rest of the family miserable. I killed several hundred birds with it and then went and lost it."[13] Though Theodore gave not even a hint as to when or where he might have lost his breech-loader—perhaps it was during the hurried carriage ride from Damascus to Beirut—there can be no doubt that the loss, to him, was a near tragedy. For three months it had been a constant companion, and at least seven more would elapse before he obtained another.

Leaving Constantinople, the Roosevelts traveled by boat and railway car to Vienna. To the active Theodore, the long trip was punctuated by boredom, more seasickness, and, on one occasion, another asthmatic attack. Life brightened soon after he had arrived in Vienna, with West Roosevelt coming from Bonn to join him. Neither of them having a gun, they reverted to their former practice of buying animals for dissection. During West's stay in Vienna, lasting six days, the two boys "skinned" several birds and some rabbits. Apparently they were profligate in the use of arsenic, for, on the day West left to return to Bonn, Theodore wrote of buying a "black cock" and of using "up all my arsenic on him."[14]

Theodore and West, during this Vienna interlude, had exercised their taxidermic skills in the hotel room jointly occupied by Theodore and Elliott. The latter, by nature a tidy individual, failed to share in Theodore's and West's disruptive activities in the room, however much they advanced the aims of science. As a result, he sought out his father and asked if it would be too expensive for him to have a room of his own. His reason became obvious when his father visited the room. Jars, bottles, and boxes containing preserved specimens stood about on tables and window ledges. The aroma of chemical pervaded the air, and, as Elliott was quick to point out, visceral parts of recently dissected animals occupied space in the only water basin. To Theodore, Sr., the room manifestly resembled a laboratory more than a hotel room, but how he, as the supreme arbiter, settled this delicate matter has not been revealed.[15] Nor have the reactions of possibly startled chambermaids! At a later date, Theodore confessed: "I suppose that all growing boys tend to be grubby; but the ornithological small boy, or indeed the boy with the taste for natural history of any kind, is generally the very grubbiest of all."[16]

"At 10 P.M. on the 14th [of May 1873]," wrote Theodore, "we two boys (with Father), left for Dresden, where we are to stay in a

German family for the summer."[17] After seeing Theodore and Elliott settled in their new home, Theodore, Sr., left for the United
States. Soon afterward, Mrs. Roosevelt and Bamie brought Corinne
to Dresden and then quickly departed for Carlsbad "to take the
cure." Thus "we three," for the first time in their lives, were free of
parental guidance, which possibly was the way Theodore, Sr.,
wanted it.

2

The idea of a summer's study in Germany for Theodore, Elliott, and
Corinne had been decided upon before the Roosevelts left New York
City. That they eventually chose Dresden over other German cities
seems to have been due primarily to the presence then in Dresden
of Lucy Elliott, widow of Mittie's half-brother Stuart Elliott, and her
two children, Maud and John. Another reason was Theodore, Sr.'s
success, with the help of the American consul in Dresden, in finding
a reputable German family willing to take the children into their
home for the summer and to teach them German. This family, a
prominent one, consisted of Herr Minkwitz, who was a member of
the German Reichstag, Frau Minkwitz, and six children, four girls
and two boys. The eldest daughter, Fräulein Anna, undertook the
job of teaching the children German. She soon established a stiff
study schedule. "The plan of the day is this," Theodore soon wrote,
"halfpast six, up and brakfast which is through at halfpast seven,
when we study until nine; repeat till halfpast twelve, have lunch,
and study till three, when we take coffee and have till tea (at seven)
free. After tea we study till ten, when we go to bed."[18]

During the summer Theodore also received instruction in drawing from "the painter Wegener, a specialist in prairie scenes and the
author of numerous books on animal life."[19] Between German lessons, Theodore made several black-and-white sketches of animals
and a few colored ones. Some of these were good enough to warrant
the conclusion that if Theodore had persisted—which he did not—
he might eventually have achieved a measure of success as an animal portraitist. But Wegener did more than teach his American pupil the fundamentals of drawing. On occasion he accompanied
Theodore on "rambles through the neighboring hills"[20] and, being a

writer of books about animals, he surely must have helped Theodore in the identification of local thrushes, warblers, and other birds.

From his outings, whether alone or with Wegener, Theodore customarily returned with animals that found quarters in the Mink-witz home. He later recorded some of the consequences. In one place he wrote: "Whenever I could get out into the country I col-lected specimens industriously and enlivened the household with hedgehogs and other small beasts and reptiles which persisted in escaping from partially closed bureau drawers." And in another place he admitted, "My scientific pursuits cause the family a good deal of consternation."[21]

For much of the information about the Dresden summer, it is necessary to consult letters written by Theodore (he had discontin-ued his diary on leaving Vienna). Rarely did Theodore write a letter without referring, in one way or another, to animals and, at the same time, interjecting a bit of humor. In late June he reported to his mother an important development: "Picture to yourself an anti-quated woodchuck with his cheeks filled with nuts, his face well-oiled, his voice hoarse from gargling and a cloth resembling in texture and cleanliness a second-hand dustman's castoff stocking around his head; picture to yourself that, I say, and you will have a good likeness of your hopeful offspring while suffering from an at-tack of the mumps."[22]

Theodore's mother may well have laughed aloud as she read this letter; certainly there was nothing in it to give her undue concern, mumps being one of the childhood diseases generally considered in-evitable and ordinarily harmless. Within a few days, however, she received another letter from Theodore, this one reporting an attack of asthma. It did not bother him much, he said, "except for the fact that I cannot speak, without blowing up like an abridged edition of a hippopotamus."[23]

Though Theodore tried to make light of his asthma, his mother was not fooled. She hurried to Dresden, and, finding that his condi-tion had worsened, bundled him off to the Swiss Alps. Theodore remained there for the better part of July, until he could breathe freely again. Before returning to Dresden, he wrote reassuringly— and zoologically—to his father: "I took several long walks today. . . . In the damp woods the 'Mavis and Merle'[24] were singing, by the wayside warblers, finches and titmice were chirping and trilling, larks rose from the wayside when the road led through fields, and throstles [thrushes] and wagtails flew in front of me while it led through forests."[25]

During this Alpine interlude Theodore's studies of the German language appreciably lagged. As a consequence, on his return to Dresden he at once asked Fräulein Anna to lengthen his daily assignments in German. In days ahead Theodore must have made exceptional progress in the language, for he was soon informing his father that, whenever not otherwise occupied, he had been spending all of his time "translating [German texts of] natural history."[26] This bit of information surprises, for technical German is difficult, and especially for one schooled briefly in the language—no more than two to three months in Theodore's case. And the information surprises even more when one learns the names of the men who wrote the natural history texts Theodore had been translating. The names are to be found in Theodore's "Zoological Record," this boyhood notebook consisting of two parts. Prefacing the first part, which is a listing of the mammals Theodore had identified in Africa, Asia, and Europe, is this statement: "Classified according to Reichenbach." Prefacing the second part, which is about reptiles and batrachians of the same area, are these words: "Classified according to Brehm." So, who were Reichenbach and Brehm, to whom Theodore was indebted? The former was Heimrich Gottlieb Ludwig Reichenbach (1793–1879), a noted German zoologist, who, beginning in 1820, served as professor of the natural history sciences in the University of Dresden. The latter was Alfred Edmund Brehm (1829–84), another celebrated German scientist. It was Brehm who established (1869) the Berlin Aquarium, among his several other outstanding accomplishments. It is impossible to say, with absolute certainty, which books of Reichenbach and Brehm Theodore had consulted in attempting to identify the specimens he had listed in his "Zoological Record." Educated guesses, however, would be Reichenbach's *Regnum Animale* and Brehm's *Thierleben*.

Theodore's mother seems to have given more thought to her son's health than to his precocity. Shortly before she and the children left Germany to return to New York City she allegedly said, in the presence of Fräulein Anna, "I wonder what will become of my

Teedie." To which the latter replied, "You must not be anxious about him, he will surely one day be a great professor, or who knows, he may become even President of the United States."[27]

3

Theodore could not say of this 1872–73 trip abroad what he had said of the previous one: that he had gained nothing in particular from it. His diary, occasional letters, and natural history notebooks supply abundant evidence that he had benefited tremendously. His diary is extremely valuable, providing a running, day-to-day account of events as they occurred and names of places visited. It contains, too, as already noted, a considerable amount of information about birds, though not nearly what is found in his natural history notebooks.

Without a close examination of Theodore's notebooks, it is next to impossible for anyone to comprehend the amount of attention he paid to the avian population of Egypt and Syria. After he had collected a specimen and prepared its skin, it became routine for him then to write a description of it. A typical description, one chosen more or less at random, is that of the green bee-eater (*Merops viridis* = *M. orientalis*):

Ad[ult] ♂ Benesoolf [Beni Suef, Egypt]. December 24th, 1872. Length 10.1 [Inches] Expanse 11.2 Wing 3.5 Tail 5.5 Bill 1.1 Tarsus 5. Middle toe .7 Hind toe .3.

Bill long, without bristles, except around the rictus, where there are a few short ones, decurved, making the culmen convex, the gonys concave. Nostrils small and round. Tarsus extremely short. Toes slender, outer one longer than inner, reaching beyond the centre of middle claw. Wing long, 2d primary longest, tertiaries slightly longer than secondaries. Tail long, nearly even, the two central tail feathers with attenuated and much elongated tips, reaching three inches beyond the rest of tail.

Colour green. Legs brown. Bill, stripe through eye, band on throat, and tips of central tail feathers black. Primaries and secondaries rich golden brown, the latter with deep the former with faint brownish tinge. The green colour is deepest on the back and wing coverts. Just below the eye there is a bright bluish green spot.

This beautiful little bird is very common on the Nile, and adds greatly to the beauty of the Egyptian scene, its vivid coloring and quick movements rendering it very conspicuous. It haunts especially the palm and sont [*Acacia arabica*] groves, but I have often seen it on the open ground. Its manners resemble to a great extent those of the flycatchers. Sitting on some lofty palm it surveys the surrounding neighborhood with a quick vivacious eye. Suddenly it swoops off through a glade of trees with such quickness as to remind one of a humming bird, and returns with an insect in its bill. This, if small, is swallowed immediately, but a large beetle usually needs a good deal of battering against the branch before it can be safely swallowed.[28]

As noted, Theodore began this description by providing both common and scientific names (the latter doubtless obtained from the Reverend Smith's work). He then continued by stating that the specimen in hand was an adult male, that it had been collected at the small Egyptian village of Beni Suef, two days' travel by dahabeah south of Cairo, and that the date had been the day before Christmas. Thereafter the description consists of three clearly defined parts: measurements, external anatomy, and personal observations. Theodore's notebooks disclose that he measured approximately fifty different species and that the number of measurements in each instance was the same as with the green bee-eater, namely seven.

Theodore's anatomical descriptions (also of some fifty other species) engender more interest. That of the bee-eater definitely impresses, for the simple reason that one is quite unprepared for Theodore's use of such technical terms as rictus, culmen, and gonys,[29] terms which, to our knowledge, he had not previously employed. By now, however, they were definitely a part of his vocabulary, and he seems to have felt obliged, in writing of the Aegypto-Syrian birds, to emulate the language of the great ornithologists of the past.

While Theodore's absorption in measurements and attention to anatomical detail may fail to capture the interest of the average reader, the same is not necessarily true of his personal observations. These fall into different categories, among them habits, protective coloration, vocalizations, flight, and food. Each merits thoughtful consideration.

Habits

As a rule, Theodore Roosevelt quickly and effortlessly noted oddities of behavior. In his "Remarks on Birds," when writing of the ziczac (*Vanellus spinosus*), he told of what a nuisance that bird could be to the hunter: "You are nearly within shot of your game, when a zic-zac observes you. It immediately starts up from the ground, and commences to utter a series of sharp, clacking cries. . . . This would be bad enough, even if it flew off immediately, but the idea of doing so never enters its head, for it soars over your head, wheels rapidly round and runs by the game, apparently for the purpose of startling it, brushes by your face, and in the meantime, its shrieks would scare a blind donkey let alone a wild animal."

In another of his natural history notebooks, "Ornithological Observations," Theodore remarked at some length on the habits of the griffon vulture (*Gyps fulvus*): "It was found in every wild locality in these lands. . . . Thus I found it alike in the lofty, snow-capped Lebanon Mts. and in the low, marshy Nile Delta; In the fertile plain of the Jordan and in the arid Nubian desert. It soars at an immense height, so as frequently to become invisible. The quickness with which a carcass will attract these birds is perfectly wonderful. Once, near Damascus, I saw two jackals pull down a goat, and although no vultures were then to be seen, in less than five minutes about eighty had gathered about its body! It hunts purely by sight."

Ever since the writings of Darwin and Waterton in South America, and those of Audubon and John Bachman[30] in the United States, the vultures have been a subject of controversy, first as to whether they possessed a sense of smell, and second—after it was established that they did—whether sight or smell was responsible for their finding food. Most of the early observers opted for sight. However, in 1927 and again in 1935, Frank M. Chapman,[31] while studying the wildlife of Barro Colorado Island, Canal Zone, ran a series of experiments in an effort to settle the controversy. It was his conclusion that, on this island, the nose of the vulture "served him better than his eyes."[32] But vultures—of which worldwide there are numerous species—differ, both as to kind and habitat. Barro Colorado Island is covered with dense tropical forest, while the region around Damascus is relatively treeless. It is difficult, therefore, to find fault with Theodore's conclusion that the vultures he observed found the freshly killed goat "purely by sight." Moreover, supporting Theodore's opinion is a recent statement by a prominent ornithologist of the American Museum of Natural History: "After the long controversy it was finally proved that some (but not all) New World vultures, in particular the turkey vulture, do have a sense of smell that aids in finding food under certain circumstances, whereas it is believed that all of the Old World vultures lack any useful sense of smell."[33]

In "Remarks on Birds" occurs another outstanding example of Theodore's close attention to bird behavior, this being a description of the roosting habits of the cattle egret. After remarking that these birds roost in great numbers in gont trees on an island near Cairo, he continued: "I used to sit on the dahabeah and watch them by the hour with an opera glass. At about half past four they would commence to arrive in parties of from ten to twenty. They would soon be seen coming from various quarters in large numbers, and the tops of the trees would be whitened by the immense multitudes perching on them, for they did not, apparently, enter in among the branches, but perched right on the top. As each flock arrived it went through various evolutions before alighting. During these movements they seemed to follow a leader as with geese and ducks."

That Theodore actually watched these birds "by the hour" is not difficult to believe. For one thing, he rarely if ever exaggerated, and, for another, he often, as his natural history notebooks attest, remained glued to a spot long enough to satisfy himself as to a particular action of a bird. It can be said, too, that Theodore's observations were his own, not one of them having been copied from the Reverend Smith's ornithological account nor, to our knowledge, from anyone else's.

Protective Coloration

In Egypt, on the borders of the desert, Theodore encountered two species of "chats" or wheatears, one apparently being *Saxicola* (*Oenanthe*) *saltatrix* and the other *Saxicola* (*Oenanthe*) *lugens.* The former, according to Theodore, was inconspicuously colored and "relied for protection more to escaping observation by its similarity in coloring to the soil than to its own vigilance." The latter, with "its bold black and white colouring," relied for protection upon alertness, instead of crouching low like the former. One day Theodore spotted one standing on a pile of stones at the moment a hawk stooped at it. It "immediately dodged into the heap, running between the stones like a rat, and remained there, of course in perfect safety until the hawk departed."[34] The likelihood definitely exists that no naturalist acquainted with these two species had earlier noted, as Theodore did, that the inconspicuously colored one instinctively sought safety by remaining motionless, while the other, boldly marked, relied upon agility to save itself.

Vocalizations

As a rule, birds sing only while nesting and thus sing rarely in winter, the season during which Theodore visited Egypt and Syria. However, in all seasons, birds utter a variety of chirps, chirrups, squawks, and other sounds. Theodore's ears, which rarely failed him when he was afield, picked up other notes. A prominent characteristic of the trumpeter bullfinch, he said, was "its peculiar, rattling, trumpet-like call or cry, from which it is named."[35] And a species of lapwing (or peewit), when alarmed, "uttered a loud 'peetweet,' like the cry of some of our sandpipers."[36]

At least two species of Old World birds sang for Theodore. One of these, identified earlier as *Saxicola (Oenanthe) lugens*, sang, Theodore wrote, "very sweetly and continuously, even at midday, being perched meanwhile on some rock or the dried stalk of a weed." The other songster was identified only as *Galerida cristata*. Of it Theodore wrote: "It was one of the few birds that sang during winter, always uttering its sweet notes while soaring in the air; but its song was not as beautiful as the skylark's."[37]

Food

While preparing his birdskins, Theodore routinely examined the stomach content of each avian species he had collected. In so doing, he could determine, among other things, whether the species was beneficial or harmful to mankind. As to the kestrel and its diet, he was soon in a position to declare: "It is, I may say, the only falcon (excepting the Fish Hawk) which deserves to be protected on account of its services to man, for its food consists principally of field mice, frogs, and occasionally the smaller birds."[38] About another hawk (*Falco cenchris*), Theodore did not feel so charitable. Its crop, he discovered, was "filled with remains of larks and lizards."[39]

As birds require food, so do humans. On February 7 Theodore reported shooting sixteen pigeons and, three days later, eleven more.

These were, of course, common pigeons, such as those found abundantly in cities large and small worldwide. Why did Theodore shoot so many of these birds, unless to provide an acceptable change in diet for passengers aboard the dahabeah? The Reverend Smith, as Theodore knew, had eaten Nile pigeons on a fairly regular basis.

On occasion Theodore, as well as others of his family, seems to have enjoyed the flesh of other Egyptian and Syrian birds. That of the hoopoe, according to Theodore, was "very good eating," also that of the laughing dove and the tattler.[40] Other birds that Roosevelt shot may also have been edible, and, if so, they too possibly went into the Roosevelt pot.

4

Roosevelt's five natural history journals detailing his experiences with Old World animals represent a tremendous amount of sustained, dedicated, and gainful labor. Demands of time and space limit the use of excerpts however. These documents, taken as a whole, disclose the youthful Roosevelt's strong-willed persistence, his eager striving to emulate his ornithological antecedents, his manifest success in widening his own faunal knowledge, his near ceaseless illustrations of observational competence, and his obvious ability, for one so young, to express himself in language adequate to rouse envy in many individuals of more advanced years.

Notes

1. Roosevelt, *Diaries of Boyhood*, 312.
2. Ibid., 313.
3. Ibid., 315.
4. Ibid., 316. According to *The Century Dictionary* (1903), the bulbul is "the Persian name of the nightingale, or a species of nightingale, rendered familiar in English poetry by Moore, Byron, and others. The same name is also given in southern and southeastern Asia to sundry other birds." To date, we have been unable to identify the "verdons" Theodore encountered near Jericho.
5. Roosevelt, *Diaries of Boyhood*, 317.
6. Ibid., 318.
7. Ibid., 319.
8. Ibid., 321. Theodore's "gardels" defeat us, though perhaps it is a word that suffered in transcription.

9. For Theodore's description of this jackal hunt, see "Zoological Record."

10. Roosevelt, *Diaries of Boyhood*, 323–24.

11. Ibid., 324.

12. Ibid., 325; Robinson, *My Brother*, 66.

13. Robinson, *My Brother*, 67.

14. Roosevelt, *Diaries of Boyhood*, 332.

15. Hagedorn, *Boys' Life*, 44–45.

16. Roosevelt, *Autobiography*, 20.

17. Roosevelt, *Diaries of Boyhood*, 335.

18. Elting E. Morison, John M. Blum, and John J. Buckley, eds., *The Letters of Theodore Roosevelt*, 8 vols. (Cambridge, Mass.: Harvard University Press, 1951), 1:10–11; hereafter cited as Morison, *Letters*.

19. Putnam, *Theodore Roosevelt*, 1:103.

20. Hagedorn, *Boys' Life*, 47.

21. Roosevelt, *Autobiography*, 20; Robinson, *My Brother*, 77–78.

22. Edmund Morris, *The Rise of Theodore Roosevelt* (New York: Coward, McCann and Geoghegan, 1979), 72.

23. Robinson, *My Brother*, 78–79.

24. The mavis is the British song-thrush (*Turdus ericetorum*) and the merle the European blackbird (*Turdus merula*).

25. Putnam, *Theodore Roosevelt*, 106.

26. Robinson, *My Brother*, 76.

27. Morris, *Rise of Roosevelt*, 73.

28. "Remarks on Birds."

29. The rictus is the gape of the mouth of a bird, the mouth opening. The culmen is the dorsal ridge of a bird's bill. The gonys is the lower outline of a bird's bill and is to the under mandible what the ridge or culmen is to the upper mandible.

30. John Bachman (1790–1874), American naturalist and clergyman, was born in Rhinebeck, N.Y., and in 1815 accepted a pulpit in Charleston, S.C. In 1831 Audubon spent a month there with him and, in due course, collaborated with Bachman in the production of *The Viviparous Quadrupeds of North America* (1845–49).

31. Frank Michler Chapman (1864–1951), American ornithologist, was born in Englewood, N.J. He is remembered as founder and editor of *Bird-Lore*, a popular magazine about birds, as head of the department of ornithology (1920–42) of the American Museum of Natural History, and as the author of *Handbook of Birds of Eastern North America* (1895), *Autobiography of a Bird-Lover* (1933), and many other books.

32. Frank M. Chapman, *My Tropical Air Castle* (New York: D. Appleton and Co., 1927), 149–66, and his *Life in an Air Castle* (New York: D. Appleton-Century Co., 1938), 85–92.

33. Dean Amadon to author, May 5, 1979.

34. "Ornithological Record."

35. "Remarks on Birds."

36. "Ornithological Observations."
37. "Ornithological Record."
38. Ibid.
39. "Remarks on Birds."
40. "Ornithological Record." The laughing dove is technically known as *Streptopelis senegalis.* The binomial for the tattler is *Tringa ochropus.*

6

"Cutting the Most Remarkable Pigeonwings"

THE TRANSAtlantic liner S.S. *Russia,* with Mrs. Roosevelt and the three children aboard, dropped anchor in New York harbor on November 5, 1873. By that date the migratory birds, except for a few stragglers, had all departed for warmer climes, and the trees, so recently extravagantly colored, were now mostly barren of their leaves. It is doubtful if Theodore immediately noticed the scarcity of birds or the defoliated trees. His mind was filled with thoughts of the new Roosevelt home he had yet to see. The carriage that conveyed the family from the docks did not travel the relatively short distance to 28 East 20th Street, Theodore's birthplace and heretofore his home. Instead, it took them north almost to Central Park, to 6 West 57th Street. Here, during the last few months, Theodore, Sr., had supervised the construction of a dwelling that, because of its size and imposing exterior, would, he hoped, better reflect his standing in the city as benefactor and philanthropist.

In building a new and larger home, Theodore, Sr., had also given special attention to needs of his children. Young Theodore, for one, was perfectly delighted on learning that increased space in the garret had been provided for his museum. At 28 East 20th Street, it will be recalled, his collection had been stored in a small closet at the end of an upstairs hallway. All of the children expressed delight when shown a fully equipped gymnasium on the top floor.[1]

Theodore was understandably eager to unpack and display his bee-eaters, wagtails, bullfinches, and other Old World birds; and, while so doing, he no doubt talked knowingly and at some length about them to any and all listeners. He was impatient, also, to question Emlen as to the present status of the Roosevelt Museum, in

70

particular about its growth during his absence. Above all, he wished to infuse new life into it. With that in mind, he soon called a meeting of the museum's directors. Minutes of that meeting, held on December 26, 1873, read as follows:

There has been no meeting for two years owing to the absence of a majority of the members in foreign countries collecting specimens.

Whereas the size of the Museum requires entire reorganization it is resolved that a new constitution be adopted.

Said new constitution having been read and signed by the directors.

It is also resolved that Mrs. James K. Gracie, Miss Elizabeth Lewis, Mr. Elliott Roosevelt and Mr. John Elliott be constituted members.[2]

It is also resolved that in consideration of the great services rendered by Messrs. Elliott Roosevelt and John Roosevelt that they be not obliged to pay any initiation fee.

It is also resolved that any of the directors be authorized to sell or exchange duplicate specimens of the Museum the proceeds to be given to the Museum.

It is also resolved that Mr. Theodore Roosevelt, Jr. President of the Roosevelt Library[3] present at the next meeting written proposition for the incorporation of the Library and Museum.

Present at the meeting:

T. Roosevelt, Jr.
J. W. [James West] Roosevelt
W. E. [William Emlen] Roosevelt

Although this meeting was characterized by apparent enthusiasm and gave promise of increased activity in the near future, the directors did not officially convene again until the following spring, on April 6, 1874, and then only briefly. The minutes of this meeting—consisting of just one sentence—read: "It was resolved that eight dollars 50/100 ($8.50) be allowed Mr. T. Roosevelt, Jr. for the purchase of ornithological specimens."

With this terse statement, the "Record of the Roosevelt Museum" came to an abrupt end. As the sole source of information available about the birth, infancy, and later development of the Roosevelt Museum of Natural History, it is an important document. If there were to be no more directors' meetings, as appears likely, it may be surmised that West and Emlen soon found and developed other and more appealing interests. But not so Theodore; he continued his collecting and taxidermic endeavors with undiminished, even accelerated, vigor and enthusiasm. In months ahead, with Theodore adding more and more specimens to the Roosevelt Museum, that institution grew steadily and substantially larger.

2

In mid-ocean, on October 28, 1873, Theodore turned fifteen, a weed of a boy shooting up to manhood. Knowledge of Theodore's appearance at that age seems to rest solely on one photograph. This is a group picture made in Dresden showing Theodore—then not quite fifteen—Elliott, Corinne, and their cousins John and Maud Elliott. In this photograph Theodore is seated, with chin in hand and face in profile. He had dressed up for the occasion, wore a white shirt, a tie, dark coat, and lighter-colored trousers. A large complement of hair, well-combed, spilled backward over his nape and coat collar. Biographers heretofore, apparently envisioning Theodore attired at all times in the clothes of the busy taxidermist, have described him as unkempt, with ill-fitting clothing befouled with blood and preservatives, and with face and hands badly in need of soap and water. One writer, apparently imagining Theodore always preoccupied with skinning birds, has said that he was "offensive to eye, ear and nostril. . . . reeked gently of arsenic."[4]

The Dresden photograph reveals Theodore's facial lineaments to be delicate, even peaked. Certainly that is true when they are compared with Elliott's, which are rounded and plump. There is, too, a suggestion of innocence about Theodore's face, as though he were posing, as he well may have been doing. Perhaps the most remarkable aspect of his countenance, no matter how closely it may be scrutinized, is its total lack of resemblance to the commanding visage of the Theodore Roosevelt of later years.

Theodore, at fifteen, was neither saint nor savage. There can be little doubt that his parents, ever concerned about his health, had been slow at times to discipline him. Maud Elliott's statement that he "thought he could do things better than anyone else"[5] may well have been true. Even his mother admitted that on occasion he was "very rude and rough in manner,"[6] though she may have been persuaded to that view by his boxing, which she regarded as a "horrible amusement."[7] Like most boys he was mischievous, though cruelty, cowardice, idleness, and untruthfulness, all traits discouraged by his father, seem to have been foreign to his nature. Serving him well in his natural history pursuits were such traits as a remarkable power of concentration and grim doggedness. One writer has emphasized yet another characteristic: "There was about him an almost terrible single-mindedness. He saw the goal and nothing else. If it seemed necessary to the interests of science to keep defunct field-mice in the family [ice box] he kept them there."[8]

At fifteen Theodore was on the threshold of manhood, and, though still an adolescent, his youthful body failed to conceal evidences of a mind in some ways keenly adult. It is not surprising, therefore, that he early began giving thought to a college education. His parents, having already fully realized "the unusual qualities of their son, the strength and power of his character,"[9] were in no real position to raise objections. After deciding that he would prefer Harvard to any other college, Theodore at once began preparing for the necessary entrance examinations.

Due in part mainly to the frequency of his boyhood illnesses, Theodore's education had been almost entirely the handiwork of tutors. At no time did he attend a public school, though he did study briefly in a nearby private school run by Professor McMullen. His record there indicated a sound mind, if not a sound body: grammar 89; arithmetic 92; geography 97; history 96; and spelling 88.[10] As a consequence of his unconventional education, Theodore had advanced beyond his age in certain subjects, notably history, geography, and zoology, but was woefully behind in Latin, Greek, and mathematics. Theodore would later write: "My first knowledge of Latin was obtained by learning the scientific names of the birds and mammals which I had collected."[11] This rather meager exposure to Latin did not lead to any appreciable increase in vocabulary or to a familiarity with the grammar and syntax of the English language. Because of his two years abroad, supplemented by Bamie's and Fräulein Anna's instruction, he could hold his own in French and German. Fortunately, Harvard required no entrance examination in spelling, a personal, perennial problem for Theodore.

To assist Theodore in preparing for the entrance examination, Theodore, Sr., chose Arthur Cutler, then a young and enterprising educator, who in 1876 would found in New York City the popular Cutler School. Theodore's study schedule under Cutler proved to be even more exacting than that required by Fräulein Anna, and it continued for more than two years. He studied six to eight hours daily, his only substantial breaks in this regimen occurring in summer when he customarily left the city for ten days or so on camping trips.[12] To his credit, Theodore kept with this schedule, right up to the day before he took the entrance examinations.

How did Theodore impress Cutler? At one time, when questioned, he spoke of his pupil's great energy and enthusiasm, and of his ability "to add up long rows of figures more rapidly than any other student he had ever had."[13] On another occasion, he emphasized "the alert, vigorous character of young Roosevelt's mind," and further said that Theodore "never seemed to know what idleness was. . . . Every leisure moment would find the last novel, some English classic or some abstruse book on natural history in his hands."[14]

Theodore may have found Latin difficult. Years later he would decry his inability to read Homer and Virgil in the original.[15] The relationship between Cutler and Theodore, at first strictly a student-teacher one, later developed into a warm, enduring friendship. "I certainly profited by my friendship with one of my tutors, Mr. Cutler," Theodore afterward wrote.[16]

During these months of intense preparation, Theodore's parents worried needlessly about his health. According to one source, Theodore regularly, in the family gymnasium, "boxed and wrestled . . . chinned himself and struggled with the parallel bars."[17] On milder winter days, he walked or skated in Central Park. One unlucky day, while skating, he fell on his head and was "senseless for several hours."[18]

3

For many years, the Roosevelt family had spent their summers either in New Jersey or in one town or another above Manhattan on the New York side of the Hudson River. In the spring of 1874 Theodore, Sr., changed the pattern. He rented a house in Oyster Bay, then a small community situated on the north shore of Long Island. Oyster Bay was less than thirty miles from New York City and could be reached either by train or by steamboat. By train the visitor took the 14th Street ferry to Hunter's Point—there then being no bridges spanning the East River—and then proceeded by railroad to Syosset, where he took a carriage to Oyster Bay six miles away.[19]

The architecture of the Long Island home must have pleased Mrs. Roosevelt and indeed may have been a factor in its selection. With its white exterior, spacious veranda, and four columns rising two stories, it bore a marked resemblance to Bulloch Hall in Roswell, Georgia, her birthplace. Its precise location was on Cove Neck, some two miles southwest of Sagamore Hill, a place which in future would play a significant role in American history. To the amusement of friends, the Roosevelts called their new summer home Tranquillity. The name, to these friends, did not exactly jibe with what they knew of activities common to the interior of the home.

Manhattan acquaintances, however, who came out to spend a weekend with the Roosevelts, returned home impressed with the setting. Joseph Hodges Choate,[20] after a visit, wrote to his wife: "I had a very delightful visit at Oyster Bay at the Roosevelts' and wish you could see their pleasant way of life there. They are only twenty-seven miles from New York and in the midst of a country which doesn't correspond in the least to your ideas of Long Island. Instead of the dreary sandy wastes of the South Shore, it is a pleasant and well wooded, rolling country, and apparently filled with good quiet people."[21]

From the start young Theodore loved Oyster Bay, for the locale offered distinct advantages, among them remoteness from urban confusion and an animal population as yet little disturbed by man. A particular advantage was the continuous presence of shore and maritime birds, the majority of which were then unknown to him. In due course Theodore became as well acquainted with surf scoters, oldsquaws, herring gulls, and red-throated loons[22]—to name just a few of the aquatic birds common to Long Island Sound—as with catbirds, chickadees, and song sparrows.

The summer of 1874—the first of three Theodore would spend at Oyster Bay before he entered Harvard—was particularly busy. On at least three days of each week, with aid from Cutler, he continued preparing for the Harvard entrance examinations. There was, also, much coming and going of visitors, many of them near Theodore's age, such as West and Emlen Roosevelt, Edith Carow, and Frances ("Fanny") Theodora Smith.[23] The presence of these guests led to much partying, as well as to swimming, boating, and horseback riding.

At no time did Theodore discontinue his body-building exercises. In addition to rowing and swimming, he competed with his cousins in such field and track events as the 100-yard dash, standing jump, running jump, and high jump. Theodore kept a record of the outcome of these events, providing evidence that he usually won. Theodore's running jump, for instance, was 13 feet and West's 12 feet 6 inches. This record (or "Sporting Calendar" as Theodore called it) listed, too, certain vital statistics: weight 124 pounds, height 5 feet and 8 inches, chest expanse 24 inches, waist 26½ inches, and forearm 10 inches.[24]

In spite of these several demands on his time, Theodore seems to have shunned no opportunity to add new specimens to his museum. From the time he first arrived in Oyster Bay, which was in late May, until late July, when he left on trips to vacation points, he was afield at least twenty-four days. Furthermore, between early September and the end of the year—after the family had returned to the city—he made the long trip from 57th Street to Oyster Bay on at least eleven different days, solely to be with the Long Island birds and in anticipation of finding specimens he had failed thus far to collect.[25]

On the majority of his field trips around Oyster Bay, Theodore presumably walked. At other times he had the choice of a boat or a horse. Whatever his method of travel, he soon became familiar with the nearby fields and woodlots, and with the principal geographical features of the island's northern shore line, among them Glen Cove, Cooper's Bluff, Lloyd Neck, Sea Cliff, Centre Island, and Huntington Bay.

Specific knowledge of Theodore's boyhood natural history adventures in the out-of-doors at Oyster Bay is derived largely from two notebooks or journals he prepared: "Journal of Natural History" and "Remarks on the Zoology of Oyster Bay." Like his previous ones of Egypt and Syria, these were crammed with biological data. They are of value to the present-day bird student in that they make it possible to recreate many of the days of long ago when Theodore sauntered through the woods and meadows of the Island, or by the waters of the Sound, listening to the songs of vireos, wrens, and warblers or to the cries of oldsquaws, loons, and gulls.

Theodore's "Journal of Natural History" consists entirely of lists of animals (mostly birds) that he, on specific days, observed and often collected. He made his first list on May 23, 1874:

Corvus americanus [*Corvus brachyrhynchos*, Common Crow]. I observed several specimens of this bird. One of these was fired at, at quite short range, several times. It flew away after each shot but as soon as we drew off returned to the same place.

Garrulus cristatus [Blue Jay]. Several specimens were seen.

Turdus migratorius [Robin]. A good many individuals were seen, and one shot, but the species was very shy.

Seiurus aurocapillus [Ovenbird]. A single individual of this species was shot. It was perched on an oak.

Turdus mustelinus [*Hylocichla mustelina*, Wood Thrush]. I found this thrush to be quite common in the woods, and also observed several specimens in orchards. It was by no means shy—not as much so as the robin.

Mimus carolinensis [Catbird]. Very common, and inquisitive. It was, with the exception of the chippy [Chipping Sparrow], the commonest bird to be seen. I found it everywhere. As soon as a cat bird saw us, it would come up to examine us, uttering a loud "pay, pay." They sang very sweetly when thinking themselves unobserved, however two specimens were killed.

Harporhynchus rufus [*Toxostoma rufum*, Brown Thrasher]. A o ♂ [Immature male] which was taken was seated in the top of a maple and was singing in a rich, sweet tone.

Icterus baltimore [*Icterus galbula*, Baltimore or Northern Oriole]. Two males (ad & o) [adult and immature] were killed in an orchard.

Tyrannus carolinensis [Kingbird]. This species was very common in the orchards and fields. It was not shy but was also not familiar. I saw a pair drive away a crow, pouncing down on him, and striking him on the head with their bills. Another couple were quarreling just as fiercely between themselves. I saw another one attack an innocent sparrow.

Troglodytes aedon [House Wren]. A ♂ & ♀ were shot in an orchard.

Dendroica discolor [Prairie Warbler]. A ♂ was shot in a cedar.

Geothlypis trichas [Yellow throat]. Quite common. It was generally seen in bushes (I saw a female in a young maple singing "peu pe twit, peeu twit.") Another attacked a nest of caterpillars, which was in a small bush. It got at the caterpillars by hanging by its feet, from a twig just above them. A ♂ & ♀ were shot.

Spizella socialis [*Spizella passerina*, Chipping Sparrow]. The most common bird to be seen, and universally distributed. 4 killed.

Zonotrichia melodia [Song Sparrow]. A single individual was observed.

Picus pubescens [Downy woodpecker]. A specimen was shot in a tall chestnut. Although hit in the brain it clung to the trunk of the tree several minutes before falling.

Sciurus carolinensis [Gray Squirrel]. Several individuals seen. Some half grown ones in an orchard were very tame and allowed of a very close approach.

Hirundo horreorum [*Hirundo rustica*, Barn Swallow]. Numerous. Saw several light on the ground by a pond.

Ortyx virginianus [*Colinus virginianus*, Bobwhite]. A single specimen seen.

This list gives a good idea of what forty or more other lists in "Journal of Natural History" were like. It demonstrates once again, through the consistent use of Latin binomials and symbols for male and female, Theodore's studious determination to be scientific. It introduces Theodore's effort, which becomes more pronounced in months ahead, to convert bird notes into words. It reveals a truth stated by one of the most brilliant ornithologists America has produced: "The true ornithologist goes out to study birds alive and destroys some of them simply because that is the only way of learning their structure and technical characters."[26]

Here and there, in ensuing lists, Theodore described events it would be a mistake to ignore. By way of illustration, on July 10 he found a nest of the white-footed deer mouse in which were one male and five females, apparently all adults. For this disproportionate combination the young Oyster Bay naturalist had a ready answer: it seemed "to indicate a state of polygamy."

Two days earlier, on July 8, Theodore wrote of collecting a young male "*Ectopistes migratorious*," namely, a passenger pigeon. In the 1870s this bird was still common in parts of the United States, notably in the Ohio and Mississippi valleys. Theodore's notebooks make it clear that it was fast disappearing from Long Island, since they contain just three other references to it, one stating simply, "now and then one is seen." But no person, certainly not Theodore, then envisioned an early extermination of this species. Neither did Frank M. Chapman, another young aspiring ornithologist, who, in 1878—just four years after Theodore had collected his first specimen—shot two of them, the only ones he ever saw in nature and, unaware of their rapidly decreasing numbers, promptly ate both.[27] In earlier years the passenger pigeon had been so abundant that estimates of their number tended to defy credibility. For example,

Alexander Wilson, while near Frankfort, Kentucky, about 1806, recorded watching an overhead migrating flock that contained, according to his count, 2,230,272,000 pigeons.[28] As is generally accepted, the last passenger pigeon on earth died on December 1, 1914, in the Cincinnati Zoo. Thus, the date of its extinction occurred almost precisely forty years after Theodore, while at Oyster Bay, had added a specimen of this species to his museum.

At about the same time Theodore began his "Journal of Natural History," he began also his "Remarks on the Zoology of Oyster Bay." The latter extends and complements the former. It is filled with personal observations on practically every aspect of avian behavior, the result of an obviously improving and more disciplined curiosity. The preface to Theodore's "Remarks on the Zoology of Oyster Bay" begins auspiciously: "In these notes I have adopted (with slight alterations) the classification of [Elliott] Coues, in his *Key to North American Birds*." Perhaps only the elder statesmen among living ornithologists can be expected fully to appreciate the significance of that prefatorial remark. Coues's *Key*, first published in 1872, won immediate praise, one distinguished ornithologist forthrightly declaring that it "stands as one of the best, if not the best, bird book ever written."[29] It exerted a tremendous influence, particularly on youthful naturalists. Ernest Thompson Seton,[30] for one, said of it: "No man can overestimate the blessing that that book has been to all the world of bird folk in America."[31] And Chapman, after obtaining a copy of the *Key*, said that he "was no longer handicapped for lack of tools. Here was a work which from preface to index offered an inexhaustible store of information . . . to a novice."[32]

In all likelihood Theodore, since he had chosen Coues's *Key* as a source for his classification of the Oyster Bay birds, would have agreed with these appraisals. Theodore's copy of Coues's *Key to North American Birds* is still extant (1982), at Sagamore Hill. As proof that he had made extensive use of it, one finds numerous marginalia in Theodore's characteristic handwriting. Further evidence of Theodore's high regard for Coues, both as an ornithologist and as a writer, is the presence at Sagamore Hill of Coues's *Birds of the Northwest* and *Birds of the Colorado Valley.*[33]

It seems safe to say that Theodore had long since taken to heart the Latin maxim, *Litera scripta manet* (i.e., the written word endures), and his "Remarks on the Zoology of Oyster Bay" lend further credibility to that rule of conduct. This journal provides comments, of greater or lesser length, on a total of 115 species of animals.

In his description of almost every species, Theodore provided (1) both scientific and common name, (2) his number for the specimen, (3) the sex, (4) date procured, (5) content of crop, (6) body length, (7) wing expanse, and (8) color of iris, bill, and legs. Of far greater importance, however, were his observations.

In both spring and fall Theodore meticulously noted the time of arrival and departure of the migrating birds. For instance, the wood thrush, traveling north, generally arrived at Oyster Bay on May 1st and left, going south, in October. Swainson's thrush, which summered and nested at higher latitudes, could be expected back on Long Island about September 20, and it stayed around, before moving on, until about October 10.

Just as Theodore familiarized himself with the timetables of birds, so did he note their habitats—at least the places where he most often found them. The brown thrasher frequented "dense woods, grown up with brushwood, and thickets," while the sharp-tailed sparrow inhabited "the salt marshes" and "sandy beaches . . . covered with coarse grass and low bushes." The song sparrow occupied a surprising variety of localities. "I know of no bird," Theodore explained, "which varies its habits to suit the locality more completely; I have seen it in company with the Yellow-wing [grasshopper sparrow] in the sandy fields of New Jersey, and the next month found it plentiful among the wooded hills of Vermont, and there as arboreal as it was terrestrial by the seacoast."

Theodore continued to study the behavior of birds and never begrudged time. Before describing the behavior of the red-throated loon, he had unquestionably spent much time watching it. "When undisturbed," Theodore wrote of this species, "it swims with its body almost entirely out of the water, merely floating on the surface; but if alarmed it immediately sinks its body, leaving only its head and neck exposed. If it thinks itself in actual danger it either flies off, rising with great difficulty and exertion, or more frequently tries to escape by diving, going very long distances with great speed, under water."

Theodore obviously enjoyed watching the Eastern kingbird in action and often did so. "It attacks," he declared, "with perfect indifference every species of bird, and is as tyrannical and bullying as it is brave. After one had attacked and routed a sparrow hawk, it suddenly attacked an unoffending bluebird. . . . Another dashed into a flock of bobolinks and scattered them as a hawk would have done. . . . The foes which it attacked with the greatest animosity, however, are the crows, and it gives those noxious birds an immense amount of trouble."

The flight of the sharp-tailed sparrow, in Theodore's words, "was firm, steady, and often protracted for quite a distance, the tail being lowered and spread." By comparison, that of the yellow-breasted chat was "in semispirals, in a queer fluttering manner, its tail hanging down, and cutting the most remarkable pigeonwings all the time." Perhaps no one will quarrel with Witmer Stone's[34] conviction that with Theodore, in all his natural history studies, "It was the habits of the animals which most appealed to him."[35]

Theodore rarely neglected the food content of the bird's crop, and this procedure supplied him with such words as herbivorous, insectivorous, graminivorous, and omnivorous, terms he often used. The crop of a prairie warbler contained "small insects, worms, etc.," while that of the passenger pigeon he had collected on July 7 contained "cherries and seeds." After he had revealed the crop content of a great-crested fly-catcher, Theodore went on to disclose another bit of information about this bird: "Judging from the condition of the ovaries of the female which I have dissected the eggs must be laid the first week in June." This unexpected revelation suggests that Theodore did a thorough job of exploring the insides of a bird.

Theodore's eyesight, seemingly so sharp and reliable while watching the flight patterns, escape routines and other activities of birds, appeared to have failed him utterly in one respect. Not once, in "Remarks on the Zoology of Oyster Bay," did he extol the beauty of plumage of a bird, not even of an oriole, tanager, or grosbeak. In his other natural history journals, he was equally quiet about color. It was a sensory lapse that defies explanation—unless Theodore's vision, even with his spectacles, was somehow chromatically deficient.

At no time, to the contrary, was there anything wanting or unpredictable about Theodore's sense of hearing. Though conspicuously mute about avian coloration, he was ever alert to, and communicative about, bird vocalizations. That was true whether the sounds were simple notes, such as the "guttural joch, joch" of the fox sparrow, the "rather jingling trill" of the dark-eyed junco, the "rollicking, bubbling notes" of the bobolink, or the "sweet and plaintive song" of the white-throated sparrow.

Among songsters, not surprisingly, Theodore had strong likes and dislikes. He regarded the chipping sparrow as the "poorest singer" he knew of, this because of "its exasperatingly monotonous notes," which continued for hours at a time. But Theodore knew no bird capable of "such horrible noises" as those of the catbird. "I do not think," he complained, "you can ever walk in any wood where there are catbirds, without promptly being informed of their presence by the monotonous and exasperating 'pay, pay' this bird meanwhile wagging its tail about as if it was really doing some good to bird-kind."

Conversely, Theodore loved certain bird melodies and often used words of his own invention in describing them. The Maryland yellow-throat had "a very bright short song, sounding like wit-te-weet, wit-te-weet, wit-te-weet, wit-te-wee." That of the American redstart consisted of "two notes: the ordinary one resembling 'tseet-see-tseetsee' loudly and quickly repeated. It also occasionally utters a few, fine 'zee, zees.'" And the song of the ovenbird consisted "of the repetition of a note of two syllables, somewhat like 'tchea, tchea, tchea, tchea, tchea' growing louder, shriller towards the end, so that while the first repetitions are full and distinct, it ends in a sort of shriek."

Theodore's description of the music of the song sparrow revealed even greater inventive originality: "Its song is loud and cheerful, if not very musical, and is uttered freely from March to October. It is short, and may be represented by 'cheet, cheet, cheet, chirr, che, che, che,' or 'cheet, cheet, cheet, cheet, chirr, che (--- $\sim$ uuuuuu or ---$\sim$).'"

Theodore truly savored the melody of the wood thrush: "Its delightful song—by far the sweetest bird music of our woods—is most often heard in the evening twilight, when it is all the more noticeable because it is the only sound to be heard, for the thrushes sing later than any other diurnal bird of this neighbourhood. In the early morning its song is given forth just as freely, but at that time it is almost drowned out by the louder, although far less melodious voices of the hosts of robins, catbirds and the like. After about the middle of August they stop singing, and during Autumn are perfectly silent."[36]

It may have been a challenge to Theodore to turn from his eulogistic description of the adult wood thrush's song to a less flattering one of the young of that species; yet he handled the problem admirably. "Early in July," he wrote, "the young begin to sing, and very queer work they make of it. The bobtailed little minstrel (in posse) usually chooses some very conspicuous twig on which to station himself, for he knows none of the modesty of his parents; and from such a perch will give forth his wheezing notes by the hour. He does not yet try the clear, belllike notes which are the especial beauty of the song of the older bird, but confines himself to imitating, with very partial success, the trills and quavers with which it commences."

Other excerpts from Theodore's "Remarks on the Zoology of Oyster Bay" could be presented, though these surely prove that Theodore's capabilities as a field naturalist, since returning from Egypt and Syria, had improved substantially, not only in the areas of observational competence, auditory alertness, and narrative talent but also, and more particularly, in that of an increasing hunger to add to his already sizable knowledge of animals.

Notes

1. Morris, *Rise of Roosevelt*, 75.
2. Mrs. James K. Gracie, before her marriage, was Anna Bulloch, Mittie's sister. She was Theodore's "Aunt Anna" and served as both nurse and tutor during Theodore's boyhood. The identity of Elizabeth Lewis has eluded us.
3. The composition of this "Roosevelt Library" is unknown, though some of the volumes doubtless still exist in Theodore Roosevelt's library at Sagamore Hill.
4. Morris, *Rise of Roosevelt*, 64. Arsenic, in its pure metallic state, is odorless, as is the oxide, a white powder, in general use today.
5. Hagedorn, *Boys' Life*, 46.
6. Putnam, *Theodore Roosevelt*, 112.
7. Ibid., 111.
8. Hagedorn, *Boys' Life*, 45.
9. Robinson, *My Brother*, 92.
10. *New York Herald*, Aug. 4, 1901.

11. Roosevelt, *Autobiography*, 19.

12. Putnam, *Theodore Roosevelt*, 126.

13. Lewis Einstein, *Roosevelt, His Mind in Action* (Boston: Houghton Mifflin, 1930), 10.

14. Morris, *Rise of Roosevelt*, 75.

15. Ibid.

16. Roosevelt, *Autobiography*, 22.

17. Hagedorn, *Boys' Life*, 50.

18. Theodore to Fräulein Anna Minkwitz, Feb. 5, 1876. See also, Morison, *Letters*, 1:14.

19. Putnam, *Theodore Roosevelt*, 117.

20. Joseph Hodges Choate (1832–1917), prominent New York lawyer and U.S. ambassador to Great Britain (1899–1905).

21. Edward S. Martin, *The Life of Joseph Hodges Choate*, 2 vols. (New York: Charles Scribner's Sons, 1920), 1:329.

22. Surf scoter (*Melanitta fusca*), oldsquaw (*Clangula hyemalis*), herring gull (*Larus argentatus*), and red-throated loon (*Gavia stellata*).

23. Frances Theodora Smith later became Mrs. James Russell Parsons and the author of *How to Know the Wild Flowers* and *How to Know the Ferns*. The latter is currently (1982) available in a reprint by Dover Books, Inc.

24. Roosevelt, *Diaries of Boyhood*, 355–57. These statistics were of Nov. 1, 1875.

25. Theodore made 1874 autumn-winter trips from New York to Oyster Bay on the following days: Oct. 10, 17, 20, 24, 31; Nov. 7, 17; and Dec. 20.

26. Elliott Coues, *Field and General Ornithology* (London: Macmillan, 1890), 15.

27. Frank M. Chapman, *Autobiography of a Bird-Lover* (New York: D. Appleton and Co., 1938), 23.

28. T. Gilbert Pearson, ed., *Birds of America*, 3 vols. (Garden City, N.Y.: Garden City Publishing Co., 1944), 2:40.

29. J. A. Allen, "Biographical Memoirs," *National Academy of Sciences* 6 (June 1909): 402. For extended coverage of Coues's *Key*, see Paul Russell Cutright and Michael J. Brodhead, *Elliott Coues: Naturalist and Frontier Historian* (Urbana: University of Illinois Press, 1981), 128–33.

30. Ernest Thompson Seton, (1860–1946), British-born artist-naturalist. He wrote many books, among them: *Two Little Savages* (1903) and *Lives of the Game Animals* (1925–28).

31. Ernest Thompson Seton, *Trail of an Artist-Naturalist* (New York: Charles Scribner's Sons, 1940), 222.

32. Chapman, *Autobiography of a Bird-Lover*, 31–32.

33. *Birds of the Colorado Valley* was perhaps a presentation copy from Coues, for, on a front page, appear these handwritten words: "Theodore Roosevelt (from the author) Jan. 1879."

34. Witmer Stone (1866–1939), naturalist, was born in Philadelphia, and for most of his life was associated with the Academy of Natural Sciences of Philadelphia. He edited *The Auk* (1912–36) and was the author of *Birds of New Jersey* (1909) and *Birds of Old Cape May* (1937).

35. William Draper Lewis, *The Life of Theodore Roosevelt* (Philadelphia: John C. Winston, Co., 1919), 390. The quotation is from chapter 25 of this work, "Roosevelt the Naturalist." It was written by Witmer Stone at Lewis's request.

36. Theodore had yet to hear the song of the hermit thrush.

7

"Above All the Birds Have Come Back"

THREE YEARS HAD in no way dimmed Theodore Roosevelt's delightful recollections of his first trip to the white pine forests and birchfronted lakes of the Adirondacks. His second visit was during the last two weeks of August 1874, not the best time of the year for an ornithologist to invade this scenic part of the state. By then the birds had ceased nesting, most of them had stopped singing, and the woods were generally quiet.

Theodore kept no diary on this trip, as he had earlier, so there exists no day-to-day account of his adventures and observations. There are, however, two natural history notebooks: "Journal of a Trip to the Adirondacks—1874" and "Notes on the Fauna of the Adirondack Mts." The former deals only with the 1874 visit, the latter with four trips: 1871, 1874, 1875, and 1877.

These two journals supply the names of the several animals Theodore encountered on his 1874 visit and provide further examples of his talents as an observer. The opening paragraph of Theodore's 1874 journal informs: "August 14. Travelled from Ausable Fork to St. Regis Lake. The ground was mountainous, and originally covered with trees but these had been burned and a dense growth of underbrush had grown up." It should occasion no surprise that Theodore headed for St. Regis Lake—actually Lower St. Regis—site of Paul Smith's establishment, where the Roosevelt family had earlier enjoyed the hospitality of its genial proprietor. Who accompanied Theodore on this trip, if anyone, is unknown. He did hire a guide, an Adirondack woodsman named Mose Sawyer. Theodore liked Mose and on future trips rehired him. Years later Mose was to recall that Theodore never smoked, drank, or cussed, was an excellent camper, and always contributed his full share to the day's work, in spite of occasional bouts with asthma. He was not interested in fishing, Mose reported, only in shooting, skinning, and mounting birds. Theodore once presented Mose with two of his mounted and arsenic-treated birds, but these came to an untimely end when Mose's cat ate them—after which the cat, too, came to an untimely end! Mose further reported that Theodore always brought books with him, and sometimes companions. He concluded his remarks about Theodore by saying, "He was a queer looker, but smart."[1]

In the preface to his "Notes on the Fauna of the Adirondack Mts." Theodore provided a good thumbnail description of the St. Regis Lake area as it was back in the mid–1870s:

The region more particularly dealt with is at an elevation of over 2000 feet, is strongly hilly, or one might almost say mountainous, and is thickly studded with small lakes and ponds whose outlets are narrow and very crooked streams. It is densely wooded; the few open places being the clearing around houses and the "slashes" where the woods have been burned. The forests are chiefly evergreen (largely intermixed with birches and maples, however); the bulk being composed of pines, balsams and spruces, with numbers of hemlocks on the ridges. In the low, level lands there are frequently extensive tamarack swamps. . . . The characteristic features of the fauna of the region are, among mammals, the presence in small numbers of the larger carnivora and furbearing species; among birds the abundance of woodpeckers, the breeding of numerous warblers, and the presence of a number of northern species, as *Picoides arcticus* [black-backed woodpecker] et *americana* [three-toed woodpecker], *Parus hudsonicus* [boreal chickadee], *Perisoreus canadensis* [gray jay], *Contopus borealis* [olive-sided fly-catcher] and *Tetrao canadensis* [spruce grouse].[2]

After two days at Paul Smith's, Theodore divided his time between the Lake Follensby area, which is six to seven miles slightly northwest of Paul Smith's, and Bay Pond, some dozen miles to the southwest. At neither of these sites did he encounter any of the larger mammals, though he would have welcomed the sight of a brown bear or a white-tailed deer. This disappointment may have been partially offset when one night he heard a wolf howl. Smaller mammals, among them squirrels, muskrats, and chipmunks, were common. Theodore thought that the chipmunks must do considerable damage in season to garden crops since he "took eighteen peas" out of the pouches of one.

Theodore listed some thirty species of birds. He had little to say about them, except for the red crossbill: "I saw several flocks. They kept among the tall trees near the water and were very restless. . . . Their flight is rapid, noisy and powerful and is usually sustained at a considerable height. . . . [They kept] to the tops of the tallest pines on whose seeds they feed. They climb about among the branches like parrots, often hanging head downwards from the cones and twigs. . . . Its ordinary note, uttered while flying, sounds like 'kip-kip.' It also chatters occasionally, uttering a loud chuck if alarmed, and while feeding keeps up a low chirping which is very ventriloquial in its effect. The males have a sweet, powerful and varied song, much like that of the purple finch." Like all bird students, Theodore was intrigued that the tips of the beaks of this bird do not meet but cross. He may not have known that this singularity—some of the earlier naturalists characterized it as a deformity—is of value to the birds, enabling them to extract the seeds of the pine cones. As explained by one ornithologist: "The bill is slipped sideways beneath the scales of a cone and then twisted, forcing the scale up so the bird can hook out the seed and eat it."[3]

In the front of the notebook Theodore had alluded to "the abundance of woodpeckers," of which there were at least five different species: downy, hairy, pileated, northern three-toed, and black-backed three-toed. Of the northern three-toed (now simply called three-toed), he wrote that he had collected two males—just that. It is surprising he said no more. For one thing, he was apparently meeting this species for the first time, for another it is rarely seen (encountering it is an event to be cherished and kept in memory), and for yet another, the northern three-toed and the closely related black-backed differ from other birds in having two toes in front, instead of the usual three, and the customary one behind. On future trips to the Adirondacks Theodore was less reticent about the birds.

2

Soon after Theodore had returned to Oyster Bay from the Adirondacks, the entire family moved back to 5 West 57th Street, where Theodore resumed his studies with Arthur Cutler, these continuing to command his attention six to eight hours daily for at least five days of each week. It was a punishing schedule, and Theodore might in time have suffered from it, if he had not known and acted upon the best possible countermeasure. As often as fall and winter weather and other factors permitted, he hurried to Oyster Bay, where he spent his hours in the out-of-doors among the birds, experience having taught him that such pleasures, more than anything else, would ease accumulated tensions. It is on record that Theodore, on October 10, while strolling along the northern coastline of Long Island, found abundant relaxation in the presence of myrtle warblers, cedar waxwings, Swainson's thrushes, and other birds. Also, on November 7 (again at Oyster Bay), he was entertained by a fox sparrow's "gutteral joch, joch notes." Again, on December 30, he wandered contentedly among Long Island golden-crowned kinglets, bluebirds, and brown creepers, and ended the day on an exultant note by collecting a fish crow, one of the rarer Long Island species that previously had eluded him.

Just two days later the Roosevelts, as well as all other families across the nation, celebrated the advent of 1875. With the date for the Harvard entrance examinations now only six to seven months away, Theodore possibly stepped up his preparations for them. However, ever mindful of his health, he routinely visited the third-floor gymnasium his father had equipped for him and the other children.

In spite of the time-consuming lessons and daily stints with boxing gloves and parallel bars, Theodore's thoughts never strayed far from his beloved birds, and on every possible opportunity he escaped to be among them. As evidence, on January 18, he traveled up the Hudson to Garrison—across the river from West Point—to be with his friend Frederick Osborn, the two entertaining high hopes of encountering and possibly collecting specimens of newly arrived northern birds. They were delighted, therefore, when they promptly located pine siskins, common redpolls, pine grosbeaks, and red crossbills.

Theodore later described an unexpected and unforgettable incident of that visit. After discharging his shotgun at a flock of red crossbills in a pine tree, he excitedly rushed forward to pick up his prizes. Unfortunately, in so doing, a twig caught his spectacles and, as Theodore reported, "snapped them I knew not where. But dim though my vision was, I could still make out the red bodies lying on the snow; and to me they were treasures of such importance that I abandoned all thought of my glasses and began a nearsighted hunt for my quarry." As a result, he failed to find his glasses and his "day's sport—or scientific endeavor—[had] come to an abrupt end."[4]

A few weeks later Theodore informed his mother that Osborn had invited him up for another outing, but, because he had a bad cold, he had had to refuse. It would appear that Theodore never again saw his friend, for four months later Fred died. Forty-three years passed and Theodore continued, distinctly, to remember him: "Among my boyhood friends who cared for ornithology was a fine and manly young fellow, Fred Osborn, the brother of Henry Fairfield Osborn. He was drowned in his gallant youth . . . but he comes as vividly before my eyes as if he were still alive."[5]

With eagerness, even impatience, Theodore looked forward to another spring, when the birds would again be winging north. Just how much his spirits rose at the sight of the first feathered arrivals may be gauged from a letter he wrote in mid-March to his mother: "Spring has come! I just begin to realize it; the birds even are commencing to come back. While in the Park [Central Park] the other day I saw great numbers of robins, uttering their cheery notes from almost every grove. That winter had only just departed was evident from the number of little snowbirds (clad in black with white waistcoats) which were about."[6]

Information is lacking as to the exact date when the entire Roosevelt family left Manhattan to spend their second summer at Oyster Bay, though it was probably not before early June. Theodore preceded the family at least twice, on April 8–10 and May 13–15. The latter visit coincided with the height of the migration season, with returning species both plentiful and vocal in every field and woods. On May 14, for instance, he identified, without difficulty, forty-one species, including twelve warblers.

In weeks immediately ahead Theodore had little time for warblers or any other birds, as he crammed for the upcoming entrance exams that he took in early July. Writing to Bamie soon afterward, he exulted: "Is it not splendid about my examinations? I passed well on all the eight subjects I tried."[7]

This communication to Bamie bore the postmark of Burlington, Vermont. To celebrate the successful issue of the Harvard examinations, Theodore had decided on another fortnight in the Adirondacks, and was traveling there by way of the Green Mountain State.

Accompanying him on this trip were Elliott and Cutler. Not surprisingly, they chose Paul Smith's as a base and from there made forays into the surrounding forested terrain, going first to Bay Pond, where they stayed August 2–6, and then to Upper Falls, Bay Pond River, where before returning to base they camped for a full week, August 7–13. In a letter to Bamie written at Bay Pond, Theodore revealed that they were experiencing annoyances that sometimes beset campers. He wrote of a three-day rain, which kept them under canvas for most of the period, of Cutler sitting in a "smudge," and of Elliott "engaged in an affair of honour with a mosquitoe."[8]

The primary objective of Elliott and Cutler on this trip was to bag a deer or other large game animal or, that failing, to pull a string of trout from one of the lakes or streams. To Theodore, this aim was secondary; as heretofore, his major purpose was to increase the size of his museum and his knowledge of the Adirondack fauna. Abundant evidence to that effect is to be found in two documents: "Journal of a Trip in Adirondack Mts., August 1875," a relatively short account of this 1875 visit, and "Notes on the Fauna of the Adirondack Mts.," mentioned earlier. The latter is, by far, the more important of the two, being replete with on-the-spot, personal observations of animals, principally birds, that he had encountered on this trip. Herein he wrote at length about a dozen or more birds; what follows is part of what he wrote about three:

Anorthura troglodytes [*Troglodytes troglodytes*, Winter Wren]—No. 585. Aug. 11th 1875. Rather common in the dense woods, but rarely seen. . . . It is often heard, however, for it possesses a gushing, ringing song, wonderfully loud for so small a creature; excepting the thrushes it is the sweetest songster of the Adirondac woods. . . . It moves by jerky hops and short flights, the tail being held perfectly erect. . . .

Zonotrichia albicollis [White-throated Sparrow]—No. 575. Aug. 6th 1875. . . . It becomes very fat in August and is at all times insectivorous. . . . It has a singularly sweet and plaintive song, uttered with clear, whistling notes; it sings all day long especially if the weather be cloudy, and I have frequently heard it at night, but its favorite time is in the morning when it begins long before daybreak; indeed, excepting the thrushes, it sings earlier than any other bird. The song consists generally of two long notes, the second the highest and with a rising inflection, followed by five or six short ones (as _/duuduu), but there are many variations. A very common one is to have but two short notes (as _/uu); sometimes the second note is broken into two (as _/uuu). It sings all through the summer.

Picoides arcticus [Black-backed three-toed Woodpecker]—No. 561. Aug. 2d 1875. Common in the dense forests and along the edges of the burnt slashes, preferring the taller trees but being found also on the stumps and among the fallen logs. In habits it greatly resembles the hairy woodpecker and like it, besides boring in the wood for grubs and beetles, picks caterpillars off the branches and sometimes takes an insect on the wing. It has quite a variety of crys, all either harsh or rolling, most of which are identical with those of the hairy.

The descriptions of the wren and sparrow emphasize again Theodore's studious attention to bird music and his obvious enjoyment of it. That of the black-backed three-toed woodpecker has been included because Theodore, heretofore, had practically ignored it. It is hardly necessary to add that Theodore's auditory powers, so evident in describing the songs of the winter wren and song sparrow, are once again superlatively keen. Conversely, as before, he completely disregards the avian plumage.

3

Soon after Theodore returned to Oyster Bay from the Adirondacks, the Roosevelts moved back to Manhattan. A full year ensued before Theodore entered Harvard. How did he spend that year? Knowledge of it depends largely on entries in Theodore's natural history journals. Without them, for example, nothing would be known of eight visits he made back to Oyster Bay that fall, where, on September 21, he encountered piping plovers, which were "occasionally piping"; on October 23, by which date most of the birds had already flown to lower latitudes, he found that hermit thrushes, as well as myrtle and blackpoll warblers, were "common"; and on November 6, when he made his final outing of the year to the Island, he reported the presence of white-throated, fox, and tree sparrows ("common"), of coots ("found either in flocks or singly"), and of a bald eagle ("one seen").

There now followed a four-month period characterized by an almost total absence of information about Theodore. Since this period included the winter months, unfavorable for more trips to Oyster Bay (hence no added journal notes), it seems reasonable to assume that he spent much of that time partying, theater-going, riding, or sledding in Central Park and, perhaps, courting eligible young women of marriageable age. Reports circulated that he and Edith Carow had reached an "understanding."

With the arrival of spring, Theodore resumed his jaunts to Long Island and his entries in "Remarks on the Zoology of Oyster Bay." Also he began yet another journal: "Field Book of Zoology." This latter, in some respects a continuation of the former, is important as a major source of information about Theodore's field activities during the spring and summer months immediately before he began his studies at Harvard. From it we quickly learn that on March 24–25—on his first 1876 trip to Oyster Bay—he recorded the presence of no more than a dozen species of birds, all of which were winter residents. On his next visit, April 17–18, the Island woods and field were full of birds, including such migrants as the bluebird, phoebe, goldfinch, and red-winged blackbird. On May 6, on his third trip back to Oyster Bay that spring, Theodore was able to report: "Nature has now assumed an entirely new face. The woods . . . have begun to bring forth buds and shoots, and indeed many of the trees and shrubs are in full blossom and the fields are even more verdant than they were. The insect world is in full life, and in rather obstreperous life too, if the flies and mosquitoes are to be taken as a criterion, *but above all the birds have come back"* (my italics).

This particular May day—when all the birds had come back—was, from first to last, a memorable one for Theodore. "At half past four in the morning," he wrote, "I was waked up by the beautiful song of the wood thrush." Soon afterward he was regaled by the "sweet plaintive" notes of the bluebird, by the "very peculiar short and unmusical warble" of the parula warbler, and by the "unmusical song" of the prairie warbler. Still later he was agreeably entertained by the antics of a male towhee in the presence of its mate: "He hopped and strutted among the twigs in a very peculiar manner, holding his head back, and with both wings and tail half spread so as to show the white marks. Sometimes the performance was varied by offering her a twig, and one of them, I could not see which, occasionally uttered a complaining whistle." Theodore concluded this description by saying that the female "appeared quite unaffected" by the amorous advances of the male.

Throughout the summer, and until September 5 shortly before he left for Harvard, Theodore was afield at Oyster Bay on no less than thirty-four days (his notebooks attesting thereto). He probably would have gone oftener, except for a steady flow of visitors requiring attention. One of them was Fanny Smith. On the very first evening after her arrival for a weekend at Tranquillity, Theodore took her "on a long moonlight row" on the Sound. On the next day he rowed her to Cooper's Bluff, and on the one following, escorted her on "a lovely ride on horseback."[9] Perhaps Theodore and Fanny, about this time, were more than mere friends. They definitely had much in common, in particular a deep and abiding love of nature, though Fanny's tastes ran to plants instead of animals. Because of Theodore's greater familiarity of birds he was able, on one occasion, to correct Fanny, who in a poem had written of thrushes perched in treetops. Theodore informed her that he had yet to see thrushes in treetops, only on branches "rather low than high." Also, in the same poem, Fanny had bobolinks "fluting from the swaying grass." Theodore regarded this as so much nonsense but, instead of saying so, politely inquired: "do you think bobolinks usually 'flute'?" He then continued: "They sing so very buoyantly, with such a babble, and so often on the wing. Now the redwings whom you mention in the preceding line do exactly what you describe."[10]

Entries of Theodore in his "Field Book of Zoology" for the summer of 1876 vary greatly in length. Quite often they are short, as when he mentions a dozen or less species. However, on two days at least he seems to have attempted a full bird count, as present-day members of the Audubon Society do in preparing annual Christmas bird censuses. On May 21 Theodore reported forty-five species and on July 24, doing better, fifty-nine.

During this summer, too, as his notebooks reveal, Theodore's emphasis on the collecting of birds diminished. Instead he paid increased attention to mammals, reptiles, amphibians, and fishes. The most likely explanation for this change was his realization that he by this time had a surplus of bird specimens and, by comparison, only a few of other vertebrate animals. Not surprisingly, in his attempts to identify the other vertebrates, Theodore sought out and obtained the most authoritative zoological texts then available, those by such distinguished scientists as J. E. DeKay[11] and D. S. Jordan.[12] In the preface to his "Notes on the Fauna of the Adirondack Mts." he wrote that in identifying fishes he had "followed the classification of Jordan in his 'Manual,'" thus naming not only the author but also the text.

At a much later date Theodore belittled his pre-Harvard natural history activities, writing: "I worked with much greater industry than either intelligence or success."[13] On other occasions Theodore Roosevelt exhibited undue modesty, but never more so than in this instance. In just a few years, mainly 1872–76, he had not only amassed an enviable collection but had also put together in notebooks a quantity of zoological information that even an Audubon or a Wilson might well have regarded as exceptional. At this early date, as Theodore's journals attest, he knew the approximate dates in spring when most of the bird migrants could be expected back in Oyster Bay from the south and, in autumn, the approximate dates of their departure. With little or no hesitation, he could have indicated the point on Long Island where this or that species could most likely be found. He could have identified on sight the majority of the species, both land and water, and, more remarkably, he could have named most on hearing their songs.

4

As the day drew ever nearer when Theodore would leave for college, the entire family must have been caught up in a flurry of excitement and anticipation. Theodore continued firm in his resolve to become a "scientific man of the Audubon, or Wilson, or Baird, or Coues type."[14] He had long talks with his father about his ambition, one that the latter, as well as others of the family, could not quite understand or accept. They seem to have been convinced all along that Theodore's youthful fascination for animals was a passing fancy, that increased maturity would cause him to turn to some other interest, just as West Roosevelt had deserted his boyhood fancy of natural history for the study of medicine. Theodore would later recall his father's advice, that "if I wished to become a scientific man I could do so," but "I must [however] be sure that I really intensely desired to do scientific work."[15]

Thus, it appears evident, Theodore's father was an eminently sensible man, making no effort to persuade his son against his will to enter the family business, as he had hoped, if not expected, from the start. But, there is reason to believe that Theodore, Sr., may have envied his own son's opportunity to obtain a college education. Purportedly, he himself had wished to do so, but that desire had been promptly squelched by *his* father, who had said college "would ruin him."[16]

Notes

1. *The Adirondack Enterprise*, Saranac Lake, N.Y., Jan. 28, 1930.

2. *Picoides americana* has been updated to *P. tridactylus*. *Parus hudsonicus*, earlier the Hudsonian chickadee, is now the boreal. The gray jay, at earlier dates, went by various names, among them, Canada jay, whiskey jack, and moose bird. *Contopus borealis* has been updated to *Nuttallornis borealis* and *Tetrao canadensis* to *Canachites canadensis*.

3. Dean Amadon to author, July 23, 1979.

4. Roosevelt, *Works, Mem. Ed.*, 6:448. After this incident Theodore never again went collecting without an extra pair of glasses.

5. Ibid.

6. Anna Roosevelt Cowles, ed., *Letters from Theodore Roosevelt to Anna Roosevelt Cowles* (New York: Charles Scribner's Sons, 1924), 4.

7. Morison, *Letters*, 1:13.

8. Cowles, ed., *Theodore to Anna*, 6.

9. Frances Theodora Parsons, *Perchance Some Day* (Privately printed, 1951), 34.

10. Ibid., 96.

11. James Ellsworth DeKay (1792–1851), naturalist, was born in Lisbon, Portugal, and died in Oyster Bay, Long Island. He is perhaps best known as the author of *Zoology of New York*, 5 vols. (1842–44).

12. David Starr Jordan (1851–1931), prominent scientist and educator, was born in Gainesville, N.Y., and in 1872 graduated from Cornell. In the years 1875–79, Jordan was professor of biology at Butler University, in 1885–91 president of Indiana University, and, 1891–1913, president of Stanford University. Among his several published scientific works were *Manual of the Vertebrates of the Northern United States* (1876)—the "Manual" Theodore reported using—and *Fishes of Middle and Northern United States* (1896–1900).

13. Roosevelt, *Autobiography*, 21.

14. Ibid., 23.

15. Ibid., 23–24.

16. McCullough, *Mornings on Horseback*, 24.

Theodore Roosevelt, age ten. (Theodore Roosevelt Collection, Harvard University)

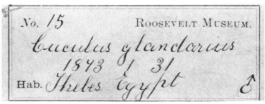

Specimen label, designed by Theodore Roosevelt shortly before he departed with his family for Egypt in October 1872. The lettering on this label was pink. (American Museum of Natural History)

Ornithological Observations

made in

Europe, Syria and Egypt

from November 1872 to July 1873

Theodore Roosevelt Jr.

Title page of one of Theodore Roosevelt's earlier natural history books. (Theodore Roosevelt Collection, Harvard University)

Theodore Roosevelt collected and mounted these birds in Egypt in the winter of 1872-73. Left to right: Egyptian spur-winged lapwing, crocodile-bird, and white-tailed lapwing. (American Museum of Natural History)

Theodore Roosevelt's boyhood attempts at animal portraiture (no date). (Theodore Roosevelt Collection, Harvard University)

Random sketches from a page of one of Theodore Roosevelt's boyhood notebooks (no date). (Theodore Roosevelt Collection, Harvard University)

Snowy owl that Theodore Roosevelt collected and mounted in 1876, now on display in the American Museum of Natural History. (American Museum of Natural History)

Theodore Roosevelt, shortly before he entered Harvard University in the autumn of 1876. (Theodore Roosevelt Collection, Harvard University)

Theodore Roosevelt at about the time of his graduation from Harvard University in 1880. (Theodore Roosevelt Collection, Harvard University)

8

"I Think I'm Getting along All Right"

THEODORE ROOSEVELT was one of 246 freshmen who in the fall of 1876 entered Harvard University; the entire student body numbered 821. He was a month shy of his eighteenth birthday; Harvard was celebrating its 240th. Theodore might or might not have agreed with Owen Wister's impressions: "When you become a freshman, you become pretty nearly nobody."[1]

Except for a tormenting fear that he might again be plagued with asthma, Theodore would have taken up residence in the college dormitory, where he had a choice of only first-floor rooms that at times might be too damp for his health. Instead, he engaged second-floor rooms at 16 Winthrop Street (now 36 Winthrop) in a private home situated between the College Yard and the Charles River. Possibly, too, conditions in the Harvard dormitory remained much the same as in the college days of Oliver Wendell Holmes, Jr., when, on extremely cold winter days, students poured water around window frames confident that it would freeze, seal the cracks, and keep out the cold air. Also, an occasional student, to obtain more warmth, would heat a cannon ball and, when the weather warmed up making the missile momentarily useless, "it was highly rewarding to roll the cannon ball downstairs; it made the proctors mad and the noise was superb."[2]

At 16 Winthrop, Theodore occupied a large, well-lighted study, with a mere alcove of a bedroom in the rear. That Bamie had preceded him to Cambridge and had used her talents to make his quarters attractive and comfortable is proved by a letter that he wrote to her soon after his arrival: "Ever since I came here I have been wondering what I would have done if you had not fitted up the rooms for me. . . . When I get my pictures and books, I do not think there will be a room in college more handsome."[3]

Needless to say, the appearance of Theodore's study soon changed. As we have learned, it had become near habitual with Theodore to clutter up rooms he occupied, whether at home, in a hotel room, or aboard a Nile houseboat. The more obvious changes in Theodore's quarters resulted from the introduction of natural history specimens. There was, too, an impromptu vivarium, which from time to time housed a varied assortment of creatures, trophies of excursions into the countryside surrounding Cambridge.

Theodore liked his Winthrop Street rooms so well that he kept them for the four full years he was at Harvard. That his landlady, a Mrs. Richardson, accepted him and his animals for those years bespeaks considerable indulgence on her part and also suggests a mutual liking and respect. Mrs. Richardson could not, of course, have regarded him as an ideal tenant. One night, for example, she lost a heart beat or two when she almost fell over a large turtle (the size of this animal tends to increase with each telling) that had managed to escape confinement and was wandering through the upstairs hallway in search of freedom.[4]

Theodore, as later described by those who remembered him as a freshman, apparently differed little physically from the boy of two or three years earlier. He was still slender, underweight, flat-chested, and frail-looking, though, as events soon proved, deceptively so. Other recollections varied tremendously: he was "quiet but eligible"; he was "crazy"; he was "a snob"; he was "friendly once you got to know him"; he was "always interesting." "His eccentricities, however," as one writer declared, "did not obscure, at least for long, the metal beneath."[5]

Theodore made few friends during his freshman year. His first, and best, was Henry Minot,[6] then a sophomore. Minot called at 16 Winthrop the day after Theodore had moved in. Through some family connection, he had learned of Theodore's interests in birds, and, having a similar interest, it was natural that he should wish to get acquainted. In succeeding pages we shall dwell at length on the friendship, both warm and enduring, that quickly developed between the two.

2

Theodore began his college life only a few years after Charles W. Eliot (1834–1926) had assumed the presidency of Harvard. Almost from the start, Eliot began to change the school's outlook. One plan, partially in effect when Theodore first appeared on campus, was the shelving of the traditional system—that of all courses prescribed— in favor of allowing certain electives. At first Eliot's proposed changes met with some opposition, one of the opponents being James Russell Lowell. According to report, Lowell reinforced his opposition by telling the story about the bartender at the Parker House in Boston, who, to improve the flavor of ducks, came up with the idea of feeding them wild celery. When later asked if his experiment had succeeded, he replied, "No, the damn ducks won't eat it."[7] Lowell's conviction was that the average student lacked the intelligence to know what was best for him. Nevertheless, Eliot's proposal of electives gained the endorsement of the Harvard Board of Overseers.

In 1876 the privilege of electives extended only to upperclassmen, so Theodore did not benefit from that license until his sophomore year. He and the other freshmen took only prescribed courses: classical literature, Greek, Latin, German, mathematics, physics, and chemistry. To no one, it would seem, did Theodore interpose any objection to these required subjects. He did, in time, inform his parents that he was experiencing some difficulty with two of the courses, writing, "I think I am getting along all right in all of my studies except one, which is Prof. Purse's Theory of Determinants. . . . My Greek has also been pretty hard."[8] Also, at no time, it would appear, did he express disappointment at being ineligible to choose any of the natural history courses.

That Theodore encountered some scholastic problems initially should not surprise, for, except his brief period in Professor McMullen's school, he had had no previous exposure to classroom instruction and discipline. In spite of these handicaps, Theodore's grades for his freshman year did not discredit the name of Roosevelt: classical literature 77; Greek 58; Latin 73; German 92; mathematics 75; physics 78; and chemistry 75 [the passing grade at Harvard in 1876 was 50].[9] Moreover, as a freshman, Theodore averaged 75 and ranked 111th, which put him in the upper half of his class.

3

As the school year progressed, Theodore and Minot met increasingly—and Theodore was shortly addressing his friend as "Hal" or

"Harry." In mid-January Theodore wrote to Bamie, saying that on the day before he had taken a train to the Minot home in West Roxbury,[10] and one month later he advised his parents: "During the spring I expect to do a good deal of collecting with Harry Minot and Fred Gardiner,[11] both of whom have similar interests to mine. . . . Our lessons will be over by the twentieth of June, and then Harry Minot and I intend leaving immediately for the Adirondacks, so as to get the birds in as good plumage as possible, and in two or three weeks we will get down to Oyster Bay, where I should like to have him spend a few days with us. He is a very quiet fellow, and would not be the least trouble."[12]

As April warmed up into May, and May into June, Theodore and Minot had their heads together almost daily. They talked of warblers, thrushes, and red-wings recently returned, and of bird music of migrants in the swamps and fields, but their conversations usually began and ended with further discussion of plans for the Adirondack visit. Theodore seems to have had no problem in selling his friend on the St. Regis Lakes as the best place to go.

With finals behind them and the school year ended, Theodore and Minot set out at once for the Adirondacks. They arrived at Paul Smith's on June 22 and spent one week together in the woods skirting Lakes St. Regis and Spitfire. At the end of that week Minot, for reasons unclear, left, though Theodore stayed on for another week, until July 9.

For Theodore, this Adirondack trip proved to be more rewarding than any of the three preceding ones. The birds, as anticipated, were in better plumage; also many of them were nesting and, consequently, still singing. From Theodore's "Notes on the Fauna of the Adirondack Mts."—the primary source of information about this 1877 trip—we learn that he was successful in locating several nests, among them those of Swainson's (olive-backed) thrush, Wilson's warbler, red-breasted nuthatch, yellow-bellied sapsucker, and black-backed woodpecker. Of this last discovery, which must have pleased him more than any of the others, Theodore wrote: "Late in June I found a female who was feeding her young, who were almost full grown and had left the nest which was high up in a hemlock tree. These nests are usually dug beneath a projecting limb."

Just as we have come to expect, even anticipate, Theodore again noted bird habits of particular interest to him. Purple grackles were seen "walking on the large lily pads in the middle of a pond, catching small frogs." Traill's flycatchers demonstrated their exceptional ability in capturing "the gnats and mosquitoes which constituted their principal food." Writing of the red-breasted merganser, Theodore passed along information of possible interest to epicures: "When hard pressed I have often made a meal of the young, and have found them at times by no means bad eating."[13]

As said, the Adirondack birds were still singing. Consequently Theodore, probably for the first time in his life, heard and enjoyed the "rich and sweet" notes of the mourning warbler, the song of the solitary vireo, which was "richer and more powerful" than that of the red-eyed, and the "sweet, powerful and varied song" of the male red crossbill. Also, one day in late June, he listened intently to a rose-breasted grosbeak "perched in a tree, singing delightfully."

It may be recalled that three years earlier, at Oyster Bay, Theodore had declared the song of the wood thrush to be superior to that of any other bird known to him; but he had yet to hear that of the hermit thrush. It was on June 23, 1877, that he apparently first heard "the purest natural melody to be heard in this or, perhaps, any land."[14] Afterward he wrote:

The song, which is uttered until the middle of August, is very beautiful and peculiar to itself; it is more continuous than that of the oliveback and to my ear even sweeter, and fully equal to the song of the wood thrush; there is a weird, sad beauty in it which attracts the attention of the most unobserving, and once heard it can never be forgotten. It sings in the early dawn, at sunset, and if cloudy often through the entire day; I have even heard it at night. Perhaps the sweetest bird music I have ever listened to was uttered by a hermit thrush. It was while hunting deer on a small lake, in the heart of the wilderness; the night was dark, for the moon had not yet risen, but there were no clouds, and as we [doubtless Minot, Mose Sawyer, and Theodore] moved over the surface of the water with the perfect silence so strange and almost oppressive to the novice in this sport, I could distinguish dimly the outlines of the gloomy and almost impenetrable pine forest by which we were surrounded. We had been out for two or three hours but had seen nothing; once we heard a tree fall with a dull, heavy crash, and two or three times the harsh hooting of an owl had been answered by the unearthly laughter of a loon from the bosom of the lake, but otherwise nothing had occurred to break the deathlike stillness of the night; not even a breath of air stirred among the tops of the tall pine trees. Wearied by our unsuccess we at last turned homeward when suddenly the quiet was broken by the song of a hermit thrush; louder and clearer it sang from the depths of the grim and rugged woods, until the sweet, sad music seemed to fill the very air and to conquer for a moment the gloom of the night; then it died away and ceased as suddenly as it had begun. Perhaps the song would have proved less sweet in the daytime, but uttered as it was, with such surroundings, sounding so strange and so beautiful amid these grand but desolate wilds, I shall never forget it.

Theodore's description of the hermit thrush's song deserves to stand alongside other classical descriptions of bird music. It was, of course, his genuine love of bird melodies, and his near worship of the serene charm of northern woods, that led him to portray this experience with such depth of feeling. And it was this same devotion that led him in after years to write: "It is an incalculable added pleasure to anyone's sum of happiness if he or she grows to know, even slightly or imperfectly, how to read and enjoy the wonderbook of nature."[15]

On leaving the Adirondacks, Theodore went directly to Oyster Bay. Here, on July 11, he reported to Minot, dispensing news about birds he had gained during his second week in the woods after Minot had left. He had, he said, found the mourning warbler, nighthawk, and Canada jay more common than expected. He concluded by correcting a mistake in identification: "The blackbirds we saw were not the *Scolecophagus* [rusty blackbirds] but the females of *Quisqualus purpureus*[16] [common grackles]."[17]

A noteworthy sequel to Roosevelt's and Minot's trip to the St. Regis Lakes' area was their joint publication of *The Summer Birds of the Adirondacks in Franklin County, N.Y.* This appeared in October 1877, as a small leaflet of four pages, without binding, title page, or wrapper. It listed ninety-seven species and had been printed, at the authors' expense, for private distribution. The leaflet had particular importance to Roosevelt—not so much to Minot[18]—for it was his first published contribution to science. Doubtless both young men applauded on reading C. Hart Merriam's[19] favorable review of it in the April 1878 number of the *Bulletin of the Nuttall Ornithological Club:* "By far the best of these recent [bird] lists which I have seen is that of *The Summer Birds of the Adirondacks in Franklin County, N.Y.* by Theodore Roosevelt and H. D. Minot. Though not redundant with information and mentioning but 97 species, it bears prima facie evidence of reliability—which seems to be a great desideratum in bird lists nowadays. Based on the sound principle of exclusion, it contains only those species which the authors themselves observed there, and consequently furnishes that which was most needed, *i.e.,* exact and thoroughly reliable information concerning the most characteristic birds of the limited region (Franklin County) of which they treat."[20]

That fall, after Theodore and Minot were back in school, the two discussed the practicality of more ambitious trips, even considering a joint excursion to the British Isles. But before anything came of these plans, Minot had to withdraw from Harvard. Writing to Bamie soon afterward, Theodore explained: "Old Hal Minot has left college; his father has taken him away and put him in a big office to study law. I am awfully sorry and so is he."[21] The two, however, stayed in touch, exchanging letters. In one of them, after telling Minot about a recent outing in the country, Theodore concluded with these wistful words: "I have greatly felt the need of someone to talk to about my favorite pursuits and future prospects."[22] Throughout the remainder of his residence in Cambridge, Theodore failed to find anyone else on campus to take Hal Minot's place.

Minot may still have been a Harvard student when in 1877 the *Naturalists' Directory,* a publication issued annually carrying the names of contemporary biologists, included a new one: "Roosevelt, Theodore, 16 Winthrop Street, Cambridge, Massachusetts. Vertebrates. Coll. Ex." Through this paid listing, Theodore informed the scientific fraternity of the day that he collected vertebrate animals and would welcome the opportunity of exchanging specimens. Whether or not the announcement brought inquiries from other collectors cannot be said, though there can be no doubt that Theodore had duplicate specimens of many species available for exchange.

4

Beyond much doubt Theodore Roosevelt, Jr., eagerly anticipated his sophomore year at Harvard. He would now be eligible to elect courses, natural history ones among them. The college, however, did require that second-year students take rhetoric, history, and themes. Theodore elected two courses in German and two in natural history. In President Eliot's day the term "natural history" embraced a variety of subjects, specifically botany, zoology, comparative anatomy, physiology, embryology, geology, geography, mineralogy, meteorology, and astronomy.

Theodore arrived at Harvard too late to take instruction from some of the school's more illustrious scientists. Louis Agassiz,[23] European-born naturalist, no longer strolled through the College Yard, "smoking his cigar in sublime disregard of law and order . . . every hair on his head bristling with energy, charm, genius."[24] No longer could Agassiz deny the evolution of man from some lesser primate. And Asa Gray,[25] though still living and still championing Charles Darwin's *Descent of Man*, no longer entered the classroom. Yet, since this eminent botanist continued to reside in Cambridge, and did so until his death in 1888, Theodore must have been familiar with his figure. Other outstanding Harvard scientists were no longer living, among them the brilliant anatomist and microscopist Jeffries Wyman (1814–72), the gifted astronomer William C. Bond (1789–1859), and the erudite mathematician Benjamin Pierce (1809–80).

The Harvard natural history staff, successors to the above, who taught Theodore Roosevelt, consisted of Nathaniel S. Shaler[26] and William M. Davis,[27] geologists; Edward L. Mark[28] and Walter Faxon,[29] zoologists; William James,[30] physiologist and psychologist; and George L. Goodale[31] and William G. Farlow,[32] botanists. Although these men were competent and respected among the American scientists of their day—Shaler because of the brilliance of his teaching, Mark for the introduction of German research methods, and Goodale for his role in bringing to Harvard the incomparable Blaschka collection of glass models of flowers—yet they were not destined to achieve the same greatness as had Agassiz and Gray.

Even before Theodore began his studies at Harvard, he probably knew that Cambridge was the home of numerous American literary figures, that most of them were Harvard graduates, and that a few still held Harvard professorships or served on the university's Board of Overseers. On almost any given day, it would have been possible for Theodore, while walking Cambridge streets or the College Yard, to have met one or more of the following: James Russell Lowell, Oliver Wendell Holmes, Jr., William Dean Howells, Ralph Waldo Emerson, Edward Everett Hale, Richard M. Dana, Henry Wadsworth Longfellow, William Brooks, and Henry Adams, grandson of the sixth president of the United States, John Quincy Adams.

Theodore did become acquainted with at least one of these personages. Writing to Bamie in mid-January 1877, he said: "Sunday night I dined with Doctor and Mrs. [Henry] Adams, and had a very pleasant time. After dinner we had some real Turkish coffee. The Doctor improves very much on acquaintance."[33] Adams was then a professor of medieval history at Harvard, though in his final year of teaching. His dinner invitation to Theodore seems to have been prompted by some previous association of his family with Theodore's.

Neither in his *Autobiograpy* nor elsewhere, including his numerous letters, as far as we have been able to determine, did Theodore allude to any of his natural history teachers at Harvard. A possible explanation of Theodore's restraint may have been supplied by a classmate, who later wrote that most of the teachers were standoffish, "thought that the students were merely something to lecture to."[34] Of his science teachers, Theodore may have been on closer terms with Shaler than any other. Students generally liked Shaler, and his natural history 4 (geology) was one of the more popular courses then offered. Agassiz-trained, versatile, companionable, and a brilliant lecturer, he was the sort to win admirers. On occasion, Theodore visited in Shaler's home, though perhaps attracted more by Shaler's daughters, in whose company he was sometimes seen, than by Shaler himself.

From various sources comes the intelligence that in the classroom Theodore talked out of turn, was argumentative, and voiced vigorous opinions. One day, for example, while Shaler was lecturing, Theodore interruped to ask a question. Shaler stopped his flow of words, answered, and then resumed. A few minutes later Theodore cut in with another question, and, once more with equal equanimity, Shaler replied. A third time Theodore interrupted. As report has it, Shaler drew himself up to his full height of more than six feet, glared at Theodore, and snapped: "See here, Roosevelt, let me talk. I'm running this course."[35]

Theodore may have been more ardent than either argumentative or disputatious. His philosophy teacher, Professor George Palmer, later recalled that Theodore spoke rapidly, "sort of spluttered as if his thoughts came faster than his mouth could express them—something like water coming out of a thin-necked bottle. Thus it might be easily interpreted that he was more disputatious and vehement in his language than he really was."[36]

Theodore's sophomore year brought to him his first great sorrow, the death of his father, on February 9, 1878.[37] Soon after he had entered Harvard, Theodore had written to his father saying: "I am sure that there is no one who has a father who is also his best and most intimate friend."[38] Expressing even better the depth of his love for his father were later letters, in particular one to his mother: "I have just been looking over a letter of my dear father's in which he wrote to me, 'Take care of your morals first, your health next and finally your studies.' I do not think I ever *could* do anything wrong while I have his letters; but it seems very sad never to write to him."[39]

At the moment of Theodore's greatest distress, Hal Minot proved his worth as a friend. In mid-February Theodore acknowledged the latter's expressions of sympathy: "*Dear old Hal*, many, many thanks . . . your sweet letter cheered us up a great deal. As yet it is impossible to realize I shall never see Father again, these last few days seem like a hideous dream. Father has always been so much with me that it seems as if part of my life had been taken away; but it is much worse for my Mother and my sisters. After all, it is a purely selfish sorrow, for it was best that Father's terrible suffering [with cancer] should end."[40]

5

The February 28, 1878, number of a short-lived periodical, *The Country*, carried a brief account of opinions recently expressed by Theodore Roosevelt, Jr., at a meeting of the Nuttall Ornithological Club, a Cambridge organization that Theodore had joined three months earlier, on November 26, 1877. A portion of the account read:

Mr. Theodore Roosevelt, Jr. of New York said that some years ago English [house] sparrows were apparently of service in New York City in destroying canker worms;[41] but last year worms were very abundant in the gardens of that city, and not interfered with by the birds. In America he had never observed them molest grain but in Egypt he had seen them feeding in the fields in flocks of many hundred, and on shooting them their crops were found to contain only grain. He had often watched them assault snow-birds, song and chipping sparrows, and had known them to kill a yellow-bellied woodpecker [sapsucker], actually mobbing it to death. . . . at West

Point on the Hudson, land owners had been obliged to shoot them as they destroyed the buds of the fruit trees and drove away the song birds.

In the spring of his sophomore year Theodore started a scrapbook, the first of more than one hundred he later compiled. The above clipping adorns page one, a memento of what became known in the 1870s and 1880s around Boston and elsewhere as "The Sparrow War." Theodore's report to the Nuttall Ornithological Club, one of several given at the meeting, was based on his own personal observations, except for possibly the West Point one, which may have been relayed to him by Fred Osborn.

The Sparrow War was bloodless, though at times suffused by considerable heat and bad feeling. It was fought over the question: Did the house sparrow, which had been introduced from England into the United States about 1850,[42] deserve indulgence and protection or censure and slaughter? On one side was a small group of men and women who took the stand that this sparrow was inoffensive, even beneficial, and merited sanctuary. The most outstanding champion of this immigrant was Dr. Thomas M. Brewer,[43] a prominent Boston physician, publisher and ornithologist. Also, he was a member of the Nuttall Ornithological Club. Many reputable and seasoned ornithologists, however, argued that the house sparrow had multiplied to the point that it had become a threat to the welfare of some of the more-cherished native songbirds, which the sparrow drove from their accustomed haunts and sometimes killed.

To many of the members of the Nuttall Ornithological Club, the facts of the case had been so unfairly and inadequately presented to the public by the press, in part swayed by the influence of Dr. Brewer, that the club called a special meeting. By so doing, it anticipated determining what action, if any, it should take. At that time the club consisted of a group of thoughtful bird students, mostly young, who in 1874 had founded the organization or who, like Theodore, had joined soon afterward. Among them were William Brewster,[44] J. A. Allen,[45] H. W. Henshaw, H. B. Bailey,[46] Charles F. Batchelder,[47] and Henry Minot, each of whom subsequently contributed significantly to the growth of ornithology in the United States.

Doubtless it was Minot who had recommended Theodore for membership. At a somewhat later date, Charles Batchelder wrote a memoir of the club, in which he appraised both Theodore and Hal

Minot: "Once in awhile—not often—there dropped in together [to meetings of the club] two undergraduates, H. D. Minot and Theodore Roosevelt, Jr.. . . . I am afraid some of us looked at the two a little askance. We recognized their ability, but both seemed a bit too cocksure and lacking in the selfcriticism that, in our eyes, went with a truly scientific spirit. But they were young, and so were we."[48]

Before adjournment of the special meeting, the club members drafted a report, critical of the house sparrow, and submitted it to the press. Some of the Boston papers, disagreeing with it, quickly attempted to discredit members of the club on the grounds that they were too youthful to be knowledgeable on such matters. One of the editorials (unsigned) was attributed to Dr. Brewer, though he disclaimed authorship. It was laden with barbs, all conspicuously aimed at Theodore: "A third [member of the Nuttall Ornithological Club], also sophomoric, draws upon an equally vivid imagination, for his facts. He tells the world that when he was in Egypt—at what age he does not tell us—he saw the house sparrow devouring grain. . . . How long has this species been known to be an Egyptian bird? He has also seen [house] sparrows persecuting little *Chippies*, birds that on Boston Common live on the best of terms with those 'ferocious foreigners,' and has even known them to mob unto death big woodpeckers and so on."[49]

The editorial lent itself to criticism, though apparently Theodore himself did not reply. Other, more experienced naturalists came to the support of the "sophomoric" youths of the club, one of the most vocal being Elliott Coues, then secretary and naturalist to the U.S. Geological Survey of the Territories. The evidence that he and others submitted, reinforced by the prestige of their names and positions, proved difficult to controvert. In years ahead the opposition languished and then expired.

5

As an undergraduate at Harvard, Theodore Roosevelt was a joiner. At one time or another he was elected to membership in such strictly campus organizations as Hasty Pudding, Porcellian, Alpha Delta Phi, Dickey, Art Club, Rifle Club, O. K. Club, and Glee Club.

Also, at about the same time he became affiliated with the Nuttall Ornithological Club, he joined the Harvard Natural History Society. In due course Theodore became vice-president of this group and, on two occasions at least, presented papers, one titled "Coloration of Birds" and the other "Remarks on the Gills of Crustaceans."

Theodore's preparation for the latter paper may have provided the substance for a story often told about him. Purportedly, he went into Boston one day, where he bought a basketful of lobsters and then, for the return trip to Cambridge, boarded a horse car crowded with passengers. At one point, with Theodore's attention altogether diverted by the pages of a book, some of the lobsters managed to ease themselves out of the basket onto the floor of the conveyance, where they created quite a stir. News of this incident soon became common knowledge and grew with the telling. It is said that it reached the ears of Shaler, who enjoyed it so much that he slapped his thigh, roared with delight, and afterward told it "over time and again."[50]

Despite the shock of his father's death and of increased demands on his time resulting from club responsibilities, Theodore's grades as a sophomore were an improvement over those as a freshman: rhetoric 94; themes 69; German 4 92; German 5 96; French 51; history 87, natural history 3 (comparative anatomy and physiology) 79; and natural history 8 (elementary botany) 89. In all likelihood, Theodore's teachers of natural history 3 and 8—James and Goodale and Farlow, respectively—regarded his grades as creditable, though not suggesting a student of exceptional scientific promise.

As Theodore neared the end of his sophomore year, he seems to have been a participant in practically every aspect of college life. In addition to activities already mentioned, he took on editorial duties with the *Harvard Advocate*, gained a place on the boxing team, and, because of a deep-rooted general interest in athletics, started the movement that led to annual track meets between Harvard and Yale.[51] The sum of Theodore's extracurricular interests strongly suggests that, to him, a sound, well-rounded, overall education took precedence over attaining all A's and B's.

And lest we forget, even momentarily, that Theodore was first and foremost an ornithologist, his notebook entry for May 6, 1878, should not be overlooked: *"Accipiter fuscus*[52] [sharp-shinned hawk].

I saw one pounce on a robin and carry it off right by the museum."
This observation, like so many others, is to be found in Theodore's
handwritten, delightfully edifying "Field Book of Zoology."

6

It was back in the summer of 1876 that Arthur Cutler, after finishing his job of preparing Theodore for the Harvard entrance examination, took off on a hunting trip to Island Falls, a small settlement
near Lake Mattewamkeag, Aroostook County, Maine. On his return
he told Theodore about his trip, stressing the beauty of the north-
woods and the abundance of fish and game. He described, in particular, an extraordinary man, William ("Bill") Wingate Sewall, a local
woodsman who had served as his guide. Theodore, Cutler insisted,
must meet Bill Sewall.

It was September 1878 before Theodore, remembering Cutler's
counsel, determined to visit Island Falls, Maine. Bill Sewall later
recalled Cutler's words about Theodore: "I want you to take that
young fellow . . . under your special care. . . . He is not very strong
. . . and if you should take such a tramp as you are in the habit of
taking sometimes, and take him with you, you never would know
that anything ailed him. . . . even if he were tired he would not tell
you so."[53]

Theodore knew nothing until later of Cutler's instructions to
Sewall, but during the summer immediately preceding his visit to
Maine his actions strongly suggested otherwise. As soon as he had
returned to Oyster Bay from Cambridge, he initiated a series of
strenuous, outdoor, body-building exercises as though impelled by
some fast-approaching deadline, these exercises including mainly
hiking, horseback riding, and rowing. Within two or three weeks, he
was rowing around Centre Island, a distance of some eight miles,
running at full speed through woods for an estimated mile, and riding increasingly longer distances on his horse Lightfoot. It was on
July 19 that Theodore really tested his physical prowess. He rowed
from Oyster Bay to Rye Beach (Rye, New York) and back, a feat requiring that he twice cross the wide expanse of Long Island Sound.
Of course, he knew in advance that the trip would be difficult, even
in the best of weather. Accordingly, he waited for a bright, cloudless
day, one when the waters of the Sound were calm. Anticipating a hot

sun, he left his bed at an early hour, departed from Oyster Bay at 5:15 A.M., and hit the sands of Rye Beach, roughly twelve miles away, at 8:15 A.M. Using good sense, he remained at Rye Beach through the hottest part of the day and did not begin his return until 4:15 P.M. Two and one-half hours later he was back in Oyster Bay. "In all," Theodore boasted, "I rowed rather over 25 miles."[54] Finally, as though still anticipating the lengthy trudges ahead through the Maine woods with Sewall, Theodore, on August 5, walked the Long Island terrain from 8:00 A.M. to 5:00 P.M., with time out only for a quick lunch and, in that period, covered some twenty-five miles. On his return Theodore declared that he had had "glorious sport and funnily enough, feel fresh as a lark."[55]

When at last Theodore left for Maine, he was accompanied by his cousins West and Emlen and a Will Thompson.[56] His diary[57] entry for September 7 reads: "I travelled [by train] all last night, reaching Mattewamkeag at 10:30, and from there took a buckboard and reached here (Island Falls) at 8 P.M.. . . . Have a pretty bad attack of asthma." The Mattewamkeag was a station on the Maine Central Railroad, the nearest stop to Island Falls, which was still thirty-eight miles away. After the overnight train ride and the difficult buckboard trip over a rough, rocky road, Theodore and his companions must have been exhausted, a fact that may have contributed to Theodore's asthmatic attack.

On reaching Island Falls, Theodore met Bill Sewall and also Wilmot Dow, Bill's nephew. A man of great physical strength, Bill was then thirty-three, with a long reddish-brown beard adorning a kindly face. Theodore was shy of his twentieth birthday and, as Sewall described him, "a thin, pale youngster with bad eyes and a weak heart."[58] Both Sewall and Dow were well schooled in most aspects of wilderness life, and especially proficient in hunting, fishing, and trapping. Sewall could also converse intelligently on a wide range of topics and, if properly primed, could even recite lines of the poets, Whittier, Scott, and Longfellow, among them.

The Harvard student and the veteran Maine woodsman seem to have liked each other at first sight. As Bill later said, "We hitched well, somehow or other, from the start."[59] Bill was drawn to Theodore because of his "amibition and grit," because he "was always good-natured," and because, no matter how tired, "he would never admit it."[60] Theodore took to Bill for several reasons, though pri-

111

marily because he was invariably kind, thoroughly reliable, and, when the going got rough, was capable of handling almost any situation, no matter how formidable.

In its abundance of small lakes and extensive virgin coniferous forests, the area around Island Falls may have reminded Theodore of the St. Regis Lakes country of the Adirondacks. Though the Maine lumbermen had already cut much of the white pine, there were still great stands of red spruce, balsam fir, and hemlock. The Island Falls region was farther north—by at least ten degrees of latitude—and more remote than the Adirondacks.

Theodore carried both rifle and shotgun and the necessities for preparing birdskins. Like his companions, he was alert to the possibility of bagging a white-tailed deer or brown bear. Relevant excerpts from Theodore's diary provide highlights of the trip:

September 8, 1879 [Sunday]—In the morning took a walk and read the Bible, learning by heart the XIX psalm, a most beautiful hymn of praise. . . .

September 9, 1878—I spent the day hunting partridges [ruffed grouse] but did not even see one.

September 10, 1878—West, Emlen, Will [Thompson], one guide (Sewall) and I in a batteau started down stream to a large lake [Mattewamkeag] at whose foot we are camped out. . . . I had several shots at pigeons[61] and ducks but missed them all.

September 11, 1878—In the morning Emlen and I paddled about Mattewamkeag Lake in the canoe [and] in the afternoon . . . tramped about ten miles through the woods after partridges; we saw only one bird but enjoyed the walk very much . . . 1 partridge (ruffed grouse).

September 12, 1878—Rainy, and we stayed in camp. . . . We have quite a varied diet of duck, partridge, trout, pickerel, &c. . . .

September 13, 1878—Rained all day, so we stayed in camp playing eucher and whist. . . . I killed a bat and a nighthawk.

September 14, 1878—Rained till noon, then it cleared and I took a fifteen mile walk with Sewall, but got nothing. . . .

September 15, 1878 [Sunday]—Read my Bible in the morning; in the afternoon . . . cleaned guns, labelled specimens, and bathed in the race of the dam.

September 16, 1878—. . . I took a thirty mile tramp . . . with Sewall. . . . we were on the go steadily from 8 A.M. to 7 P.M. I saw no game whatever . . . but enjoyed the walk greatly. 1 red rabbit,[62] 1 merganser,[63] 1 ruffed grouse.

September 17, 1878—West and I with Dow took the canoe and

paddled to the upper end of the lake. . . . We three camped out in a wigwam. 1 dippy duck,[64] 1 wood duck.

September 18, 1878—The three of us got up at four in the morning, and started after ducks before daylight, and saw nothing. When I got back to the old camp I took Will Dow and tramped about ten miles through the woods. . . . 1 merganser, 1 ruffed grouse.

September 19, 1878—I walked about fifteen miles. . . . about three miles were through a succession of cedar swamps . . . I killed a spruce partridge [spruce grouse] . . . and a birch partridge[65] on a hemlock ridge.

September 20, 1878—I took a ten mile walk with Sewall. I saw nothing in the woods, but after a rather neat stalk killed a duck in a small lake.

September 21, 1878—Emlen and I went out shooting in the afternoon. . . .The leaves are now beginning to turn and the woods are perfectly beautiful. I have enjoyed this week very much; the trip so far has been a great success. 1 ruffed grouse.

September 22, 1878 [Sunday]—I spent the day much as last Sunday.

September 23, 1878—Broke camp and started for Island Falls in the batteau—a clumsy looking craft. I spent the afternoon tramping through the woods with West. 1 ruffed grouse.

September 24, 1878—I took a twenty-five mile tramp through the woods with Dow, shooting a logcock [pileated woodpecker] and two partridges. I have had wonderfully bad luck regards shooting . . . but nevertheless have enjoyed the trip greatly.

September 25, 1878—Spent the day driving around in a buckboard with Will Dow, getting out whenever we saw a partridge. . . . I saw a fox.

September 26, 1878—We drove in a wagon to Mattewamkeag [station] where we took the night train to Boston; tomorrow the other three fellows go on to New York, while I go out to Harvard.

Theodore had spent a total of eighteen days in the Maine woods. His diary, viewed one way, suggests that the trip for him had been a disappointment. He had shot poorly, had seen no animal larger than a fox, and had collected just two mammals and only a few birds, on average, about one each day. He could hardly have exclaimed with delight when attaching a specimen label to a bat or a ruffed grouse, or even to a "dippy duck." However, if viewed in another way, the diary argues the opposite. On September 18, it will be recalled, Theodore had matched strides with Bill Sewall through the Maine woods for a distance of thirty miles, which, Sewall later maintained, "was a goodfair walk for any common man."[66] It was another personal triumph for Theodore, to equal his earlier feat of rowing across Long Island Sound from Oyster Bay to Rye Beach and back. But Theodore's diary entries—on at least two dates—bespeak his enjoyment of the trip, notably those of September 21 saying, "I have enjoyed this week very much; the trip so far has been a great success," and of September 24 (nearing the end of his visit): "I have had wonderfully bad luck regards shooting . . . but nevertheless have enjoyed the trip greatly."

It is no contradiction that thousands of sportsmen, whether anglers or hunters, regularly anticipate vacations in wilderness areas hopeful of returning home with a haunch of venison or a string of trout, but are not unduly disappointed if unsuccessful. For these individuals, it is enough that they can get away from irksome, monotonous routines to find a measure of physical and mental reconditioning in surroundings generous with clean air, tall trees, rushing mountain streams, and a terrain abounding in colorful plants and animals. Beyond question, Theodore Roosevelt was such a man; he had just proved it in the company of Bill Sewall and in the future would prove it again in the company of other individuals, among them John Burroughs and John Muir.

Notes

1. Owen Wister, *Roosevelt, the Story of a Friendship* (New York: Macmillan, 1930), 2.

2. Catherine Drinker Bowen, *Yankee from Olympus* (Boston: Little, Brown, 1945), 120.

3. Cowles, *Letters from Theodore Roosevelt*, 12.

4. R. W. G. Vail, "Your Loving Friend, T. R.," *Collier's*, Dec. 20, 1924.

5. Putnam, *Theodore Roosevelt*, 1:136.

6. Henry Davis Minot (1859–90), ornithologist, was born in West Roxbury, Mass., and was a brother of the anatomist, Charles Sedgwick Minot. He is best remembered as the author of *The Land and Game Birds of New England* (1877).

7. Putnam, *Theodore Roosevelt*, 1:132.

8. Morison, *Letters*, 1:18.

9. For a complete listing of Roosevelt's Harvard grades, see ibid., 25–26.

10. Cowles, ed., *Theodore to Anna*, 18.

11. Frederic Gardiner graduated from Harvard in 1880—in the same

class with Roosevelt—and then went into the ministry. He later became headmaster of Yeates Institute, a boys' preparatory school in Pennsylvania.

12. Ibid., 12.

13. In a letter of Aug. 8, 1979, to author from Dean Amadon the latter said: "In the early days there was confusion as to the breeding status of the two larger species of merganser in the Adirondacks. It is now believed that the nesting birds are all (plus a few of the small hooded merganser) common mergansers, hence the young that T. R. speaks of eating were probably not red-breasted."

14. Pearson, ed., *Birds of America*, 3:234.

15. Theodore Roosevelt, *Outdoor Pastimes of an American Hunter* (New York: Charles Scribner's Sons, 1905), 339.

16. *Quisqualus purpureus* has been updated to *Q. quiscula.*

17. Morison, *Letters*, 1:28–29.

18. At about this same time Minot had published a more ambitious work, *The Land and Game Birds of New England* (Boston: Estes & Lauriat, 1877).

19. Clinton Hart Merriam (1855–1924), American naturalist, was born in New York City. He studied at the Sheffield Scientific School (Yale) 1874–77 and in 1879 received an M.D. degree from College of Physicians and Surgeons, Columbia. He later became the first head of the U.S. Geological Survey.

20. In due course this paper, of which a limited number were printed, became a rarity. On Mar. 26, 1923, for instance, a copy was offered for auction by the American Art Galleries, New York City, with their exhibition catalog containing this description: "Excessively rare first edition of Roosevelt's first published work. . . . and any collection of the writings of Colonel Roosevelt must remain incomplete without it."

21. TRCHL. See also Paul Russell Cutright, *Theodore Roosevelt the Naturalist* (New York: Harper & Brothers, 1956), 18.

22. Cutright, *Roosevelt the Naturalist*, 18–19.

23. Louis Agassiz (1807–73), celebrated naturalist, was born in Switzerland. After attending European universities, in 1846 he came to the United States, where he was elected to the position of professor of zoology at Harvard in 1847.

24. Bowen, *Yankee from Olympus*, 116.

25. Asa Gray (1810–88), brilliant American botanist, was born in Paris, N.Y., and in 1831 graduated in medicine at Fairfield College. In 1842 he was appointed Fisher professor of natural history at Harvard. His most important publication was *Manual of the Botany of the Northern United States* (1847).

26. Nathaniel Southgate Shaler (1841–1906), geologist and paleontologist, was born in Newport, Ky. In 1862 he graduated from the Lawrence Scientific School (Harvard) and was professor of geology at Harvard from 1868 to 1887.

27. William Morris Davis (1850–1934), geologist, geographer, and me-

teorologist, was born in Philadelphia, and in 1869 received a B.S. degree at Harvard. In 1879 he was appointed assistant to Shaler. Davis continued to teach at Harvard and in 1890 was given a full professorship (in physical geology).

28. Edward Laurens Mark (1847–1946), zoologist, was born in Hamlet, N.Y. In 1871 he received an A.B. from the University of Michigan and in 1876 a Ph.D. from the University of Leipzig, Germany. In 1877 he joined the Harvard natural history staff as an instructor and in time achieved a full professorship.

29. Walter Faxon (1848–1910), zoologist, was born in Roxbury, Mass. He studied at Harvard, receiving an A.B. in 1871 and a Sc.D. in 1878. In 1874 he was appointed curator of invertebrates at the Museum of Comparative Zoology (Harvard) and in 1880 joined the Harvard natural history staff. Subsequently, he was advanced to a full professorship.

30. William James (1842–1910), physiologist and psychologist, was born in New York City. In 1867–68 he studied in Germany and the following year received his M.D. at Harvard. He taught at Harvard, beginning in 1872, first as a physiologist. He later achieved enduring fame as a psychologist.

31. George Lincoln Goodale (1838–1923), botanist, was born in Saco, Me. In 1860 he received an A.B. from Amherst and in 1863 an M.D. from Harvard. In 1873 Harvard appointed him assistant professor of botany and in 1878 made him a full professor.

32. William Gilson Farlow (1844–1919), botanist, was born in Boston. He obtained an A.B. from Harvard in 1866 and in 1870, also from Harvard, an M.D. He began teaching at Harvard in 1874. Of interest was his publication in 1880 of *Apples of the United States.*

33. Morison, *Letters,* 1:22.

34. TRCHL.

35. Donald Wilhelm, *Theodore Roosevelt as an Undergraduate* (Boston: John W. Luce, 1910), 35.

36. TRCHL.

37. The death of Theodore Roosevelt, Sr., was due, according to New York newspapers, to a malignancy of the intestinal tract.

38. Cowles, ed., *Theodore to Anna,* 12.

39. Ibid., 28–29.

40. Morison, *Letters,* 1:31.

41. Cankerworms are larvae of moths, of which there are two species: fall cankerworm (*Alsophila pometaria*) and spring cankerworm (*Paleacrita vernata*).

42. For more about the introduction of the house sparrow into the United States, see Pearson, ed., *Birds of America,* 3:18.

43. Thomas Mayo Brewer (1814–80), ornithologist and publisher, was born in Boston and in 1835 graduated from Harvard Medical School. Chief among his published works was *North American Oology* (1857).

44. William Brewster (1851–1919), ornithologist, was born in Wake-

field, Mass., and became curator of ornithology in the Museum of Comparative Zoology. He was also one of the founders of the American Ornithologists' Union.

45. Joel Asoph Allen (1838–1921), zoologist, was born in Springfield, Mass., studied at Harvard under Louis Agassiz, and in 1865 accompanied Agassiz to Brazil. In 1870 he was appointed assistant ornithologist to the Museum of Comparative Zoology; he served as curator of birds and mammals at the American Museum of Natural History, New York City (1884–1912).

46. Henry Balch Bailey (1853–1928), ornithologist and businessman, was born in Boston and was an original member of the Nuttall Ornithological Club.

47. Charles Foster Batchelder (1856–1954), naturalist, was born in Cambridge, Mass., and in 1878 graduated from Harvard. In the years 1899–1947 he edited *Proceedings of the New England Zoological Club*.

48. Charles F. Batchelder, *An Account of the Nuttall Ornithological Club* (Cambridge: Nuttall Ornithological Club, 1937), 36.

49. Ibid.

50. Wilhelm, *Roosevelt as an Undergraduate*, 13.

51. Hagedorn, *Boys' Life*, 55.

52. *Accipiter fuscus* has since been updated to *A. striatus*.

53. William Wingate Sewall, *Bill Sewall's Story of T. R.* (New York: Harper & Brothers, 1919), 2–3.

54. Putnam, *Theodore Roosevelt*, 145–46.

55. Ibid., 146.

56. Will Thompson remains unidentified except for a reference to him as "Dr. W. Thompson" in Morris, *Rise of Roosevelt*, 9.

57. Roosevelt's diary here referred to was one he kept from Jan. 1, 1878, through Dec. 31, 1880, and randomly thereafter through 1884. Since the majority of the entries were made while Roosevelt was at Harvard, and to distinguish it from his "Diaries of Boyhood," it will be cited hereafter as "Roosevelt, Harvard Diary."

58. Sewall, *T.R.*, 2.

59. Ibid., 3.

60. Ibid., 3–4.

61. Presumably these were passenger pigeons (*Ectopistes migratorius*).

62. This "red rabbit" was apparently the varying hare (*Lepus americanus*), the coat of which varies seasonally.

63. Either the common merganser (*Mergus merganser*) or the red-breasted one (*M. serrator*).

64. Possibly Sewall's vernacular for the pied-billed grebe (*Podilymbus podiceps*).

65. "Birch partridge" may be another common name for ruffed grouse (*Bonasa umbellus*).

66. Ibid., 3.

9

"I Really Have My Hands Full"

BACK AT HARVARD, now a junior, Theodore enrolled in nine courses, a heavier program than in any previous year. Of the nine, four were required: themes, logic, forensics, and metaphysics; the others, Italian, German, philosophy, natural history 1, and natural history 3, were electives. This academic load at once posed potential difficulties for him. Writing to his mother in early October, he admitted: "My studies do not come very well this year, as I have to work nearly as hard on Saturday as on any other day—that is, seven or eight hours. Some of them are extremely interesting, however, especially Political Economy [i.e., philosophy] and Metaphysics. These are both rather hard, requiring a good deal of work, but they are even more interesting than my Natural History courses, [one of them being] rather dry, but the other I like very much, though it necessitates ten or twelve hours work a week."[1]

The "dry" natural history course was probably natural history 1, a combination of geography, meteorology, and geology—with little or nothing about animals. In light of events soon upcoming, Theodore's statement that he found his course in political economy even more interesting than either of his natural history courses must not be disregarded, particularly in view of two other letters he shortly wrote, one to Bamie and the other to Corinne. To Bamie, on October 13, he said: "I must try and see Mr. Choate this year; it is time for me to think what I shall do when I leave college."[2] And, on November 10, to Corinne: "[This fall] I really have my hands full, especially now that my political economy professor [J. Lawrence Laughlin] wishes me to start a finance club, which will be very interesting indeed and will do us all a great deal of good, but which will also take up a great deal of time."[3]

Theodore's references in these letters to his conferring with Mr. Choate, to his enjoyment of the political economy course, and to his obvious pleasure in having been asked to form a finance club all point in the same direction: Theodore was experiencing misgivings about his original intention of devoting his life to science. He had not as yet, however, arrived at a definite decision and did not do so until some months later. In fact, it was not until he had fallen in love with Alice Lee, or so it would appear, that he finally made up his mind. In time Alice Lee would, of course, become the first Mrs. Theodore Roosevelt.

2

Taking advantage of his 1879 Harvard spring recess, Theodore again took off for Maine and the agreeable companionship of Bill Sewall. He was in no way deterred by the fact that winter conditions at this time, the first two weeks of March, still prevailed in Aroostook County. He went by himself on this visit and was met at Matte-wamkeag station by Sewall, who then drove him to Island Falls in a sleigh through three to four feet of snow. Again, instead of para-phrasing Theodore's diary entries, we let him speak for himself:

March 1, 1879—I tried snowshoeing for the first time, went about six miles, making the rounds of Will Dow's "lucivee" [Canada lynx] traps which however contained nothing. . . . We saw many tracks of lucivee, foxes, otters and rabbits, and found a porcupine up in a hemlock.

March 2, 1879 [Sunday]—Read my Bible in the morning. In the afternoon took a tramp through the woods. I can not get used to the extreme beauty of the snow-covered pine and spruce forests. The cold does not bother me at all in the woods, but if there is any wind it is very disagreeable in the open.

March 3, 1879—I went off on a tramp through the woods with Will Dow. . . . I saw an Arctic [three-toed] woodpecker by a stream and some Hudsonian chickadees in a spruce wood, and the whisky jacks [gray or Canada jays] came round at lunch time.

March 4, 1879—I spent the day tramping through the woods with Bill Sewall. . . . but the only living creatures [seen] were a couple of chickadees and a woodpecker.

March 5, 1879—I spent the day snowshoeing through the woods as usual and with my usual ill success as regards game, but otherwise I am enjoying myself to the utmost; but the asthma keeps me up a good deal at night. . . . By trapping we have caught a lucivee and a fox.

March 6, 1879—Sewall, Dow and I started with a pung [box sleigh] and a shaggy, lean horse for a logging camp some thirty miles distant, reaching it after dusk. When we started, the thermometer was 10° below zero. . . . I saw several flocks of snow buntings, a red crossbill, and a small party of grosbeaks which were very tame and confiding.

March 7, 1879—Dow and I started out early in the morning. . . . [in] the afternoon . . . we roused a caribou in a dense, low spruce wood. I caught a glimpse of him as he vanished not thirty yards distant, but had no chance to fire. We followed the tracks till dusk, when we went into camp. The night was very cold and we had but little food and no blankets and so were pretty uncomfortable in spite of a huge fire.

March 8, 1879—Before sunrise we again started on a caribou trail, the thermometer being below zero. . . . Followed till mid-day and then gave up the chase.

March 9, 1879 [Sunday]—I was pretty well fagged out by my two days chase after the caribou and have been lying back and resting all day. I have not been bothered [again] by the asthma.

March 10, 1879—Sewall and I while hunting through the woods found a small deer yard. We approached it from different sides, and I saw the buck first, getting a shot first, but I tripped up at the moment and missed it. It then broke out of the yard and ran. After following at full speed for about a mile I got another shot and killed it with the rifle.

March 11, 1879—Started back for Island Falls . . . the roads were frightful. . . . Heard some more birds (buntings) singing beautifully. Reached Island Falls in time for tea.

March 12, 1879—In the morning went the rounds (7 miles) of the lucivee traps, which contained nothing, but we saw a coon cross the road ahead of us. . . . About 10 A.M. we started for Mattewamkeag Lake, at the foot of which we camped out for the night. On the way down I picked up a couple of spruce partridges in a swamp.

March 13, 1879—We broke camp pretty early and reached Island Falls in time for dinner.

March 14, 1879—Spent the entire morning hunting partridges without seeing one. . . . I have never passed a pleasanter two weeks. The skins of the fox, lucivee, coon and buck make quite a set of trophies, and we have shot enough partridges and rabbits to eat—not to mention the venison. I have collected a good many specimens.

March 15, 1879—Started for Mattewamkeag [station] in a sleigh at 5 A.M. Took the night train for Boston. I am now going to study all the time to Easter, doing double work to make up for the holiday.[4]

Theodore could hardly wait to tell his mother of the joys he had experienced during this trip. Writing from Cambridge the next day after his return, he said: "I enjoyed every moment. The first two or three days I had asthma, but, funnily enough, this left me entirely as soon as I went into camp. The thermometer was below zero pretty often, but I was not bothered by the cold at all, except one night when I camped out on the trail of a caribou. . . . I have never seen a grander or more beautiful sight than the northern woods in winter. The evergreens laden with snow make the most beautiful contrast of green and white, and when it freezes after a rain all the trees look as though they were made of crystal. . . . My trip was a success in every way."[5] One writer, after weighing Theodore's 1879 Maine hunting exploits against his obvious, all-inclusive love of nature, discerningly commented: "The hunter had not eclipsed the naturalist."[6]

Sometime in March 1879, perhaps near the time Theodore had been chasing a woodland caribou, there came from the press *Notes on Some of the Birds of Oyster Bay, Long Island*, by Theodore Roosevelt, Jr. This was a most modest piece, being just one page in length and listing only seventeen birds that Theodore had collected and regarded as rare to Long Island or, for one reason or another, as of special interest. Writing at a much later date, Theodore alluded to "certain boyhood ornithological publications" that had reported "such items as, for instance, that on one occasion a fish-crow, and on another an Ipswich sparrow, were obtained by one Theodore Roosevelt, Jr. at Oyster Bay."[7] These two birds were among the seventeen listed in *Notes*. Apparently Theodore had been more excited about their acquisition than about any of the others and, it would appear, with good reason. Respecting the fish crow, we have been advised, "Certainly much less was known about it in the 1870s than at present [and] it may have been rarer when Theodore was a boy."[8] As to the Ipswich sparrow, that bird had not been recognized as a species until 1872.[9] It may be that Theodore regarded the acquisition of his Ipswich sparrow more highly than any other specimen in his boyhood collection. Thirty years later he was able clearly to recall intimate details of the event: "At Oyster Bay on a desolate winter afternoon many years ago [1878]. . . . I shot an Ipswich sparrow on a strip of ice-rimmed beach, where the long coarse grass waved in front of a growth of blueberries, beach-plums, and stunted pines."[10] Of the remaining birds Theodore had listed in his 1879 paper, four were warblers, the prairie, golden-winged, pine, and Connecticut. Another was the mockingbird, which then must have been a rare visitor as far north as Long Island. He seemingly included the common black-capped chickadee in order to put on record an observation heretofore unpublished: "With us, [the black-cap] is very fond of using the fur of the pine mouse as lining [for its nest]." Though just another bird list, and a relatively inconsequential one at that, it nevertheless caught the eye of J. A. Allen, who reported: "Several of the species are given as rare to the locality, while the observations respecting others are of interest."[11]

Through reading Theodore's letters and diary entries written between his return from Maine and the end of his junior year, it is evident that athletic, social, and club responsibilities increasingly demanded his attention. Yet, in spite of these demands, Theodore's third year at Harvard terminated well academically, his grades being: German 82; Italian 82; themes 76; forensics 60; logic 85; metaphysics 87; philosophy 89; natural history 1 92; and natural history 3 97. With a grade average of about 83, Theodore ranked thirteenth in his class. His overall record might well have been even higher if, now and then, he had resisted the companionship of girls, especially that of "pretty Alice,"[12] who was, of course, Alice Lee of fashionable Chestnut Hill.

3

As the summer of 1879 wore on, Theodore developed a stubborn urge to rejoin Bill Sewall in Island Falls, and the urge led to reality when Arthur Cutler and Emlen Roosevelt agreed to accompany him. On August 22, from Chestnut Hill, Theodore wrote Corinne: "It is just after breakfast, and I am writing in Mrs. Lee's parlour. I am going to Maine this evening."[13]

Theodore, Emlen, and Arthur arrived at Mattewamkeag station in mid-morning of the next day. Both Bill Sewall and Wilmot Dow were there to welcome them and to drive them to Island Falls. During the next two days the men made preparations for a trip to Mt.

Katahdin. Theodore's verbatim account of the trip to the foot of Mt. Katahdin, its ascent and its descent (requiring four days), follows herewith:

August 26, 1879—Emlen, Arthur Cutler, Will Dow, Bill Sewall and I started for Mt. Katahdin. Drove twenty-three miles, and then carried our packs about ten [more], when we went into camp. I carried about forty-five pounds, including my guns and ammunition. Crossing a stream I lost one of my shoes. Fortunately I had brought a pair of moccasins tied to my pack.

August 27, 1879—Walked up to the head of Katahdin Lake where we camped. I got along very well with my pack. Killed four ducks . . . also picked up a couple of partridges. We caught a few trout. Black flies are pretty bad, but they do not bother me yet.

August 28, 1879—After lunch we started for Katahdin [5,268 feet high]. . . . We caught about 100 trout at [a] nearby brook, then got lost, and after tramping through frightful ground till after dark camped out by a small water hole, tired and hungry—but happy. There are plenty of fresh tracks of both bear and caribou, but we saw nothing living except the usual woodpeckers, chickadees, jays, &c.

August 29, 1879—Started before daylight, walking straight through the woods, and then up Katahdin; it was very difficult walking, and both Emlen and Arthur gave out before making the summit, the view from which was beautiful. I find I can endure fatigue and hardship nearly as well as the lumbermen. . . . Reached our camp at Katahdin Lake [at the foot of the mountain] about dusk. . . . It is raining and we are all soaked through.

Four days later Theodore and the others were back in Island Falls, with Theodore writing, "I have enjoyed the trip exceedingly— am in good condition." Since neither Emlen nor Arthur had been able to reach the top of Mt. Katahdin, it is obvious that they were not in the best of condition. Certainly, as a preparation for the climb, neither had walked long distances, nor in one day, had rowed across Long Island Sound and back.

Apparently Emlen and Arthur had joined Theodore in Maine solely to undertake the Mt. Katahdin outing. In any event, once back in Island Falls, they left for home. Theodore stayed on, having made arrangements in advance with Bill Sewall to visit the Munsungan Lakes region of Aroostook County. Theodore's diary entry for September 4 reads: "Spent the day preparing for the Munsungan trip. I shall go . . . alone with Bill Sewall. For provisions I take tea, pork and hardtack, and some flour; we have a shelter tent, two blankets and some cooking utensils; and one complete change of under-clothing each."

Theodore's diary fails to make entirely clear the route he and Sewall followed to the Munsungan Lakes area, so that some clarification seems in order. On leaving Island Falls, they traveled almost due north to the approximate site of the present-day town of Oxbow, Maine. En route, they crossed the watershed between the Penobscot River, whose waters flow south into the Atlantic, and the Aroostook River, which flows northeast from Oxbow to empty into the St. John's River. Having reached the Aroostook River, which they did on September 5, they went by dugout canoe up that stream some twenty miles, traveling slightly southwest instead of north, until they came to the mouth of the Munsungan River, a southern tributary of the Aroostook. They then ascended the Munsungan, roughly an additional twenty miles, until they arrived at the Munsungan Lakes. At that point, they were only about sixty miles south and east of the Canadian border, and thus in one of the more remote parts of the Maine wilderness.

The events of the days (September 6–9) when Theodore and Bill paddled, poled, pushed, and pulled the heavy dugout up the Aroostook and Munsungan rivers to the Munsungan Lakes are told in Theodore's own words:

September 6, 1879—Started . . . in a pirogue or dugout. . . . We went about 20 miles up the Aroostook, paddling sometimes, poling most of the way. The scenery is very beautiful and wild. I saw no trace of man, but also no trace of game. Trout was plentiful however. Pitched camp before dark. . . . Black flies, mosquitoes and midges pretty plentiful. I don't mind them much.

September 7, 1879 [Sunday]—We started as usual, there was no use of laying up; but I compromised by not shooting or fishing. We poled up the Aroostook till lunch time, when we were near the mouth of the Munsungan. Up this we had to wade, dragging our boat. The water was up to our ankles, now to our hips. It was heavy work, moreover it was raining heavily, and toward dusk we pitched camp, drenched through and tired out. Midges bad.

September 8, 1879—Rained hard all day. We started early; for several hours it was rapid, shoal water, through which we waded, dragging the heavy dugout over the rocks and shallows. Then we got into deeper, dead water, but this was nearly as bad owing to the beaver dams and log jams which we had to cut through or pull around. There were some falls we had to get up, taking everything out of the boat; then we pulled up through more dead water, then poled through the lower Mansungan lake and half way up the middle one, where we camped. Tired out and wet through, hungry and cold—but we are having a lovely time.

September 9, 1879—Rained all day, but we paddled up the middle lake and then walked (through most frightful ground) to the head of the upper one. On the way I saw a few partridges, an old moose track, a recent bear track, and a few old signs of deer and caribou. On the lake are a few loons and fish ducks.[14] As game is so scarce, I shall go right back to Island Falls, instead of staying up here, as I had intended. As wet through as usual, and rather tired. . . . The work is very hard, but I am enjoying the trip greatly.[15]

Four days later, on September 13, Theodore and Bill were again back in Island Falls, their return route having been essentially the same as the one going north. On the way, according to Theodore, they subsisted mainly on food they shot (or caught): one wood duck, one black duck, one red rabbit, eight ruffed grouse, and several trout. The last three days they traveled on foot, on the first, fifteen miles, on the second, "over twenty," and on the third, twenty-five.

Having just completed the most ambitious, arduous, and harrowing of his three trips in Maine, it might logically be expected that Theodore would hurry to catch the first train to Boston and Cambridge—and to Alice Lee. But not so; instead he extended his stay twelve more days, until September 24, spending most of them in the woods with Sewall, in a last-ditch effort to bag at least one of the larger game animals. It should be more than ever evident by now that Theodore possessed a doggedness uncommon to most men and, at the same time, a spirit remarkably attuned to the out-of-doors, especially to the beauty of the great virgin, coniferous forests of Aroostook County, Maine.

A brief look back at Theodore's three Maine trips reveals that he spent a total of sixty-nine days in that state, most of them in the company of Bill Sewall, and traveled in excess of one thousand miles. During those days he collected a sizable number of birds, mostly ruffed grouse, spruce grouse, and ducks, but only a few mammals, among them a raccoon, a fox, a Canada lynx, and a deer. He did, as we know, get a tantalizing glimpse of the rear end of a caribou as it fled to safety.

When Theodore, at the end of this third trip to Maine, shook the hands of Bill Sewall and Will Dow, not one of them had even the slightest notion that their next meeting would be on the High Plains of the Dakotas.

4

Theodore arrived back in Cambridge on September 25. He was now a Harvard senior, with all the rights and privileges customarily pertaining to that academic summit. One privilege allowed him to ease his course load. Instead of taking nine courses, he chose five: one prescribed (forensics) and four electives (Italian, political economy, natural history 4, and natural history 6). Like other college seniors, Theodore wanted leisure to enjoy the months of his final scholastic year. In particular, he sought time to be with Alice Lee.

At some imprecise moment during his senior year, Theodore abandoned his original intention of becoming "a scientific man of the Audubon, Wilson, Baird or Coues type." The specific time may have occurred immediately preceding February 13, 1880. On that date, Theodore wrote to Hal Minot:

Dear Hal: I write to you to announce my engagement to Miss Alice Lee; but do not speak of it till Monday. I have been in love with her for nearly two years now; and have made everything subordinate to winning her; so you can perhaps understand a change in my ideas as regards science, &c. *Your aff friend*[16]

What did Theodore mean in this letter by stating that he had subordinated everything to winning Alice Lee—unless she had refused to marry him if he persisted in his resolve to make science his life's work? Is it unreasonable to assume that the young lady, with the blood of the Lodges and Higginsons in her veins, had turned up her already slightly tilted nose, when Theodore, in proposing marriage, had nothing more glamorous to offer in the way of a career than a lifetime devoted to long hours in museum laboratories redolent with smells of formaldehyde or to excursions into wilds populated with all manner of scary things? Or did she, with uncanny intuition, persuade him that his life's work lay in broader, more rewarding fields?

Months before Theodore wrote the above letter to Minot, there were intimations of an approaching break with science. It will be recalled that Theodore had written Bamie of his wish to consult with Mr. Choate and to his mother about his enjoyment of political science courses taught by J. Lawrence Laughlin. Not until years later did Laughlin look back upon "an interesting conference" he once had with Theodore: "He came to me to discuss whether it would be better for him to specialize in natural history or to take more economics. He gave no indication that he was thinking of a public career. My advice was that the country at that time especially needed men trained to think correctly on public questions and that those questions were nine-tenths economics. I cannot say that my advice influenced him, but he did continue economics in his senior year."[17]

Other, earlier evidence of a possible shift away from natural history exists. On February 7, 1878, he made his final entry in his "Field Book of Zoology"[18] and, soon afterward, severed his connection with the Harvard Natural History Society, giving as his reason "a press of other duties in my studies and in outside societies."[19] Also, in a December 1878 diary entry, Theodore wrote that if he continued in science he would have "to study three years abroad," an outlook that, just to think about, made him "perfectly blue."[20]

As to whether any of this earlier indecisiveness was attributable to Alice Lee is conjectural. It can be said, however, that, when Theodore later made public his explanation for abandoning natural history, he included no mention of Alice, saying, instead:

I did not [continue in science] for the simple reason that at that time Harvard, and I suppose our other colleges, utterly ignored the possibilities of the faunal naturalist, the outdoor naturalist and observer of nature. They treated biology as purely a science of the laboratory and the microscope, a science whose adherents were to spend their time in the study of minute forms of marine life, or else in section-cutting and the study of the tissues of the higher organisms under the microscope. This attention was, no doubt, in part due to the fact that in most colleges then there was a not always intelligent copying of what was done in the great German universities. . . . My taste was specialized in a totally different direction, and I had no more desire or ability to become a microscopist or section-cutter than to be a mathematician. Accordingly I abandoned all thought of becoming a naturalist.[21]

It was true, of course, that Harvard did not then offer courses requiring field work and, in consequence, ignored the background that Theodore desired and thought should have been provided. However, Theodore's explanation of his reason for abandoning natural history failed, as we have noted, to tell the complete story. It included nothing about his developing interest in political economy nor his misgivings concerning years of postgraduate study abroad, and no allusion to Alice Lee. Furthermore, when Theodore's Harvard natural history teachers were later interviewed they expressed surprise. Dr. Mark, for one, saying that Theodore, to his recollection, had never complained to him about the way things were run in the department.[22] Also, in his several letters to family and friends (Minot among them), he gave not even a hint that he was disappointed over Harvard's inattention to field work; indeed, from his letters one may build up a pretty fair case for the opposite point of view, Theodore every so often writing of his enjoyment of this or that natural history course.

Another factor, one easily overlooked, may have had a bearing on Theodore's decision to abandon science as a career, namely, a lack of encouragement. The members of his own family, including his father, had been skeptical about his intention from the beginning. Not one of his Harvard teachers, as far as is known, had encouraged his ambition. From what Charles F. Batchelder later wrote, no member of the Nuttall Ornithological Club—excepting Minot of course—nurtured his aspirations. And certainly Alice Lee, whose varied interests did not include animals, not even birds, supplied no encouragement. As a consequence, Theodore's decision, when he was finally forced to make it, may have been neither difficult nor painful. But what was the alternative? Shortly before Theodore's graduation from Harvard, he told a friend: "I am going to try to help the cause of better government in New York City; I don't exactly know how."[23]

Although Theodore Roosevelt thus abandoned natural history as a future vocation, he never lost his love for the birds and other wilderness creatures. Indeed, that love remained a strong and well-disciplined—even sustaining—force until he died. Strong and sustaining, too, were his many friendships with naturalists, one of the first being with Minot. In letters to Minot during Theodore's later years at Harvard—after Minot had been forced to withdraw from college—Theodore provided meaningful evidence of their warm and steadfast friendship. Excerpts follow:

16 Winthrop St., Camb.
Jan. 11th, '79

Dear Old Hal: I was particularly delighted to hear from you again, my dear old friend and sympathizer. It will be lovely to see you again in the spring. . . . I did some quite good work last summer and this winter, got my first Ipswich sparrow. . . . *Your Loving Friend, Theodore Roosevelt*

Oyster Bay, Long Island, N.Y.
July 27th, '79

Dear Old Hal: I suppose you are having a lovely time now; if I could have only gone with you. What lovely excursions we could have made!

I have been spending the last month in boating with my cousins about the Sound; and before I go back to Harvard I shall spend all six weeks or so in the [Maine] woods. I have not done much collecting this summer, for, as you know, I don't approve of too much slaughter. . . . *Yours ever, Teddy R.*[24]

16 Winthrop St., Cambridge
Sept. 20th, 1879

Dear Old Hal: . . . . I think I can certainly get away to the White Mts. for a Saturday and a Sunday [with you] this October. . . . I spent most of last summer at Oyster Bay, but was up in Maine for four weeks; I had some perfectly absurd things happen to me up there, which I shall tell you when we next meet. I have started work again with a will; last year I did pretty well in my studies, and I want to keep up in my average. . . . *Yours ever, Ted*

[Oyster Bay, L.I., N.Y.]
July 5th, 1880

Dear Old Hal: I had just answered your letter when I heard of your great loss [the death of your mother]; so I tore my letter up, but now don't think me intruding too soon upon your sorrow if I write to you. Dear old fellow, I shall never forget how your sympathy comforted me in the hour of my trouble. . . . In my life I have known great sorrow and great joy, and though the joy has far overbalanced the sorrow, yet I have suffered keenly enough to be able to sympathize with others. . . . I will write you again soon; good-by, old friend. Your Loving Teddy[25]

What additional letters Roosevelt wrote to Minot—there *must* have been others—seemingly have been lost. Meanwhile, Minot became associated with a railroad, and in due course he was elevated to the presidency of the Eastern Railroad of Minnesota. Though deeply engrossed in this profession, he retained a deep interest in birds, and, it is said, looked forward to periods of leisure when he would again be able to get away and enjoy the companionship of his woodland friends. On November 13, 1890, near New Florence, Pennsylvania, he was killed in a train wreck.

5

Meanwhile, Harvard senior Theodore Roosevelt was busying himself more than usual. In addition to the demands of his teachers, of his several club organizations, of a Sunday School class that he taught regularly—and had taught since early in his freshman year—and by the *Harvard Advocate* for which he provided occasional copy, there was also his eager, continuing pursuit of his adored Alice. Moreover, and astonishingly, Theodore had started writing a book: *The Naval War of 1812*.

Being so engaged, and in so many directions, it can be no surprise that Theodore's grades as a senior failed to measure up to those of his junior year: Italian 70; forensics 65; political economy 78; natural history 4 (geology) 91; and natural history 6 (advanced zoology) 89. Shaler taught the geology course, and Faxon the advanced zoology.

Writing later about his Harvard scholastic record, Roosevelt said that he had been just "a reasonably good student."[26] He was, of course, minimizing his record. He graduated twenty-first in a class of 161 and received a diploma ornamented with the academically coveted words *magna cum laude*. He was also elected to Phi Beta Kappa and was accorded "Honorable Mention" in natural history. Roosevelt's scholastic rating, incidentally, was equal to those of two other distinguished Harvard graduates, Ralph Waldo Emerson and James Russell Lowell.

Roosevelt often belittled his mental capabilities, not only as a student, but also as a naturalist, author, historian, and whatever. He wished to leave the impression with the American public that he was just an average citizen, who had succeeded through diligence and hard work as any man of average intelligence might do. It would have been a most egregious political error, as he saw it, for him to have divulged the truth, namely, that he had been a youthful prodigy and, as a man, an intellectual heavyweight.

Theodore terminated his residence at 16 Winthrop Street, Cambridge, on June 30, 1880, the same day that he graduated from Harvard College. How did he fit into the select, diversified group of Harvard alumni? According to a reporter for the *Pioneer Press* of St. Paul, Minnesota, who, some months later, had a good look at him: "He is not at all an ideal Harvard alumnus, for he lacks that ingrained conceit and grace of manner that a residence at Harvard insures. Although of the old Knickerbocker stock, his manner and carriage are awkward and not at all impressive."[27]

For Theodore Roosevelt, Jr., the 1880 Harvard Commencement exercises could not have been the totally happy series of events he had anticipated. Only a day or two before commencement, to satisfy a college requirement, he had visited the Harvard physician, Dr. Dudley A. Sargeant, for what he had thought would be another satisfactory routine physical examination. To his dismay, it did not turn out that way. Dr. Sargeant had informed him that he had an ailing heart, that he should shun strenuous exercise, even to running up stairs, and that he should choose an occupation as free as possible of violent exertion. As later reported, Theodore hesitated only momentarily before he told Dr. Sargeant: "I am going to do all the things you tell me not to do. If I've got to live the sort of life you have described, I don't care how short it is."[28] Still today, in the files of the old Harvard gymnasium one may find Theodore's card, on which Dr. Sargeant had written, "Irregular heart."[29] So, without doubt, the college physician had detected irregularities in Theodore's heart beat, though some irregularities, such as extra systoles, may not necessarily signify an organically unsound heart.

After leaving Dr. Sargeant's office, Theodore made a quick but well-considered decision; he would maintain complete silence about the physician's adverse report. As a result, he told none of his family, and not even his Alice, with whom he would soon exchange marriage vows. Some sources would have it that he never did tell them. Throughout the graduation activities, Theodore fairly radiated good health and happiness, secure in the knowledge that Alice and his family, blissfully unaware of the doctor's findings, were enjoying to the full each and every event.

Following his graduation, Theodore seemingly made another decision: he would prove Dr. Sargeant wrong—or die in the attempt. As long as uncertainty existed, he could not, in good conscience, marry Alice. Until mid-July, he spent much of his time at various places along the Maine coast, among them Bar Harbor and Mt. Desert Island. Here, beginning at once, Theodore daily subjected his heart to strenuous tests: tennis, hiking, boating, and swimming.

On July 16 Theodore and Elliott left for the Midwest on a hunting trip, visiting Illinois, Iowa, and Minnesota. It was while in the vicinity of Moorhead, Minnesota, that he walked across prairie lands, not stopping until he had covered thirty miles.[30]

Apparently satisfied that this feat had proved Dr. Sargeant wrong, on October 27 (his birthday) Theodore married Alice Lee. The marriage by no means deterred him, however, from future endurance tests. In May of the following year, while with Alice in Switzerland on a delayed honeymoon, he climbed the Matterhorn, doing so, he informed Bill Sewall, because an Englishman had told him he could not do it.[31]

If Theodore thereafter entertained any lingering doubts as to the soundness of his heart, he surely dispelled them, once and for all, on the Fourth of July, 1882. On that date, in Chestnut Hill, he played ninety-one games of tennis.[32] Ninety-one games is the equivalent of a five-set match with such scores as 9–7, 6–3, 10–12, 8–10, and 14–12. Moreover, by the time the match ended Theodore and his opponent must have exchanged forehands and backhands for no less than four or more hours. (There were then, of course, no tie breakers).

Even before this date, Theodore Roosevelt possibly felt that he was ready to take on the world. And why not? He had earned a Harvard College diploma inscribed *magna cum laude*, he had won the hand of his beloved Alice, he had climbed the Matterhorn, and had proved to himself that his heartbeat was steady and strong. But, if queried as to the kind of world he would prefer to take on, it is our guess that, if he had answered truthfully, he would have asserted a preference for an animate world characterized by a superabundance of animals and plants.

Notes

1. Morison, *Letters*, 1:33–34.
2. Ibid., 34.
3. Ibid., 35–36.
4. Roosevelt, "Harvard Diary."
5. Morison, *Letters*, 1:37.
6. Putnam, *Theodore Roosevelt*, 160.

7. Roosevelt, *Autobiography,* 21.

8. Robert Cushman Murphy, department of ornithology, the American Museum of Natural History, to author, Aug. 11, 1944.

9. The Ipswich sparrow (*Passerculus princeps*) was first described by C. J. Maynard, in the *American Naturalist* 6 (Oct. 1872): 637–38. Theodore obtained his specimen six years later, on Dec. 28, 1878. See Roosevelt, *Works, Mem. Ed.,* 6:472.

10. Roosevelt, *Works, Mem. Ed.,* 3:362.

11. *Bulletin, Nuttall Ornithological Club,* July 1879.

12. Morison, *Letters,* 1:38.

13. Ibid., 40.

14. Evidently the common merganser, sometimes called fish duck.

15. Roosevelt, "Harvard Diary."

16. Morison, *Letters,* 1:43.

17. J. Laurence Laughlin, "Roosevelt at Harvard," *Review of Reviews* (Oct. 1924): 397.

18. Roosevelt's "Field Book of Zoology" was, as earlier indicated, the last of his boyhood natural history journals. His final entry read: "*Aegiothus linaria* [*Acanthis flammea,* common redpoll]. A small flock were seen."

19. TRCHL.

20. Roosevelt, "Harvard Diary." See also Putnam, *Theodore Roosevelt,* 177.

21. Roosevelt, *Autobiography,* 24–25.

22. This was Dr. Mark's recollection, when in 1943 I visited him in his Cambridge home. He was then in his ninety-seventh year.

23. William Roscoe Thayer, *Theodore Roosevelt* (Boston: Houghton Mifflin, 1919), 21.

24. Here, perhaps for the first time, Theodore used the name "Teddy." We seem to recall having read that Roosevelt disliked that nickname, though perhaps in later years only.

25. For these letters from Roosevelt to Minot, see Vail, "Your Loving Friend, T. R.," 8–45.

26. Roosevelt, *Autobiography,* 23.

27. Hermann Hagedorn, *Roosevelt in the Bad Lands* (Boston: Houghton Mifflin, 1921), 89.

28. Hagedorn, *Boys' Life,* 63–64.

29. Putnam, *Theodore Roosevelt,* 198.

30. Ibid., 207.

31. Sewall, *T.R.,* 9.

32. Morison, *Letters,* 1:56.

10

"Shall Send You the Skins"

DURING THE MONTHS immediately following his marriage to Alice Lee, Theodore lived in ecstasy, was doubtless never happier in his life. Leaving Boston on the day after the wedding, he and Alice went directly to Oyster Bay where for two weeks they had Tranquillity to themselves, except for two maids and a manservant. The days passed all too quickly, the result of daily horseback rides, tennis, rowing, and long buggy rides. As the honeymoon neared its end, Theodore informed his diary: "I am living in a dream world, how I wish it could last forever."[1]

But, of course, the "dream world" could not go on. It ended on Saturday, November 13, with the bride and groom moving to 6 West 57th Street. Here they were lovingly welcomed by Mittie, and here they would live through the winter, while Theodore attended classes at the Law School of Columbia University.

Theodore, it appears, had by now resolved to pursue a legal career, perhaps as a result of talks with his Uncle Robert, himself a lawyer. Having made that decision, Theodore reasoned that, even if he did not open a law office, the knowledge and self-discipline he would acquire in obtaining a law degree would benefit him whatever profession he ultimately chose.

The Columbia School of Law was then located in the old Schermerhorn building on Great Jones Street some fifty-four blocks (about three miles) down Fifth Avenue from 57th Street. Punctually, each morning on class days, Theodore left home at 7:45 and, at 8:30, having walked the entire distance, arrived at the law school in time for his first class. In the afternoon he walked directly back to 57th Street, except when he took the time to stop at the Astor Library to obtain additional data for his advancing studies on the naval history of the War of 1812 or at his Uncle Robert's office to read law. This

134

round trip of some six miles from home to law school, made in all kinds of weather, Theodore would explain, constituted his only form of exercise when he attended law school.[2]

Throughout this winter Theodore crammed many activities into his days besides his legal studies. He attended numerous dinners, receptions, balls, and musicals and, in so doing, introduced his bride to New York society. He enjoyed even more, however, the winter days when, with snow on the ground, he often took Alice on long sleigh rides through Central Park or on Riverside Drive. Between times, Theodore had been elected a trustee of the Orthopedic Hospital and of the New York Infant Asylum and, by mid-January, had begun showing up at meetings of the Republican Club.

At the end of the school year Theodore and Alice sailed for Europe on a second honeymoon, this one lasting more than four months. During this visit Theodore did not write home about throstles, wagtails, kestrels, and other birds, as he had on previous trips abroad. Instead, he commented on such topics as his unbounded admiration for the genius of Rembrandt, his dislike of the work of Rubens, and his love of the fluviatile attractions of Venice. Also, in addition to climbing the Matterhorn, he took Alice to the London Zoo, where he became momentarily speechless when Alice asked him who had shaved the lions—her explanation for the animals' manes.[3]

Back in New York in late September, Theodore resumed his daily walks to Columbia Law School. Succeeding events occurred in almost breathtaking speed. Theodore increased his attendance at meetings of the Republican Club, and on October 28—one month after his return from Europe and one day following his twenty-third birthday—he was nominated by the Republicans as their candidate to the New York State Assembly. On November 6 he was elected to that office.

Since his graduation from Harvard, Roosevelt had regarded himself as a literary and legal figure; he was now, as a consequence of election to the Assembly, also a political figure.

2

It was on April 25, 1882, five months after Roosevelt's election to the New York Assembly, that Spencer F. Baird, then holding office of secretary of the Smithsonian Institution, wrote Roosevelt:

Dear Sir: Dr. [Elliott] Coues has sent me your letter [to him] offering certain specimens to the Smithsonian Institution. In reply I beg to say that the same will be very acceptable to us even should there be nothing actually new, for they will give us the opportunity at least of supplying some Museum at home or abroad, and of obtaining in exchange a possible rarity. . . .

May I ask what relation you are to my much esteemed friend Robert B. Roosevelt or Mr. Theodore? Yours respectfully

In this manner began a brief exchange of letters between the aging secretary of the Smithsonian and a young New York State legislator, who would in time take up residence in the White House. At this date Baird seems to have been ignorant of Roosevelt's boyhood activities as a naturalist, of his founding at the age of nine his own natural history museum, of his early acquired skills as a taxidermist, of his amazing industry in enlarging his museum—this enlargement furthered by collecting abroad as well as at home—and of his biological studies at Harvard. Beyond question, in offering to give his specimens to the Smithsonian, Roosevelt had come to the decision that, having assumed heavy responsibilities in the political arena, he could no longer provide his specimens with the care they demanded. On receipt of Baird's letter, Roosevelt replied at once, and on "State of New York, Assembly Chamber," stationery:

April 27th, 1882

Dear Sir: I am a son of Theodore Roosevelt and a nephew of Robert B. I am very much obliged for your kind letter, and shall send you the [bird]skins; would your collection include Egyptian skins, as I have some of them? Very truly yours.

On the next day Baird answered:

April 28, 1882

Dear Sir: I shall be very happy indeed to have the Egyptian skins, referred to in your letter, as well as others, from different parts of the world, which you may be disposed to contribute to the Museum.

I am very glad to know something of your personality. I was well acquainted with your father and, in common with all his other friends, esteemed him most highly. Yours truly.

Roosevelt lost little time in having his specimens boxed and shipped to Baird. One month later the latter assured the donor that his gift had arrived:

May 26, 1882

Dear Sir: I have great pleasure in acknowledging the arrival of the collection referred to in your letter of April 27. I was by no means prepared for so admirable or extensive a contribution, and beg to thank you very much for it. There are many specimens in the series which will be of great service to us in extending and completing the collections of the several compartments.

I need hardly say that whatever [else] you can furnish in the way of specimens of natural history will always be gladly received. Yours truly,[4]

It should be appended here that Baird had joined the Smithsonian staff in 1850, and Joseph Henry,[5] the Institution's first secretary, had at once given him the responsibility of enlarging the Smithsonian's then lean natural history collection. In this job Baird exceeded Henry's expectations, due largely to the former's tremendous capabilities in inspiring young men to espouse natural history as a career and then, after proper training—and an assist from the War Department—in getting them placed in remote parts of the continent most suitable for the collecting of plants and animals unknown to science. As a consequence, the Smithsonian's cabinets filled rapidly, and Baird's opportunities for exchanges increased. No one then living was better qualified to pass judgment on the worth of a collection, including Roosevelt's, than Baird.

An early move by Baird, after he had assumed his duties at the Smithsonian, was to institute the practice of keeping accession records for all acquisitions. As a result, with the arrival of Roosevelt's collection, some staff member at the Smithsonian, using pen and ink, made a detailed record of each specimen Roosevelt had entrusted to the museum.

This Smithsonian accession record has a wealth of information. It contains, for each specimen, a species number, Latin binomial, the conventional symbol indicating sex, and date and place of acquisition. For example, data recorded for the robin, the first bird on the list, reads: "[No.] 464—*Merula migratoria*, ♂ ad[ult], Oyster Bay, L.I., Apr. 8, 1875." This information about the robin—and that of other birds in the collection—had been copied verbatim from Roosevelt's pink-lettered specimen label attached to the robin. The only thing missing is the common name, Theodore having long since opted for the Latin binomial instead. Whoever at the Smithsonian had been delegated to prepare the handwritten accession record of

Roosevelt's gift may well have found the task tedious. The transcribed data covered twenty-five, legal-sized pages. Also, and more significantly, the Latin binomials on these pages add up to a total of 622, this being the number of birdskins Theodore Roosevelt in 1882 had presented to the Smithsonian.

Looking closely, one finds additional facts of interest in the accession record: (1) fifty-three of the 622 skins had been acquired by Roosevelt in the Old World; (2) of the fifty-three, thirty-one had come from Egypt, six from Syria, five from Austria, one from Germany (Bonn), one from France (Paris), and two from England (Liverpool); (3) the skins prepared in the United States had originated, for the most part, in three localities: Oyster Bay (at least 500), the Adirondacks (ca. eighty-five), and Garrison, New York (between fifty-five and sixty); and (4) the collection included a large number of duplicate specimens, for example, twelve of the myrtle warbler, eighteen of the prairie warbler, and fifteen of the white-throated sparrow.

From time to time, at later dates, Smithsonian ornithologists extended their record of Roosevelt's gift by explaining how they disposed of supernumerary specimens. This information was written on pages dextrally adjoining the twenty-five oversized pages already mentioned. Thus we learn that Baird sent duplicates not only to other institutions (colleges, universities, and museums) but also to specific individuals, with the expectation of improving, through exchanges, both the quality and quantity of the Smithsonian holdings. As a result of this added intelligence, it is possible to name the principal recipients and the approximate number of duplicate skins each received. Some 200 of them ended up in the hands of individuals, three in particular: William H. Fox,[6] who acquired eighty-seven, Joseph H. Batty,[7] who obtained fifty-five, and Richard B. Sharpe,[8] who got twenty-five. All three of these men were ornithologists and well known to Baird, Fox and Batty being early members of the American Ornithologists' Union, and Sharpe, an Englishman, being affiliated with the British Ornithologists' Union as well as keeper of the department of birds in the British Museum. Both local and foreign institutions received Roosevelt duplicates. Among those at home were Indiana State University, Oberlin College, Illinois Wesleyan, Utah State, and the American Museum of Natural History. Among foreign recipients were museums in England, France, Norway, India, Pakistan, Japan, New Zealand, and Argentina.

A most interesting feature of the accession record is its disclosure of the names of duplicate skins sent to overseas museums, the names of those institutions, and the dates of shipments. Specific examples follow herewith:

Hylocichla fuscescens [Veery], ♂ ad., Oyster Bay, L.I., Sept. 5, 1877. . . . Sent to Bergen Museum [Norway], June 23, 1886.

Troglodytes aedon [House Wren]. ♂ ad., Oyster Bay, L.I., May 24, 1874. . . . Sent to Karachi Mus. [Pakistan], June 25/86.

Dendroica fusca [Blackburnian Warbler]. ♂ ad., St. Regis Lake [Adirondacks], N.Y., June 26, 1877. . . . Sent to La Plata Mus. [Argentina], 1895.

Loxia curvirostra [Red Crossbill]. ♂ ad., Garrison [N.Y.], Dec. 30. 1874. . . . Sent to R. B. Sharpe [British Museum], Dec. 15/84.

Melospiza melodia [Song Sparrow]. ♀ ad., Oyster Bay, L.I., Mar. 25, 1876. . . . Sent to Paris Mus. Nat. Hist. [France], March 23/86.

Agelaius phoeniceus [Red-winged Blackbird]. ♂ ad., Oyster Bay, L.I., June 10, 1876. . . . Sent to Madras Mus. [India], Nov. 9/87.

Dumetella carolinensis [Catbird]. ♂ ad., Oyster Bay, L.I., June 28, 1876. . . . Sent to J. F. Cheeseman, Auckland Mus. [New Zealand], Oct. 31/85.

Certhia familiaris [Brown Creeper]. ♂ ad., Oyster Bay, L.I., Oct. 25, 1875. . . . Sent to Tokyo Mus. [Japan], Sept. 27/87.

Pinicola enucleator [Pine Grosbeak]. ♀ ad., Garrison [N.Y.], Jan. 20, 1875. . . . Sent to Albany Mus., S. Africa, in 1897.

The Smithsonian was eminently successful in exchanging Roosevelt's duplicate skins, the number of them sent to individuals and institutions in expectation of obtaining "possible rarities" exceeding 300. For various other reasons, the original number of 622 was further reduced. The accession record alludes here and there to "Destroyed" and "Lost on loan." A late invoice of Roosevelt's skins at the Smithsonian revealed the present number to be 220.[9]

3

Theodore Roosevelt did not give his entire collection of boyhood natural history specimens to the Smithsonian. At later date(s) he presented a lesser number to the American Museum of Natural History, New York City. Accession records at that institution list approximately 125 birdskins and four mounted birds: a snowy owl and three Egyptian species (a spur-winged lapwing, a crocodile bird, and a white-tailed lapwing).

Since Theodore Roosevelt's father played an important role in the founding of the American Museum, a question at once intrudes: why did his son not give the bulk of his boyhood collection to that museum, instead of to the Smithsonian? Any answer is conjectural, though Roosevelt's decision may well have turned on the fact that in 1882 the Smithsonian, founded in 1846, was definitely a more prestigious institution than the American Museum, not founded until 1869. Also, Roosevelt's self-esteem, an attribute not entirely absent from his character, could have been a factor. It is altogether possible that he took pride in reporting to acquaintances, including fellow legislators, that the fruits of his boyhood natural history labors had found a home in the Smithsonian Institution.

Among Roosevelt's boyhood bird specimens, one stands alone, his stuffed snowy owl (*Nyctea scandiaca*). For years this specimen has been on display, under a protective glass dome, at the American Museum, and here thousands of visitors have stopped to admire it and to comment on the fact that it had been stuffed and mounted by a teenager who later became president of the United States. The snowy owl is the most beautiful of all the owls, the plumage of the male being pure white except for occasional brownish spots. In the Western Hemisphere it breeds from far within the Arctic Circle and comes south only in winters. In 1876 one came south to Oyster Bay, Long Island, and never returned; and because it failed to return it today stands on exhibit in one of the world's great museums, a mute testimonial to the youthful industry and taxidermic talents of Theodore Roosevelt.

At least two more of Roosevelt's juvenile bird specimens exist today, and in yet another location, his birthplace at 28 East 20th Street, New York City. One is a purple finch and the other a starling, and both are mounted.[10] Roosevelt collected the former on Long Island and the latter in Egypt, which was as good a place as any to collect starlings in 1872 (the year Roosevelt obtained his specimen), since that species had not as yet been introduced into the United States.

On several counts, Theodore Roosevelt's boyhood collection of birds may justifiably lay claim to a goodly measure of distinctions:

(1) it was the product of a youth, who, born with an intense love of animals, early determined "to be a scientific man of the Audubon, or Wilson, or Baird, or Coues type"; (2) it was the obvious result of near incredible industry and perseverance; (3) it could boast of specimens collected in the Old World (in such distant countries as Egypt, the Holy Land, and Syria); (4) it exhibited a superb knowledge of ornithology, this having been largely obtained through a painstaking study of advanced texts by such professional naturalists as Baird and Coues; (5) it had elicited praise from the then secretary of the Smithsonian; and (6) it was the unique achievement of a youngster, who would take up residence at 1600 Pennsylvania Avenue, Washington, D.C.

4

Although Roosevelt had parted with his sizable collection of natural history specimens, two events, both occurring soon after his election as an assemblyman, provide immediate and unassailable proof that animals were still much on his mind—as they forever would be. At no time in his life did he lose, even momentarily, his love for the birds and other creatures inhabiting the out-of-doors.

The first event took the form of an essay that Roosevelt called "Sou'-sou'-southerly." This was a spirited and colorful account of a trip that he and Elliott made one wintry day in December in a twenty-one-foot, jib-and-mainsail boat on Long Island Sound. They were afloat from dawn to dusk, came close at times to capsizing on submerged rocks, and encountered everywhere great flocks of water birds: loons, coots, ducks and sou'-sou'-southerlies, this last name being one of several vernaculars applied to the oldsquaw (*Clangula hyemalis*). The essay could have been written only by one whose heart quickened at the sight of wings in action and warmed to the timber of mingled bird cries. Consider, for example, Roosevelt's opening paragraph:

Of all the waterfowl, that in the winter throng the half-frozen seas of Long Island Sound, the sou'-sou'-southerly is the most plentiful and most conspicuous. When the October weather begins to grow cool and sharp, and the northwest winds blow over the steel-gray waters till they are tossed into long, foam-capped billows, then, for the first time, small parties of these birds appear, their bold, var-

ied coloring and harsh but not unmusical clangour at once attract-
ing the attention of anyone who may be out sailing over the Autumn
seas. In the clear fall days they can be seen a long distance off, and
even before they can be seen, can be heard the loud "ha'-ha'-wee,
ha'-ha'-wee," from the real or fancied resemblance of which calls to
the words "sou'-sou'-southerly" they derive that one of their numerous titles with which I have headed this article.

The second event had its origin with a letter, one that Roosevelt
wrote to C. Hart Merriam soon after his Long Island Sound adventures. It was in response to an article Merriam had published about
the carnivorous habits of one of the insectivores, the short-tailed
shrew.[11] On reading this letter, Merriam learned that Theodore Roosevelt was himself an authority on this tiny mammal, that, in fact,
he had earlier written an essay about it, one he had titled "*Blarina
talpoides* (Short-tailed Shrew)." Merriam learned, too, that Roosevelt's observations on this shrew had closely paralleled his own,
even to a common agreement that "in proportion to its size, the
male shrew is as formidable as any of our beasts of prey." Roosevelt
knew this to be true, for at one time he had kept a male in a cage,
for several weeks running, and had daily watched its behavior, witnessing at one time its ferocity when killing and devouring a seven-
inch garter snake.

Thus the evidence mounts that Theodore Roosevelt, even
though he already had a foot in "the great bear pit of politics,"[12]
could no more have disassociated himself from the fascinating world
of animals than least sandpipers could forever renounce the sandy
beaches fronting the oceans.

Notes

1. Roosevelt, "Harvard Diary."
2. McCullough, *Morning on Horseback*, 232.
3. Morison, *Letters*, 1:48.
4. These letters of Baird and Roosevelt are currently in files of the
Smithsonian Archives, Washington, D.C.
5. Joseph Henry (1797–1878), American scientist and first secretary of
the Smithsonian Institution, a post he held 1846–78.
6. William Henry Fox (1857–1921), American naturalist, was born in
Washington, D.C., and in 1884 received an M.D. degree from Columbian
College, now George Washington University.
7. Joseph H. Batty (ca. 1846–1906), naturalist and taxidermist, was

born in Springfield, Mass., and later collected extensively in the West and in Central America, with many of his specimens going to the American Museum of Natural History.

8. Richard Bowdler Sharpe (1847–1909), British ornithologist, became keeper of the department of birds in the British Museum and, jointly with Henry E. Dresser, wrote *A History of the Birds of Europe* (1871–96).

9. Bonnie Farmer, technician, Department of Birds, Smithsonian Institution, to author, July 12, 1978.

10. The existence of these two birds at 28 East 20th Street, New York City, was verified by a letter of Apr. 6, 1979, to me from John W. Ryan, Jr., museum technician, Theodore Roosevelt Birthplace.

11. TRCHL. See also Cutright, *Roosevelt the Naturalist*, 36–37.

12. McCullough, *Mornings on Horseback*, 251.

11

"The Country Is Growing on Me"

IN OCTOBER 1882 Roosevelt was renominated to the New York State Assembly and in November reelected. During the winter that followed, he and Alice, in addition to accepting a strenuous involvement in social and political events, moved from 6 West 57th Street into a home of their own at 55 West 45th Street.

The State Assembly of 1883 adjourned on May 4. Three weeks later, on May 28, Theodore was a guest of honor and speaker at a meeting of the Free Trade Club of New York City. Of signal importance to his future was Theodore's introduction at this meeting to a retired naval officer, H. H. Gorringe, who had recently returned from a visit to the Little Missouri country of Dakota Territory. Roosevelt and Gorringe were attracted to each other immediately, Gorringe to Roosevelt because of the latter's recently published book on the naval War of 1812, and Roosevelt to Gorringe, when Gorringe assured him that buffalo were still obtainable in the valley of the Little Missouri River. Elliott had earlier described to Theodore his successes in Texas hunting buffalo, and Theodore, ever since, had been wanting to kill one himself. Before Roosevelt and Gorringe separated, after the adjournment of this meeting, they agreed to make a trip together in the fall to the Little Missouri.

In late August Roosevelt informed Gorringe: "I am now being forced to make my plans in regard to the political campaign this Autumn, and so I am anxious to fix, as near as is convenient to you, what will be about the dates of our departure and return. I am fond of politics, but fonder still of a little big game hunting."[1] Such was Theodore's seeming eagerness to get a buffalo—or bison as he later tried to persuade his countrymen to call it—that when circumstances prevented Gorringe from joining him he made the trip by himself.

One of the more fascinating, memorable, and illuminating chapters in Theodore Roosevelt's colorful, many-sided life began on September 8, 1883, at three o'clock in the morning, when he stepped from a Northern Pacific train into the darkness enveloping the small cattle-town of Little Missouri in the Badlands of Dakota Territory.

Theodore had arrived in the Dakota Badlands in the last days of its original state, while it was still "a land of vast silent places, of lonely rivers, and of plains where the wild game stared at the passing horsemen."[2] The old-timers had already noticed two most conspicuous changes: the Indian villages had largely given way to the white man's towns; and the buffalo, once darkening prairie from above the Canadian border to the Rio Grande, had dwindled from a mass of millions to a few scattered herds. In most other ways the Little Missouri Badlands probably looked as they had since the Pleistocene.

This region, soon to become almost as familiar to Theodore Roosevelt as the fields bordering Long Island Sound, is situated in what is now southwestern North Dakota. It is drained by the Little Missouri River, which here flows north before turning east to empty its waters into the Missouri. Numerous creeks feed the parent stream from both east and west, creeks bearing romantic-sounding names, among them Prairie Dog, Black Tail, Little Cannonball, Coyote, and Medicine Hat—all "sharp names that never get fat."[3]

On either side of the Little Missouri rise steep, jagged buttes, on the slopes of which grow stunted pines and cedars and sprawling clumps of sagebrush. These add touches of green to a colorful, stratified background made up of reds, blacks, purples, browns, and yellows, each of the different layers of sandstone, clay, and marl possessing its own distinctive hue. To Bill Sewall, who would soon follow Roosevelt to the Badlands, the composition of the colors was like "a great rag rug such as the women made down in Maine, of all kinds and colors of rags."[4] Theodore's more poetic imagination produced this thought: "When one is in the Badlands he feels as if they somehow *look* just exactly as Poe's tales and poems *sound*."[5]

Back from the river, on either side, are the land areas alluded to specifically as the Badlands, regions slashed and scored by the knives of the elements. For countless eons these climatic weapons had been at work, dissecting the original landscape into all manner of fantastically shaped eminences, with broken, intervening fissures branching in all directions, their sides sometimes gentle slopes, at other times sheer cliffs.

Separate from the Badlands is the prairie, level or undulating terrain, stretching to the horizon. In the spring this land is bright and green. In places, according to Roosevelt, a man could "gallop for miles at a stretch with his horse's hoofs sinking at every stride into the carpet of prairie roses, whose short stalks lift the beautiful blossoms but a few inches from the ground."[6] For the greater part of the year, however, the prairie land, for lack of rain, is dry and brown. In more arid parts sagebrush, prickly pear, and other cacti prevail.

The summers in this region may bring near intolerable heat, and the winters excessive cold. General Alfred Sully, after leading a summer expedition into the Dakotas, was asked his opinion of the Badlands. He replied that he "didn't know they were like anything, unless it was Hell with the fire gone out."[7] After Bill Sewall had there experienced temperatures as high as 125° F. in the shade, he was convinced that a few of the fires still burned. Also, before Bill left the Badlands, he had shivered through days when the thermometer registered 40° below zero.

2

The morning following Theodore's first night in the West, which he had spent in Little Missouri's only hotel, he inquired about obtaining a guide and was directed to a young man named Joe Ferris. Joe did not care much for the looks of the young dude from New York City and at first refused to act as a guide; he agreed only after Theodore made him a cash offer he could not afford to turn down.

Eager to begin the hunt, Theodore helped Joe to load a buckboard with provisions and hunting gear, and in mid-afternoon they headed south, following the course of the Little Missouri. They made their first stop at the Maltese Cross Ranch (also known as Chimney Butte), eight miles away, where Joe lived with his brother Sylvane and Bill Merrifield. The Ferris brothers and Merrifield were transplanted Canadians, who had moved to Dakota Territory only two or three years before Roosevelt's arrival. All three men were still

146

in their twenties, quiet-mannered, self-reliant individuals who had as yet no inkling of the roles that they were destined to play in the life of Theodore Roosevelt. Years afterward Roosevelt said to a friend: "If you want to know what I was like when I had bark on you ought to talk to Bill Sewall and Merrifield and Sylvane Ferris and his brother Joe."[8]

Theodore spent the night at the Maltese Cross Ranch. The next morning he almost failed in his attempt to get a saddle horse for the hunt, Sylvane and Bill seemingly having doubts as to whether he would return it; they had not liked his looks anymore than Joe had. In the end Theodore had to buy a mount; it was cash or nothing. Mounted, Theodore and Joe continued on up the Little Missouri, heading for the mouth of Little Cannonball Creek, some forty-five miles south, and the abode of Gregor Lang and his son Lincoln, who had only recently emigrated from Ireland. Theodore and Joe reached the Lang home at dusk and were warmly welcomed. Theodore found Gregor Lang to be an educated, intelligent, and well-informed man, who liked to express whatever was on his mind. That evening the two talked until midnight.

Roosevelt's buffalo hunt was a combination of foul weather, misfortune, and indifferent shooting. For one solid week rain fell. Each morning Joe Ferris, who could take punishment if need be but saw no reason for courting it, suggested that hunting would be difficult and it might be well to wait until the weather cleared. Each time Theodore replied that he had come to the West to hunt and that was what he proposed to do. Day after day they rode in drizzle or downpour, through rocky defiles, up slippery slopes, and across bleak, rolling prairie, without so much as seeing a buffalo. Each evening, wet to the skin and plastered with sticky gumbo mud, they returned to the Langs' modest quarters. Of the two, it was Ferris who tired first and turned in. Theodore and Gregor Lang sat up till all hours discussing literature, politics, history, cattle-raising, and natural history. At the conclusion of these talks, Theodore refused Lang's offer of a bunk and instead rolled up in his blankets on the floor.

Roosevelt did not get his buffalo until near the end of his second week of hunting. It was a large bull, one with a remarkably good head. He was elated even though he faced the difficult task of removing the beast's skin and head to be shipped to a New York taxidermist. With that task done Theodore, such was his delight, gave Joe $100.[9]

Even before the two weeks had ended, Joe Ferris had been obliged to revise his original opinion of Roosevelt. During those days the latter had uncomplainingly endured cold, hunger, thirst, and fatigue and had been the victim of several perverse accidents, such as having his head split open when his gun struck it, and later being tossed over the head of his horse. Throughout it all, Theodore never once complained; on the contrary, he was cheerful. On one occasion he awoke to find himself lying in four inches of water, sat straight up, and, seeing Joe, exclaimed: "By Godfrey, but this is fun!"[10] "He was a plumb good sort,"[11] Joe was shortly confessing to fellow cowpunchers. And Joe's enhanced regard for Roosevelt was in no wise diminished when the latter disclosed to him Dr. Sargeant's diagnosis, namely, that he had a weak heart and violent exercise might prove fatal.[12] Of the men Roosevelt came to know on this trip, his first to the Badlands, it was Gregor Lang, however, who was most impressed: "He is the most extraordinary man I have ever met. I shall be surprised if the world does not hear from him one of these days."[13]

Before Roosevelt left the Badlands for home, he made a sudden decision: he would go into the cattle business. He named Bill Merrifield and Sylvane Ferris as his managers and gave them a check in the amount of $14,000 with which to acquire stock. Some of his family thought the decision ill-advised and could not understand it. Lincoln Lang did: "Clearly I recall," he later wrote, "his wild enthusiasm over the Bad Lands. Just as they had gripped me, the wild romantic, arcadian charm of the region had reached for and made him his own. It had taken root in the congenial soil of his consciousness, like an ineradicable, creeping plant, as it were, to thrive and permeate it thereafter, causing him more and more to think in the broad-gauge terms of nature."[14]

Roosevelt had indeed fallen in love with the Badlands. Carrying Lincoln Lang's thoughts a bit further, his abrupt decision to become a rancher was simply his way of providing a sound, practical reason for returning to this region, where he could again ride through sagebrush and cactus, watch the sundogs hanging in the red dawn, explore further the prairie lands stretching endlessly for "leagues of dreary sameness,"[15] and continue the active outdoor existence which he had so recently sampled and so thoroughly enjoyed.

Theodore's long train ride back to New York gave him ample time to reflect on all that he had just seen and experienced. Uppermost in his thoughts now and then were surely those concerning the scarcity of the buffalo and other large game animals in the valley of the Little Missouri. From previous experience, both in the Adirondacks and the Maine woods, he knew that this reduction in numbers had been due to the indiscriminate slaughter by the guns of "Man the destroyer,"[16] to use Roosevelt's later term.

3

Roosevelt did not return to the Little Missouri valley until June 10, 1884, nine months after he first went there. During those months much happened in his life, so much, in fact, that scores of pages could here be written about that period—and have been elsewhere. The majority of those pages, as to be expected, have been filled with accounts of Theodore's triumphs and reverses in the New York State Assembly. However, many additional ones have been devoted to personal tragedy. On February 13 Theodore's mother died, and on the following day, at two o'clock in the afternoon, compounding tragedy, Alice died, after giving birth to a daughter.[17]

"Theodore is in a dazed, stunned state. He does not know what he does or says," Arthur Cutler advised Bill Sewall.[18] Nevertheless, evidencing tremendous self-discipline and courage, Theodore, three days after the double funeral, was back in Albany, at his seat in the House. Reflecting thereafter his unassuaged grief, Theodore never once alluded to Alice, not to anyone. And in his autobiography, one of almost 600 pages, he did not so much as mention her. (At least one of Roosevelt's kinsmen has criticized this silence, saying that it should "belong on the debit side in any evaluation of his character."[19])

4

It may be said that with Roosevelt's return to the Badlands, in June, a new chapter in his life opened; the earlier buffalo hunt there had been merely a prelude. A letter of June 17 from Theodore to Bamie sets the stage:

Well, I have been having a glorious time here, and am well hardened now (I have just come in from spending thirteen hours in the saddle). For every day I have been here I have had my hands full. First and foremost, the cattle have done well, and I regard the outlook for making the business a success as being *very* hopeful. . . . In the autumn I shall bring out Sewall and Dow and put them on a ranch with very few cattle to start with. . . . I have never been in better health than on this trip. . . .

The country is growing on me, more and more; it has a curious, fantastic beauty of its own, and as I own six or eight horses I have a fresh one every day and ride on a lope all day long. How sound I do sleep at night now! There is not much game, however; the cattle men have crowded it out and only a few antelope and deer remain. I have shot a few jackrabbits and curlews, with the rifle, and I also killed eight rattlesnakes.[20]

In addition to this statement about the cattle-raising, Theodore told Bamie that his stock, in spite of a loss of "25 head to wolves, cold, etc.," was in "admirable shape" and that he had about 150 calves. Because of this optimistic outlook, Theodore proceeded to give Bill Merrifield and Sylvane Ferris an additional $26,000 with which to purchase 1,000 more head of cattle, and then he bought the property, some thirty-five miles downstream from Little Missouri, on which Sewall and Wilmot Dow, after their arrival, would build the Elkhorn Ranch house. This structure became home to Roosevelt during all of his later visits to the Badlands.

Theodore obviously thought he could afford such expenditures. He had inherited $125,000 from his father, a sum from which he should have realized an annual income of some $8,000. But Theodore, since his father's death, had been anything but frugal; during his final years at Harvard he seems to have spent at least $10,000 to $12,000 annually, which was twice President Eliot's salary of $5,000.[21] Since his marriage, he had lavished his money on Alice, particularly during the lengthy European honeymoon and, more recently, on the purchase of a home at 55 West 45th Street. Therefore it is in no way surprising that there was much headshaking when his New York kin learned of his latest expenditures.

With these fiscal arrangements behind him, Theodore turned to a more agreeable matter. He confided to Lincoln Lang that he would like to have a buckskin suit. To acquire the suit, Lang escorted Theodore to the home of a Mrs. Maddox, who, after taking his measurements, told him to return in two weeks. Few acquisitions ever gave Roosevelt such lasting satisfaction. He had himself photographed in it, recurringly boasted of its comfort and durability, for years wore it on hunting trips, and eventually passed it along to one of his sons. "It was the dress," Theodore declared, "in which Daniel Boone was clad when he first passed through the trackless forests of the Alleghenies and penetrated into the heart of Kentucky; it was the dress worn by grim old Davy Crockett when he fell at the Alamo."[22]

Theodore ended this particular trip to the West on June 10. When he returned, early in August, he brought with him Sewall, Dow, and their wives. From Little Missouri they went at once to the "good place for a ranch," where the two Maine woodsmen immediately began construction of the Elkhorn Ranch house. Roosevelt later described the completed building as "a long, low ranch house of hewn logs, with a veranda, and with, in addition to the other rooms, a bedroom for myself, and a sitting room with a big fireplace. I got out a rocking-chair—I am very fond of rocking chairs— and enough books to fill two or three shelves, and a rubber bathtub so that I could get a bath. And then I do not see how any one could have lived more comfortably."[23]

5

During the years 1884–92 Roosevelt divided his time between New York City and the Dakotas. In the earlier part of that period he was more often to be found in the West than in the East. He came to know the prairies and the Badlands in all seasons, and he left a factual and enviable record of his observations and experiences, a record which, when published, filled three meaty volumes: *Hunting Trips of a Ranchman* (1884), *Ranch Life and the Hunting Trail* (1888), and *The Wilderness Hunter* (1893).[24] These three books constitute a most important historical trilogy of the West, and they met with such success that, for a time at least, Roosevelt seriously considered making writing his life's principal work. "Mind you," he informed Brander Matthews,[25] "I'm a literary feller, not a politician, nowadays."[26]

The three volumes, despite their seeming accent on hunting, set a new style in this particular genre. They were far from being just a hunter's narrative of trophies bagged, as most of the hunting books of the time were. In addition to accounts of the chase, they provided vivid pictures of windswept prairie, baldface mountains, and endless forests. They provided, too, charmingly worded vignettes of birds and small mammals and comprehensive biographies of big game, from buffalo and elk to bighorn, grizzly, antelope, and mountain goat.

These biographies included abundant detail not previously found in books of this kind. Certainly nothing so thorough and rewarding about the private life of the grizzly bear had yet appeared as that in the chapter on this animal in *The Wilderness Hunter*; and no previous treatise on the bighorn sheep had equaled Roosevelt's in *Ranch Life and the Hunting Trail*. Indeed, no writer until then combined quite so well the offices of the hunter with those of the naturalist. As one critic said, his books were "tinglingly alive, masculine, and vascular."[27] No reviewer, however captious, ever contended that Roosevelt's books about the West were dull. Yet none of the trilogy quite measured up to Theodore's aspirations. Writing to Owen Wister, he said: "I wish I could make my writings touch a higher plane; but I don't well see how I can, and I am not sure that I could do much by devoting more time to them. I go over them a good deal and recast, supply or omit, sentences and even paragraphs, but I don't make the reconstruction complete the way that you do."[28]

During his literary apprenticeship, a period coinciding roughly with his years in the Badlands, Roosevelt was prone to an extravagance of statement—"He fairly lived in an atmosphere of superlatives," one writer declared[29]—and was guilty of occasional grammatical lapses. For instance, he split infinitives with abandon. When he learned, after becoming president, that Yale's Professor Thomas Lounsbury[30] countenanced the splitting of infinitives, Roosevelt wrote to him: "Here have I been laboriously trying to avoid using them in a vain desire to look cultured and now I shall give unbriddled rein to my passion in the matter."[31]

Roosevelt mentioned by name just four of the books taking up space on his shelves at Elkhorn Ranch: T. S. Van Dyke's *Still Hunter*, Colonel Richard Dodge's *Plains of the Great West*, John Dean Caton's *The Antelope and Deer of America*, and Elliott Coues's *Birds of the Northwest*.[32] No person who loves sport, he said, could afford to be without them. However, the information on animals and plants that Roosevelt displayed on the pages of his trilogy came less from books than from his personal observations. Commenting on Roosevelt's wide knowledge of zoological literature, Stewart Edward White[33] once said: "He preferred to argue from experience rather than authority, though he seemed to have read and to possess on file in the front of his mind about everything that had been said on the matter."[34]

The men who reviewed Roosevelt's books of the West were reminded of the works of earlier celebrated naturalists. One said that *Hunting Trips of a Ranchman* "could claim an honourable place on the same shelf with Waterton's[35] *Wanderings* and Walton's[36] *Compleat Angler.*"[37] And another reviewer concluded: "Among American writers who have attempted to describe nature, few, save Thoreau and Burroughs, have been so successful as Mr. Roosevelt."[38] George Bird Grinnell[39] was impressed with "the freshness and spirit" of *Hunting Trips of a Ranchman* and, in those and other respects, was reminded of Francis Parkman's[40] *The Oregon Trail.* He did think, though, that Roosevelt had occasionally been guilty of "accepting as fact some statements made in books, and others by men with whom he had talked, who were either bad observers or careless talkers."[41]

The *New York Tribune*, assessing the merits of Roosevelt's animal biographies in *Ranch Life and the Hunting Trail*, declared that they were "full of information about the habits of game, especially the mountain sheep, white goat and blacktail deer. There is not a dull line between the covers of this splendidly printed and made volume, and Mr. Remington's[42] illustrations are full of fire and spirit."[43]

The Wilderness Hunter, the last of the western trilogy to come from the press, was a more finished product than either of its notable predecessors—at least in its treatment of the trans-Mississippi biota. It appeared in 1893, by which time Roosevelt could count a full ten years since he had first looked upon the extravagant terrain of the Badlands. As the years had slipped by, he had not only increased his knowledge of the western fauna but had also sharpened his faculties of observation, reflection, and self-criticism. Declared the *London Field:* "It has seldom been our good fortune to read such an entertaining account of sport in the United States as that which is contained in *The Wilderness Hunter.*"[44] To which the *Philadel-*

phia Telegram added: "No song of bird or flower or the shyest plant which grows escapes his appreciative notice."[45]

6

Theodore Roosevelt had three vantage points from which to make the acquaintance and widen his familiarity with the western fauna and flora: (1) the restricted area limited to Elkhorn Ranch and immediate environs; (2) the expansive terrain of prairie and Badlands encircling Elkhorn Ranch; and (3) the vast acreage of mountain range and forest to the west.

The veranda of the Elkhorn Ranch house proved to be a superb observation post for Roosevelt. One of the mose sensitive passages in *Ranch Life and the Hunting Trail* reads:

Throughout June the thickets and groves about the ranch house are loud with bird music from before dawn till long after sunset. . . . Late one evening I had been sitting motionless on the veranda, looking out across the water [of the Little Missouri] and watching the green and brown of the hilltops change to purple and umber and then fade off into shadowy gray as the somber darkness disappeared. Suddenly a poorwill[46] lit on the floor beside me and stayed some little time; now and then uttering its mournful cries, then ceasing for a few moments as it flitted around after insects, and again returning to the same place to begin anew. The little owls[47] call to each other with tremulous, quavering voices throughout the livelong night. . . . From the upper branches of the cotton-wood trees overhead . . . comes every now and then the soft, melancholy cooing of the mourning dove, whose voice always seems far away and expresses more than any other sound in nature the sadness of gentle, hopeless, neverending grief.[48]

The river that flowed slowly beside the ranch house attracted many birds. On hot summer evenings Theodore often watched the greater prairie chickens[49] and horned larks come down to drink, and during spring and fall migrations he looked on as flocks of Canada geese, snow geese, pintails, mallards, shovelers, black-necked stilts, willets, blue-winged teal, long-billed curlews, golden plover, and other avian species spiraled down to light on the river's surface. At other times he observed strings of sandhill cranes flying above the river, "their gutteral clangour being heard very far off," and sometimes these same birds formed rings and went through "a series of antics, dancing and posturing to each other."[50]

Ranchmen along the Little Missouri tolerated the company of smaller, sometimes unwelcome, mammals, among them the pack rats.[51] Of these creatures, Roosevelt wrote: "[They] are larger than our house rats, with soft gray fur, and bushy tails, like squirrels; they are rather pretty beasts and very tame, often coming into the shacks and log-cabins of the settlers. . . . [they] were christened pack-rats on account of their curious and inveterate habit of dragging off to their holes every object they can possibly move." From the hole of one of these eager rodential kleptomaniacs, Roosevelt once saw taken "a small revolver, a hunting knife, two books, a fork, a small bag, and a tin cup."[52]

At times a cat-sized, black and white carnivore, the skunk, invaded dwellings, and sometimes all too commonly. One year, according to Roosevelt, there "was a perfect plague of them all along the river. . . . At every ranch-house dozens were killed, we ourselves bagging thirty-three, all slain near the house, and now, to our unspeakable sorrow, in it."[53] Roosevelt had a particularly sound reason for killing the skunks, one in addition to reducing their numbers. He knew that at night these creatures sometimes bit sleeping men and women, that occasional ones were rabid, and that "at certain times the bite of the skunk is surely fatal, producing hydrophobia."[54]

7

Astride his horse, Roosevelt within minutes could climb from his ranch house to the prairie above. During his periods of residence in the West, he visited the prairie almost daily, mainly, as he said, to obtain food for his cowhands. As he became better acquainted with its flatness, semiaridity, lack of trees, interminable grass covering, and the animal life common to it, his fascination for it grew, and he could write: "Nowhere, not even at sea, does a man feel more lonely than when riding across the far-reaching, seemingly never-ending plains. . . . Nowhere else does one seem so far off from all mankind. . . . All objects on the outermost verge of the horizon, even though within the ken of his vision, look unreal. . . . A mile off one can see, through the strange shimmering haze, the shadowy white outlines of something which looms vaguely up till it looks as large as the canvas-top of a prairie wagon; but as the horseman comes nearer it shrinks and dwindles and takes clearer form, until it at last changes into the ghastly staring skull of some mighty buffalo long dead and gone to join the rest of his vanished race."[55]

Roosevelt's numerous forays onto the prairie made him familiar with the animals common to it, especially the game animals; such as the pronghorn antelope, the white-tailed and black-tailed (mule) deer, and the sharp-tailed and sage grouse. In one or another of his western books he provided full-length chapters about each of the above. But his knowledge extended also to the smaller prairie creatures, among them the coyote, gray wolf, prairie dog, pocket gopher, black-footed ferret, lynx (both bay and Canada), cottontail, and porcupine, and even to such reptiles as the horned toad and prairie rattler.

The rattlesnakes, which in places abounded, drew from Roosevelt the comment: "In the narrow ravines . . . the only living things were the rattlesnakes, and of these I have never elsewhere seen so many. Some basked in the sun, stretched out at their ugly length of mottled brown and yellow; others lay half under stones or twined in the roots of the sage-brush, and looked straight at me with that strange, sullen evil gaze, never shifting or moving, that is the property only of serpents and of certain men."[56]

Roosevelt's trilogy abounds in examples of his exceptional capabilities as observer and describer. Space allows the inclusion of only a few examples. For instance, he capably illuminated a peculiarity of the prairie chicken: "When on the ground it has a rather comical look, for it stands very high on its legs, carries its sharp little tail cocked up like a wren's, and when startled stretches its neck out straight; altogether it gives one the impression of being a very angular bird."[57]

Roosevelt's eyes, as we know, were singularly insensitive to the coloration of birds, but not so to the footwork of the plains' deer: "The white-tail runs at a rolling gallop," he explained, "striking the ground with the forward feet first, the head held forward. The black-tail, on the contrary, holds its head higher up and progresses by a series of prodigious bounds, striking the earth with all four feet at once, the legs held nearly stiff."[58]

Roosevelt soon learned of the near morbid curiosity of the pronghorn. One rainy day on the prairie he wore "a great flapping yellow slicker," which was "about as unlikely a garb as a hunter could possibly don. It fascinated a band of antelope which, on seeing this strange sight, immediately huddled up and stood gazing at it."[59] This experience may have reminded him of a somewhat similar one described by John James Audubon. While on the Yellowstone River in 1843, the great artist-naturalist had decoyed antelope within sixty to seventy yards of him by the simple expedient of lying flat on his back and kicking his heels in the air.[60]

Roosevelt's hearing served him as well on the Little Missouri plains as it had on Long Island Sound or in Adirondack forests. Out on the prairie near Elkhorn Ranch, he found the sharp-tailed grouse everywhere. Now and then these birds gathered in dancing rings, and at such times Roosevelt was able to creep up on them and to experience the pleasure of watching them shuffling round each other, wings outspread, all the time keeping up a curious clucking and booming that accorded well with their odd gyrations. To Roosevelt, the "hollow booming" of the male sharp-tails was "one of the most attractive sounds of the prairie."[61]

Roosevelt enjoyed the clucking and booming of the sharp-tails, but not to the extent he enjoyed the song of the Missouri skylark (less euphemistically called Sprague's pipit). The melody of this small brown and gray-streaked bird of the High Plains exceeded that of any other western songster, in Roosevelt's opinion, and moved him to write:

Nothing was in sight in the way of game, but overhead a skylark was singing, soaring up above me so high that I could not make out its form in the gray morning light. I listened for some time, and the music never ceased for a moment, coming down clear, sweet and tender from the air above. Soon the strains of another answered from a little distance off, and the two kept singing and soaring as long as I stayed to listen, and when I walked away I could still hear their notes behind me. In some ways the [Missouri] skylark is the sweetest singer we have, only certain of our thrushes rival it, but though the songs of the latter have perhaps even more melody, they are far from being so uninterrupted and well sustained, being rather a succession of broken bursts of music.[62]

Roosevelt recognized that other connoisseurs of bird music might disagree with his appraisal of the skylark's melody: much, he rationally emphasized, depended on the mood of the listener, the character of his surroundings, and other factors. To him, the skylark's song was intimately associated "with the sight of dim hills reddening in the dawn, with the breath of cool morning winds, with the scent of flowers on the sunlit prairie, and with all the strong thrill of eager and buoyant life."[63]

8

Those who have read Roosevelt's consequential trilogy know that, during the years he routinely invaded the Dakota Badlands, he made six trips into the mountains lying to the west: in 1884 to the Big Horn Mountains of Wyoming, in 1886 to the Coeur d'Alenes of Idaho, in 1888 to the Selkirks of British Columbia, in 1889 to the Bitterroots of Wyoming and Idaho, in 1890 to Yellowstone National Park and in 1891 to the Two-Ocean Pass country of Wyoming.

These were ambitious trips, each demanding much advanced preparation. The first, to the Big Horns, necessitated a journey of almost two months duration and travel of at least 600 miles. Roosevelt took with him two companions, Bill Merrifield and a teamster, and, for transport, a ranch wagon and seven horses, the wagon being primarily for the return of trophies. Since the men expected to live largely off the land, they took essential foods only: flour, bacon, coffee, sugar, and salt. They arrived at the base of the Big Horns at a point near old Fort McKinney. Here they left their ranch wagon, continuing by pack train as they climbed to higher elevations. The main purpose of this trip and of all the subsequent ones was to obtain trophies, more specifically the heads of the larger western game animals. By this date Roosevelt was enthusiastically embracing the avocation of many other wealthy hunters, that of acquiring animal heads, antlered or otherwise, with which to adorn walls of homes or offices.

Because Roosevelt had never before visited any of the western mountains, the Big Horn trip had, as he said, "the added zest of being also an exploring expedition."[64] Thus Roosevelt would be familiarizing himself not only with topographic features of the land but also with its animals and plants. He later stated explicitly: "The true still-hunter should be a lover of nature as well as of sport, or he will miss half the pleasure of being in the woods."[65]

If Roosevelt himself had not been "a lover of nature," the accounts of his hunting trips into the Big Horns and the Rockies might well have been replete with little else but endless, conventional details of the chase, and of little interest to anyone except the sportsman. Instead, they teem with instances of his irrepressible enthusiasm for the wilderness and its inhabitants. Almost without exception, wherever Roosevelt paused in the western mountains, he took time to put into words his sentiments about the animals most recently encountered. For example, at the end of one day in the Big Horns, he reflected: "I by degrees came to feel as if I had a personal interest in the different traits and habits of the wild creatures. The characters of the animals differed widely, and the differences were typified by their actions; and it was pleasant to watch them in their homes, myself unseen, when . . . I came upon them going about the ordinary business of their lives."[66]

Being a newcomer to the high country of the West, Roosevelt encountered many species of animals he had not seen before. Of these, some naturally interested him more than others. He was particularly attracted to Clark's nutcracker and Lewis's woodpecker, for, as he said: "Their names commemorate their discoverers, the explorers Lewis and Clarke,[67] the first white men who crossed the United States to the Pacific." Roosevelt then went on to describe the nutcracker as "an ash-colored bird with black wings and white tail and forehead," and Lewis's woodpecker as a "dark-green bird, with white breast and red belly."[68]

The Big Horns yielded their share of birds Roosevelt had not previously seen, but so did the Selkirks, Bitterroots, and other mountains of the West, among them the lark bunting, blue grouse, McCown's longspur, and white-tailed ptarmigan. But the one bird that Roosevelt encountered in the Rockies that elicited the most elaborate comment was the dipper or water ousel. His discovery of it, in a small, swift-flowing stream in the Selkirks, coincided with the sighting of a water shrew:

I was sitting on a stone by the edge of the brook, idly gazing at a water-wren [a dipper] which had come up from a short flight. . . . Suddenly a small animal swam across the little pool at my feet. . . . It was a water-shrew,[69] a rare little beast. I sat motionless and watched both the shrew and the water-wren—water-ousel, as it rightly should be named. The latter, emboldened by my quiet, presently flew by me to a little rapids close at hand, lighting on a round stone, and then slipping unconcernedly into the swift water. Anon he emerged, stood on another stone, and trilled a few bars, though it was late in the season [September] for singing; and then dove again into the stream. I gazed at him eagerly; for this strange, pretty waterthrush is to me one of the most attractive and interesting birds to be found in the gorges of the great Rockies. Its haunts are romantically beautiful, for it always dwells beside and in the swift-flowing mountain brooks; it has a singularly sweet song; and its ways render it a marked bird at once, for though looking much like a somber-colored, ordinary woodland thrush, it spends half its time under the water, walking along the bottom, swimming and diving, and flitting through as well as over the cataracts.[70]

The dipper belongs to one of the most unique of avian families (Cinclidae), being the only representative of that family in the United States. Its habits have long interested ornithologists, particularly so following John Muir's delightful description of them.[71]

Roosevelt's ears were attuned to the vocalizations of an occasional mammal, as well as to those of the birds. On hearing for the first time the bugling of the elk, he almost rhapsodized about it: "It is a most singular and beautiful sound, and is very much the most musical cry uttered by any four-footed beast. When heard for the first time it is almost impossible to believe that it is the call of an animal; it seems far more as if by an Aeolian harp or some strange wind instrument. It consists of a series of notes uttered continuously, in a most soft, musical, vibrant tone, so clearly that they can be heard half a mile off. Heard in the clear, frosty moonlight from the depths of the rugged and forest-clad mountains the effect is most beautiful; for its charm is heightened by the wild and desolate surroundings. It has the sustained, varied melody of some bird songs, with, of course, a hundred-fold greater power.[72]

It was during these expeditions into British Columbia, Idaho, Montana, and Wyoming that Roosevelt obtained his abundant knowledge of the large game animals. Also, he experienced many exciting moments. He watched two giant elk in mortal combat; he stood off the charge of a huge wounded grizzly; and he came close to losing his life when he fell over a cliff. Of course, he succeeded in obtaining most of the trophies he had sought, namely, heads of the bighorn, elk (wapiti), Rocky Mountain goat, grizzly bear, and caribou. It was characteristic of Roosevelt—if not expected—that, after bagging his caribou prize, he could write: "It was one of those moments that repay the hunter for days of toil and hardship; that is if he needs repayment, and does not find life in the wilderness pleasure enough in itself."[73]

When one of the worst winters in the memory of the oldest inhabitants of the Dakota Badlands—the winter of 1886–87—struck the Little Missouri area, killing off the cattle by the thousands, Roosevelt's experiment in ranching came to an abrupt end. From the financial reverse suffered, one in the neighborhood of $50,000, he did not recover until years later.

But Roosevelt's years in the West brought fruitful gains as well as grievous losses. To a friend he later posed this question: "Do you know what chapter or experience in all of my life I would choose to remember, were the alternative forced upon me to recall one portion of it, and to have erased from my memory all the other experiences?" He then answered the question himself: "I would take the memory of my life on the ranch with its experiences close to Nature and among the men who lived nearest her." [74]

Roosevelt had sound, practical reasons for holding inviolate in memory his "experiences close to Nature" while a resident of the West, reasons which would later surface, and rekindled, make of him our country's foremost conservationist. He had witnessed the Little Yellowstone in flood, and the resultant damages. He was familiar with the erosive power of water, as seen on the barren, plantless walls of the Badlands gorges. He had viewed to the west the extensive semiarid lands, which lacked only water to make them bloom. He had visited farther west the great stands of pine, fir, spruce, and hemlock that, if struck by fire, could quickly be utterly destroyed. And, above all else, he had been spectator to the rapid, remorseless destruction of the buffalo and other game animals, this causing him to cry out, "The frontier has come to an end, it has vanished." [75]

Notes

1. Putnam, *Theodore Roosevelt,* 309.
2. Roosevelt, *Autobiography,* 93
3. See Stephen Vincent Benet's "American Names."
4. Sewall, *T.R.,* 16.
5. Roosevelt, *Hunting Trips of a Ranchman* (New York: G. P. Putnam's Sons, 1886), 12.
6. Roosevelt, *Ranch Life and the Hunting Trail* (New York: The Century Co., 1888), 36.

7. Sewall, *T.R.*, 15–16.

8. Hagedorn, *Roosevelt in the Bad Lands*, x.

9. Ibid., 45. Roosevelt shipped the head to a New York taxidermist. Afterward it found a home at Sagamore Hill. As of 1982 it adorns one of the walls of the Trophy Room with the legend: "Pretty Buttes, N.D., September, 1883."

10. Ibid., 36.

11. Ibid., 28.

12. Ibid., 39.

13. Ibid., 45.

14. Lincoln A. Lang, *Ranching with Roosevelt* (Philadelphia: J. B. Lippincott, 1926), 104–5.

15. Roosevelt, *Hunting Trips of a Ranchman*, 279.

16. Ibid., 295.

17. According to existing medical records, Roosevelt's mother died of typhoid fever and Alice of Bright's disease, a form of nephritis. The daughter, born to Theodore and Alice on Feb. 12, was named Alice. In due course she became Alice Roosevelt Longworth.

18. Sewall, *T.R.*, 11.

19. Nicholas Roosevelt, *Theodore Roosevelt, the Man as I Knew Him* (New York: Dodd, Mead & Co., 1967), 25.

20. Morison, *Letters*, 1:73–74.

21. McCullough, *Mornings on Horseback*, 205.

22. Roosevelt, *Ranch Life and the Hunting Trail*, 81.

23. Roosevelt, *Autobiography*, 95–96.

24. Additional sources dealing with Roosevelt's years in the West are his *Autobiography*, Hagedorn's *Roosevelt in the Bad Lands*, and Lang's *Ranching with Roosevelt*.

25. Brander Matthews (1852–1927), American man of letters, professor of literature at Columbia (1892–1900), and author of such works as *The Historical Novel* (1901) and *A Study of the Drama* (1910).

26. H. F. Pringle, *Theodore Roosevelt, a Biography* (New York: Harcourt, Brace and Co., 1931), 115.

27. Statement by Brander Matthews. See Roosevelt, *Works, Mem. Ed.*, 14:xii.

28. Wister, *Roosevelt, the Story of a Friendship*, 41.

29. F. E. Leupp, *Atlantic Monthly* 109 (1893): 643.

30. Thomas Raynesford Lounsbury (1838–1915), scholar and literary critic, was professor of English in Yale's Sheffield Scientific School (1871–1906).

31. Cutright, *Roosevelt the Naturalist*, 55.

32. Roosevelt, *Hunting Trips of a Ranchman*, 12.

33. Stewart Edward White (1873–1946), American novelist. In 1911 he met Roosevelt in Africa and afterward recounted his African experiences in *The Land of Footprints*.

34. Roosevelt, *Works, Mem. Ed.*, 2:xxi.

35. Charles Waterton (1782–1865), British naturalist, explorer, and author of *Wanderings in South America* (1825).

36. Izaak Walton (1593–1683), English naturalist and author of *The Compleat Angler* (1653).

37. *London Spectator*, Jan. 16, 1886.

38. *Chicago Unity*, Sept. 24, 1886.

39. George Bird Grinnell (1849–1938), American naturalist and editor. Grinnell served as naturalist with General George Custer's 1874 expedition to the Black Hills and with Colonel William Ludlow's 1875 reconnaissance of Yellowstone National Park. In the years 1880–1911 he edited *Forest and Stream* magazine.

40. Francis Parkman (1823–93), American historian and author of *The Oregon Trail* and other distinguished works.

41. Roosevelt, *Works, Mem. Ed.*, 1:xiv–xv.

42. Frederic Remington (1861–1909), American artist. Remington illustrated Roosevelt's *Ranch Life and the Hunting Trail* with some seventy-five of his vigorous sketches.

43. From an undated clipping in TRCHL.

44. *London Field*, Nov. 25, 1893.

45. *Philadelphia Telegram*, July 26, 1893.

46. The poorwill (*Phalaenoptilus nuttalli*), and not to be confused with the whippoorwill (*Caprimulgus vociferus*). The poorwill is unique in that of all birds it is the only one known to hibernate, a fact first noted by Captain Meriwether Lewis in October 1804 near the South Dakota–North Dakota line.

47. Presumably the pygmy owl (*Glaucidium gnoma*).

48. Roosevelt, *Ranch Life and the Hunting Trail*, 38–39.

49. The greater prairie chicken (*Tympanachus cupidopinnatus*) once had a smaller eastern relative, the heath hen (*T. c. cupido*). The latter is now extinct; it was last sighted in 1932 on Martha's Vineyard.

50. Ibid., 42.

51. The pack rat is one of several species of wood rats. Roosevelt's description of the one at Elkhorn Ranch as having a bushy tail would seem to prove that it was the bushy-tailed wood rat (*Neotoma cinerea*), a.k.a. the pack rat.

52. Roosevelt, *Hunting Trips of a Ranchman*, 12–13.

53. Roosevelt, *Ranch Life and the Hunting Trail*, 41.

54. Roosevelt, *Hunting Trips of a Ranchman*, 66.

55. Ibid., 211–12.

56. Roosevelt, *Ranch Life and the Hunting Trail*, 148.

57. Roosevelt, *Hunting Trips of a Ranchman*, 73.

58. Ibid., 135.

59. Roosevelt, *Ranch Life and the Hunting Trail*, 135–36.

60. John Francis McDermott, *Up the Missouri with Audubon, the Journal of Edward Harris* (Norman: University of Oklahoma Press, 1951), 150.

61. Roosevelt, *Hunting Trips of a Ranchman*, 73.

62. Ibid., 225.

63. Roosevelt, *The Wilderness Hunter* (New York: G. P. Putnam's Sons, 1893), 65.

64. Roosevelt, *Hunting Trips of a Ranchman*, 296.

65. Ibid., 312.

66. Ibid., 311.

67. Roosevelt, like many others of that and earlier dates, misspelled Clark. It was Elliott Coues, who in his 1893 edition of the Lewis and Clark journals first settled the question of the spelling.

68. Roosevelt, *Wilderness Hunter*, 173–74.

69. Probably *Sorex palustris*.

70. Ibid., 135–36.

71. John Muir's classic account of the dipper (*Cinclus mexicanus*)—or water ousel, as he called it—first appeared in Muir's *The Mountains of California* (New York: The Century Co., 1894), ch. 13. His account has since been praised by some ornithologists as the most superb description of a bird ever written.

72. Roosevelt, *Hunting Trips of a Ranchman*, 310.

73. Roosevelt, *Wilderness Hunter*, 151.

74. Frederick G. Wood, *Roosevelt as We Knew Him* (Philadelphia: John C. Winston Co., 1927), 12.

75. Roosevelt, *Wilderness Hunter*, 11–12.

12

"I Must Have a B & C Dinner"

A NUMBER OF significant events in the life of Theodore Roosevelt occurred in the years 1880–1900, most of which have no direct bearing on this study. However, in the interests of chronology and biographical integrity, it seems expedient here to include them, though briefly.

In 1880, after Theodore's marriage to Alice Lee, he had bought sixty acres of land on Cove Neck, a thumblike headland between Oyster Bay Harbor and Cold Spring Harbor. Here also, in 1883, before leaving for his buffalo hunt in the Badlands, he had purchased sixty-five additional adjoining acres.[1] On this property Roosevelt began construction of a home he called Leeholm. Not long afterward Alice died, and, when in 1885 the house was completed, he changed its name to Sagamore Hill.

According to Roosevelt himself, "Sagamore Hill takes its name from the old Sagamore Mohannis, who, as chief of his little tribe, signed away his rights in the land two centuries and a half ago."[2] In the time of Peter Minuit, early in the seventeenth century, the western half of Long Island was inhabited by the Canarsee Indians, a small Algonquian tribe. "Sagamore Mohannis"—Sagamore is another name for chief—may therefore have been a Canarsee.

Sagamore Hill stands on an elevation, on the east side of Cove Neck, about three miles from the town of Oyster Bay. Why did Roosevelt build there? He later gave a reason, a convincing one: "Many birds dwell in the trees round the house or in the pastures and the woods near by, and of course in winter gulls, loons and wild fowl frequent the waters of the Bay and Sound. We love [Sagamore Hill during] all the seasons: the snows and bare woods of winter; the rush of growing things and the blossom-spray of spring; the yellow grain, the ripening fruit and tasselled corn, and the deep, leafy shades that are heralded by 'the green dance of summer'; and the sharp fall winds that tear the brilliant banners with which the trees greet the dying year."[3]

The house, Queen Anne style, was built of wood and brick, the wood was painted a mustard color, the brick was red, and the trim was painted dark green. It was a three-storied dwelling of twenty-three rooms and eight fireplaces. When friends hinted to Roosevelt that the house, viewed from the outside, was something of an architectural monstrosity, he had a ready reply: "I had to live inside and not outside the house; and while I should have liked to 'express myself' in both, as I had to choose, I chose the former."[4] In one significant respect Sagamore Hill had a distinct bearing on Roosevelt's life as naturalist and conservationist. From 1887, when he first occupied it, until his death in 1919, it was, year in and year out, a most congenial and enviable place to visit, and, of visitors, none was more welcome than the naturalists, among them John Burroughs, Frank M. Chapman, and William Beebe.

In December 1886, in London, Roosevelt married Edith Kermit Carow, and after a honeymoon on the continent the two took up residence at Sagamore Hill. Then and thereafter, to Theodore and Edith, there was no place like Sagamore Hill, not even the White House; and it became the home of the five children born to them: Theodore, Jr. (b. September 13, 1887), Kermit (b. October 10, 1889), Ethel (b. August 13, 1891), Archibald (b. April 9, 1894), and Quentin (b. November 19, 1897).

Since 1963, Sagamore Hill, like Mount Vernon, Monticello, the Hermitage, and other homes of former presidents of the United States, has been a National Historic Site administered by the Department of the Interior. By and large, Americans who today visit Sagamore Hill have been attracted by reports of its extraordinary interior that, except for minor alterations, is much the same as on the day in 1919 when Theodore Roosevelt died. Herein one finds no resemblance to the homes of Washington, Jefferson, and Jackson, or, indeed, to the interior of any other home. Most conspicuous are trophies of the chase: game heads adorning walls and robes scattered about on floors. Also conspicuous are books, these occupying shelves—often to ceilings—in practically every room in the house, even in the Gun Room on the third floor. Present among these, and still in excellent condition, are several (such as those by Spencer F. Baird and Elliott Coues) that Theodore regularly used back in the 1870s when he was identifying birds and other animals.[5]

Other major events in the life of Roosevelt during the 1880s and on through the 1890s followed in swift and almost uninterrupted succession. In 1886 he ran for mayor of New York City and was defeated. In 1887 he and George Bird Grinnell took the first steps in forming the Boone and Crockett Club (more of this later in this chapter). In 1889 he was appointed, by President Benjamin Harrison, as civil service commissioner, a post he held for six years. In 1895 he was made police commissioner of New York City. In 1897 he left that position to serve as assistant secretary of the Navy under William McKinley. In 1898, at the outset of the Spanish-American War, he resigned the naval appointment and, with Leonard Wood, formed the first U.S. Volunteer Cavalry regiment, soon to be known as the Rough Riders. This regiment landed in Cuba in June 1898 and on July 1 charged to victory up San Juan Hill. Just two months later, with the war ended, the Rough Riders were mustered out at Montauk Point, Long Island, and in November Colonel Theodore Roosevelt, celebrated leader of the Rough Riders, was elected governor of New York State.

Also, throughout this pivotal and episodic period, Roosevelt was uncommonly busy as an author. In addition to the western trilogy, he published *Thomas Hart Benton* (1887), *Gouverneur Morris* (1889), *Winning of the West* (4 vols., 1889–1906), *New York* (1891), and *Oliver Cromwell* (1900), not to mention numerous contributions to periodicals.

2

The Boone and Crockett Club was the outgrowth of long and serious talks, beginning early in 1887, between Roosevelt and Grinnell, editor of *Forest and Stream* magazine. The two had known each other only casually until Roosevelt called upon Grinnell in his New York office to discuss the adverse remarks the latter had made in reviewing *Hunting Trips of a Ranchman*. Grinnell later recalled that they "talked freely about the book, and took up at length some of the statements," after which he "saw my point of view."[6]

Grinnell's experiences of the West had begun earlier, and lasted longer, than Roosevelt's. In 1874, for instance, he had served as naturalist with General George Custer's expedition to the Black Hills and, two years later, he was with Colonel William Ludlow during the latter's reconnaissance of Yellowstone National Park. Then, and later, he "had travelled over much country and seen much of the native life between the Missouri River and the Pacific coast."[7] Grinnell had liked the freshness, spontaneity, and enthusiasm of *Hunting Trips of a Ranchman*, but its author "had the youthful . . . tendency to generalize from his own observations and to conclude that certain aspects of nature were always and in all places as he had found them in one place."[8]

After the initial meeting in Grinnell's office, others followed, and a lasting friendship developed between the two men. At these later meetings, they talked about "the broad country" they both loved, and Roosevelt, after listening to Grinnell's recital of experiences with western birds, mammals, and Indians, would inject his own vigorous, running comment. Roosevelt, said Grinnell, "was always fond of natural history, having begun, as so many boys have done, with birds; but as he saw more and more of outdoor life his interest in the subject broadened and later it became a passion with him."[9]

Vaguely at first, and then more clearly, Roosevelt and Grinnell foresaw the dangers threatening the large game animals inhabiting the great expanse of the western plains, the unspoiled forests of the Rocky Mountains, and the many other faunally rich parts of the nation. As Grinnell put it: "We regretted the unnecessary destruction of game animals, but we did not know all it meant, nor had we the vision to look forward and imagine what it portended. So though we discussed in a general way the preservation of game, it must be confessed—in the light of later events—that we were talking of things about which we knew very little. We wanted the game preserved, but chiefly with the idea that it should be protected in order that there might be good hunting which should last for generations."[10]

Although Roosevelt and Grinnell did not immediately envision what the unnecessary destruction of game animals foreshadowed, they did become more and more convinced that some action should be taken, and soon, to initiate the protection of these animals. Thus, in the fall of 1887 Roosevelt proposed to Grinnell that they take the lead in forming a club to consist of worthy sportsmen, who were also experienced big-game hunters. When Grinnell approved the proposal, Roosevelt took the first step by inviting to dinner at his Manhattan residence the following men: Elliott Roosevelt, West Roosevelt, Archibald Rogers, E. P. Rogers, J. Coleman Drayton, Thomas Paton, J. E. Jones, Rutherford Stuyvesant, and, of course, Grinnell.[11]

At this meeting, in December 1887, the Roosevelt-Grinnell proposition that a club be formed consisting of experienced "American hunting riflemen" met with unanimous approval, and a January date was set for the formal organization of the club. At this January meeting the organization received its name, "The Boone and Crockett Club," a constitution was adopted, Theodore Roosevelt was elected president, and Archibald Rogers, secretary. Twenty-four men attended this organizational meeting, fourteen of them in addition to those present at the December dinner.[12]

The Boone and Crockett Club, in time, became a powerful instrument in furthering the preservation of our nation's natural resources. However, the conservation movement, as an organized, creative, and highly motivated force, had its origin in the 1870s concurrently with the publication of four magazines: *American Sportsman* (1871), *Forest and Stream* (1873), *Field and Stream* (1874), and *The American Angler* (1881).

Of these four periodicals, *Forest and Stream* quickly emerged as the most innovative and influential, due principally to its founder and editor, Charles Hallock, and to his nature editor and business partner, George Bird Grinnell. Charles Hallock (1834–1917), a graduate of Yale (A.B., *extra ordinem*, 1871), an experienced newspaper reporter, and a man deeply concerned about the future of his country's environment, was well equipped to edit *Forest and Stream*, and did so most capably for seven years. In those years he added to his stature as a concerned environmentalist by publishing such books as *Camp Life in Florida: A Handbook for Sportsmen* (1876) and *Hallock's American Club List and Sportsmen's Glossary* (1878). Like Hallock, Grinnell was also a Yale graduate (A.B., 1870, and Ph.D., 1880), and was of particular value to Hallock because of his extensive knowledge of the western fauna, knowledge Hallock lacked.

Forest and Stream, with offices in New York City, produced its first issue on August 14, 1873. As this and future issues proved, the thinking of Hallock and Grinnell was far ahead of their time. Not only did they, in editorials and feature articles, stress diminishing game, but also the need for scientific management of forests, uniform game laws, improved fish culture, reduced water pollution, and domestication of fur-bearing animals. They even advocated the protection of watersheds as a means of flood control.

Editorials of *Forest and Stream* were directed primarily at the "true sportsmen," the men who hunted for pleasure (never for profit), who in the field allowed game a sporting chance, and who, as one writer put it, "possessed an aesthetic appreciation of the whole context of sport that included a commitment to its perpetuation."[13] Hallock and Grinnell could not possibly have anticipated the response of the "true sportsmen" to their editorial warnings and exhortations. Almost at once, and in all parts of the nation, hunters and fishermen began uniting to form sportsmen's clubs. The movement developed so rapidly that by 1878, just five years after the inception of *Forest and Stream*, thirty-four clubs of anglers had been formed and 308 other clubs whose memberships included both fishermen and hunters. Within these groups, as their constitutions severally attested, there shortly developed a genuine commitment to the perpetuation of wildlife and their habitats and an increased awareness of the sportsmen's responsibilities to other aspects of conservation. Thus these clubs, generally well organized, enthusiastic, and highly motivated, were actually responsible, more so than any other bodies, for initiating and spearheading the conservation movement in the United States.

Before the advent of Hallock and Grinnell there were, of course, many individuals who had expressed themselves in respect to one aspect or another of needed conservation. Both George Washington and Thomas Jefferson, among others, were worried about soil erosion, soil exhaustion, and the rapid destruction of timber from Virginia farms. Indeed, the situation became so acute that, as one historian has written, "there were no more rails for fencing, and both Washington and Jefferson imported thousands of hawthorn cuttings for hedge fences."[14] Another concerned individual was Henry William Herbert, who in 1831 came to the United States from England. Using the pseudonym of "Frank Forester," he was soon writing articles for *Sporting Magazine* and other periodicals of the 1830s. In each of his pieces he lamented the commercial exploitation of wildlife and urged sportsmen to band together to protect the animals and their environment. A more important figure of somewhat later date was George Perkins Marsh, who, as a result of his published *Man and Nature* (1864), has been called "the fountainhead of the conservation movement."[15] Not to be overlooked either was Robert Barnhill Roosevelt, Theodore's uncle. He wrote several books about hunting and fishing and was a pioneer in urging cleaner streams already alarmingly polluted. In one instance, for example, he complained that "streams in the neighborhood of New York [City] that formerly were alive with trout are now totally deserted . . .[and] the shad that a few years ago swarmed up the Hudson River in numbers incomputable, have become scarce."[16] Each of these men and many others revealed their environmental worries, with some of them warning of impending calamities unless steps were soon taken to prevent the ever-increasing, remorseless destruction of our natural resources. Unfortunately, to most Americans, they were only "voices crying in the wilderness." Were not the forests, wildlife, and other natural resources inexhaustible?

During the period of greatest activity in the forming of the sportsmen's clubs, namely in the late 1870s, Theodore Roosevelt was, of course, a student at Harvard and deeply engrossed in his studies and extracurricular events. He never joined one of the sportsmen's clubs, though he may well have been an early subscriber to *Forest and Stream,* as he definitely was just a few years later. Even if he had been approached to join, he probably would have demurred, on the valid ground that, as a member already of many campus clubs—and the Nuttall Ornithological Club—it would not have been in his best interests to join another.

The year 1880 was important to both Roosevelt and Grinnell; the former graduated from Harvard and soon thereafter, with Elliott, visited the Red River of the North, where he obtained his first glimpse of the western plains. Grinnell bought out Hallock and thus became the owner and editor-in-chief of *Forest and Stream.* This acquisition by Grinnell of *Forest and Stream* was, as one writer has declared, indeed "a monumental event in the history of conservation." Grinnell edited the magazine for thirty-one years (1880–1911) and, through immense personal effort, including a flood of editorials, "made his influence on conservation incalculably great."[17]

Grinnell persistently directed his *Forest and Stream* editorials at the sportsmen, fully conscious of the fact that many American males—and females—had at one time or another either hunted or fished and were thus better informed about animals than those who had not. In his scholarly, factual, and thought-provoking book, *American Sportsmen and the Origins of Conservation* John F. Reiger at one point lists eighty prominent Americans of the last century, who had gone afield with rifle or fishing pole. The list reads like a "Who's Who" of American leaders of the 1880s. As to be expected, Reiger included Theodore Roosevelt among the eighty, but more than that, proved that our twenty-sixth president had moved in exceptionally good, even distinguished, company including former presidents Chester A. Arthur, Grover Cleveland, and Benjamin Harrison; artists John James Audubon and George Catlin; authors William Cullen Bryant, James Fenimore Cooper, and Washington Irving; political leaders Daniel Webster and Horace Greeley; historians Francis Parkman and Frederick Jackson Turner; and naturalists Alexander Wilson, Spencer F. Baird, Elliott Coues, George Bird Grinnell, C. Hart Merriam, Ernest Thompson Seton, John Burroughs, and Frank M. Chapman.[18] The only prominent American naturalist of that period unlisted was John Muir. Reiger could have extended his list, even to eight times eighty, but he had made his point: that before the advent of the twentieth century practically everybody hunted or fished and that it was virtually unknown then for a voice to be raised protesting these outdoor pastimes.

The years from 1873, when Hallock and Grinnell joined hands to battle for the preservation of our natural resources, until 1887, when Roosevelt and Grinnell verbally contracted to form the Boone and Crockett Club, numbered just fourteen; yet in that time, as noted, Hallock and Grinnell had busied themselves in laying durable foundations upon which, before long, the multistoried edifice of conservation would be built.

3

The constitution of the Boone and Crockett Club outlined (in Article II) the following objectives:

(1). To promote manly sport with the rifle.

(2). To promote travel and exploration in the wild and unknown, or but partially known, portions of the country.

(3). To work for the preservation of the large game of this country, and so far as possible to further legislation for that purpose, and to assist in enforcing the existing laws.

(4). To promote inquiry into and to record observations on the habits and natural history of the various wild animals.

(5). To bring among the members interchange of opinions and ideas on hunting, travel and exploration; on the various kinds of hunting rifles, on the haunts of game animals, etc., etc.[19]

These were the initial objectives of the club, and for a time each received its due share of attention. "Gradually, however," as Grinnell subsequently wrote, "the settlement of the country and the sweep of population to the westward made it more and more difficult to carry out the two first-named, while the same causes magnified the importance of the third and fourth of these objectives."[20]

Article VI of the club's constitution declared: "This Club shall consist of not more than one hundred regular members,"[21] and Article III explained: "No one shall be eligible for Regular Membership who shall not have killed with the rifle, in fair chase, by still hunting, or otherwise, at least one adult male individual of each of three of the various species of American large game." Article IV listed the acceptable species as follows: "Black bear, grizzly bear, brown bear,[22] polar bear, buffalo (bison), mountain sheep, woodland caribou, barren ground caribou, cougar, muskox, white goat, elk (wapiti), pronghorn antelope, moose, Virginia deer, mule deer, and Columbia black-tail deer."[23] By the time of the club's first meeting Roosevelt had already shot at least seven of these species. Before many years passed he would shoot others, though he never did succeed in bagging the polar bear, musk ox, or barren-ground caribou.

As Grinnell had said, the club soon began to place greater emphasis on the third and fourth objectives of the organization. The first evidence of a more serious intent was the formation of a Committee on Parks, instructed "to promote useful and proper legislation towards the enlargement and better government of the Yellowstone National Park." In taking this step the club was attacking a problem vital to the entire nation. When Congress had acted to create Yellowstone National Park in 1872, it had failed to include in its action a law enforcement provision, which would have insured protection of the park's forests, wildlife, and other assets. Ten years later, by which time the Northern Pacific Railroad had extended its lines to the park, thus making the entire Yellowstone area easily accessible to the public, there was still no protection. Soon thereafter a real threat to the park developed when certain unprincipled, covetous promoters realized its possibilities as a pleasure resort. Forming a syndicate, these promoters succeeded in obtaining from the Department of the Interior provisional leases on ten plots of land, each of 640 acres, strategically located at points of greatest scenic interest. This syndicate, calling itself the Yellowstone Park Improvement Company, at once began to "improve" the park by bringing in a sawmill, which began cutting timber for the construction of hotels and other buildings, while the imported labor further "improved" the Park by defacing, and sometimes removing, irreplaceable geyser formations and by killing buffalo, elk, and other game animals.

Fortunately these activities of the syndicate did not go unnoticed by Grinnell and others, such as U.S. Senator George G. Vest,[24] Arnold Hague[25] of the U.S. Geological Survey, William Hallett Phillips,[26] and Archibald Rogers, all of whom would soon become members of the Boone and Crockett Club. From 1883 through 1892, bills framed by Senator Vest to stop these disconcerting threats failed to gain congressional approval. On four different occasions the bills passed the Senate, but a strong lobby managed to defeat them in the House, through the expedient of attaching a rider, which would have allowed a railroad right of way through the park. This rider ultimately proved to be the undoing of the Yellowstone Park Improvement Company, as members of the Boone and Crockett Club and far-seeing congressional leaders successfully fought it.

In April 1890 Grinnell wrote the *New York Tribune* saying that Theodore Roosevelt "could now be counted among the [forest] reserve's most enthusiastic defenders" and that he had no other "motive in this matter, except the proper preservation of the Park."[27] Roosevelt soon proved the truth of Grinnell's statement. In January 1891 he held a Boone and Crockett Club dinner at the Metropolitan Club, Washington, D.C., to which he invited a small galaxy of notables, his main purpose being to gain additional converts to the cause of protecting Yellowstone. As president of the club, Roosevelt presided at the dinner table, with Secretary of War Redfield Proctor[28] at his left, Speaker of the House Thomas B. Reed[29] to his right, and, across the table from him, Secretary of the Interior John W. Noble,[30] Smithsonian Secretary Samuel P. Langley,[31] and Grinnell. Elsewhere were seated such other dignitaries as Henry Cabot Lodge, Hague, and Phillips.

In a business meeting preliminary to the dinner, Roosevelt and Grinnell presented two resolutions, both of which won unanimous approval: (1) "That the Boone and Crockett Club, speaking for itself and hundreds of [other] clubs and associations throughout the country, urges the immediate passage by the House of Representatives and Senate of the bill for the protection and maintenance of the Yellowstone National Park," and (2) "that this Club declares itself emphatically opposed to the granting of a right of way to the Montana Mineral Railroad or to any other railroad through the Yellowstone National Park."[32]

Following the dinner Roosevelt spoke and then invited questions or comments. A significant response came from Langley of the Smithsonian, who said that from what he had heard "the large game of the continent would be practically exterminated, except in such preserves as the Yellowstone Park, within the life of the present generation of men." As a result of this and other similar comments, Grinnell was soon writing in *Forest and Stream* that the dinner had been a success and that he was now "more hopeful than . . . for two or three years" that the bill then pending in Congress would pass.[33] However, the continuing efforts of the railroad lobby developed sufficient opposition in the House to defeat it again.

More than a year passed; then, on December 8, 1892, *Forest and Stream* published another editorial by Grinnell, this one titled "A Standing Menace." In it Grinnell severely attacked a newly conceived railroad proposition—the "standing menace"—which, if sanctioned, would remove 622 square miles from the northeastern part of the park and return it to the public domain. Roosevelt was outraged, as a letter he at once wrote to Grinnell reveals:

I have just read the article, "A Standing Menace," printed in the *Forest and Stream*, in reference to the attempts made to destroy the National Park in the interests of Cooke City.[34] I heartily agree with this article. It is of the utmost importance that the Park shall be kept in its present form as a great forestry preserve and a National pleasure ground, the like of which is not to be found on any other continent than ours; and all public-spirited Americans should join with *Forest and Stream* in the effort to prevent the greed of a little group of speculators, careless of everything save their own selfish interests, from doing the damage they threaten to the whole people of the United States, by wrecking the Yellowstone National Park. So far from having this Park cut down it should be extended, and legislation adopted which would enable the military authorities who now have charge of it to administer it solely in the interests of the whole public, and to punish in the most vigorous way people who trespass upon it.[35]

The "Cooke City" proposition failed, a primary reason being Grinnell's continued, persuasive hammering away on the general theme of protection to Yellowstone, supported by the Boone and Crockett Club, with Roosevelt as its president. Their efforts were substantially reinforced when a poacher in the park was caught in the act of skinning several buffalo that he had just killed. This incident was first reported in the March 24, 1893, number of *Forest and Stream* and thereafter quickly made headlines in papers across the country. Almost over night there was a general outcry denouncing the deed and calling for action to prevent future recurrences. By this time, too, many Americans had begun to regard the buffalo as a symbol of the West and treated the incident as an omen of the buffalo's impending extinction. Additionally, and more important, these same people were being persuaded that the inexhaustibility of our natural resources was a myth that should be interred with the bones of the dodo, the auk, and other extinct animals.

Just a few days after Grinnell's weekly had reported the illicit killing of the buffalo in Yellowstone, Iowa Congressman John F. Lacey,[36] perhaps sensing that the time was propitious, introduced into Congress a newly worded Yellowstone bill. This bill, which became known as the Lacey Act or the Park Protection Act, promptly passed both houses of Congress, and, on May 7, 1894, was signed into law by President Grover Cleveland.[37] In due course Grinnell would write: "This [Lacey Act] was the ultimate reward of a number of men who, for a dozen years, had been working for the protection and betterment of the Yellowstone National Park. It may fairly be said that since then that great reservation has never been exposed to any special dangers."[38]

For the successful passage of the park bill, in the final analysis, the major share of praise should manifestly go to Grinnell, though in the later years of the fight he had been ably supported by other members of the Boone and Crockett Club, notably Theodore Roosevelt and an associate member of the club from Oskaloosa, Iowa, the Honorable John F. Lacey.

4

The conditions that Grinnell, Roosevelt, Hague, and others had found to exist in Yellowstone had much to do with the origin of the forest reserves, or national forests as they are called today. Almost at once these same men realized that similar problems existed in stands of timber throughout the Rockies and the Cascades from Canada to Mexico. Thus was born the incentive to protect the western forests generally. It will be recalled that Roosevelt, in his letter to Grinnell about the "standing menace," had said: "So far from having the Park cut down, it should be extended."

Members of the Boone and Crockett Club, in their future endeavors to save stands of timber north, south, east, and west of Yellowstone were soon joined by members of the American Forestry Association, by B. E. Fernow, chief of the Division of Forestry in the Department of Agriculture, and by F. H. Newell of the Geological Survey. As a result of their combined efforts on March 3, 1891, Congress passed "An Act to Repeal Timber Culture Laws and for Other Purposes," the bill upon which our present national forest system is based. The "meat" of the bill, to employ Grinnell's word, is to be found in Section 24, which reads: "That the President of the United States may, from time to time, set apart and reserve in any State or Territory having public lands bearing forests, any part of the public lands, wholly or in part covered with timber or undergrowth, whether of commercial value or not, as public reservations, and the President shall, by public proclamation, declare the establishment of such reservations and the limits thereof."[39] When Congress passed this bill, Benjamin Harrison was president and John W. Noble his secretary of the interior. Seemingly, it was due to Noble's influence that Harrison signed the bill and then, of even greater import, set aside the first forest reserve, the Yellowstone Park Timber Reserve. This forest, east and south of Yellowstone National Park, and entirely within Wyoming, contained 1,239,040 acres.[40]

Theodore Roosevelt, now into his fourth year as president of the Boone and Crockett Club, lost no time in transmitting the club's congratulations to Harrison and Noble:

Resolved, That this Society most heartily thanks the President of the United States and the Honorable John W. Noble, Secretary of the Interior, for having set apart, as a forest reserve, the large tract situated in Wyoming, at the headwaters of the Yellowstone and Snake Rivers, and for having set apart the Sequoia Park,[41] for the preservation of the great trees of the Pacific Slope.

That this Society recognizes in these actions the most important steps of recent years for the preservation of our forests and measures which confer the greatest benefits to the people of the adjacent states.

Resolved, That copies of this resolution be sent to the President of the United States and the Honorable Secretary of the Interior.

By the President of the Club: The Honorable Theodore Roosevelt.[42]

Obviously Theodore Roosevelt had had a hand, as had others of the Boone and Crockett Club, in the passage of the forest reserve bill, and in years immediately ahead he followed closely all that Grover Cleveland and William McKinley had been able to do through it. Of far greater importance, however, was what the bill enabled he himself to accomplish during his own administration. Just how important was this forest reserve bill? According to the distinguished American historian, Charles A. Beard, it was "one of the most noteworthy measures ever passed in the history of the nation."[43]

5

In 1913 Grinnell wrote and published a history of the Boone and Crockett Club.[44] This is a most important document, since it describes the club's contributions not only toward passage of laws to protect Yellowstone National Park and to create this country's first forest reserves, but also toward the passage of other measures.

The club, for example, early in 1889, instructed its Committee on Parks to support actively proposed legislation to create a zoological park in the nation's capital. There being in this case no opposition from lobbyists, Congress, the next year, established the

National Zoological Park.[45] Roosevelt played an important role in the creation of this institution and perhaps an even more important one soon afterward in the establishment of the New York Zoological Gardens, more often referred to simply as the New York or Bronx Zoo. Writing late in 1894 to Madison Grant,[46] a fellow member of the club, he said: "I saw Grinnell, and he seemed to think your proposal [to found a New York Zoo] was a very good one, but he also seemed a little doubtful as to whether I should appoint a committee when I have no explicit authority to do so. However, I think I'll go ahead and do it; I should like some advice from you as to the committee. Grinnell should be put on simply as an advisor, also [Elihu] Root,[47] but neither of these can do much work. Now, beside yourself, what other two men ought I to put on?"[48] This committee, with Grant as its chairman, promptly drafted a bill, which the New York legislature passed, with only minor modifications, early in April 1895. About one month later the New York Zoological Society was founded, with nine Boone and Crockett Club members named to its Board of Directors. Soon afterward, following a gift by the city to the society of 261 acres in the southern extremity of Bronx Park, the zoo was officially opened to the public. Roosevelt was delighted with Grant's achievement: "I congratulate you with all my heart upon your success with the Zoo bill. Really, you have done more than I hoped. I always count myself lucky if I get one out of three or four measures through."[49]

Early in its existence the Boone and Crockett Club took steps to prohibit the unsportsmanlike practice of hounding deer into water, where hunters in boats easily killed the animals, either by shooting them, hitting them over the head with clubs, or slitting their throats. In mid-January 1894 Roosevelt wrote Grinnell: "Don't you think the executive committee [of the Club] plus Madison Grant . . . might try this year to put a complete stop to hounding in the Adirondacks? Appear before the Legislature, I mean. I wish to see the Club do something."[50] The club's efforts in this direction ultimately got results. In 1897 the governor of New York signed a bill that prohibited for five years both hounding and jacklighting (the shooting at night of game blinded by the glare of artificial lights). At the expiration of the five years the prohibition became permanent. Other states soon followed New York's example, discontinuing these same practices.

The Boone and Crockett Club, with Grinnell as chief advocate, also played an important role in the formation of Glacier National Park. Grinnell, as one writer has pointed out, "had explored and hunted in this spectacular country before the Club was founded, and in 1901 he published an eloquent article in *Century* magazine . . . urging that it be made a national park. Nine years later, his hope was realized."[51]

Yet another accomplishment of the Boone and Crockett Club should be acknowledged. At the 1889 annual meeting of the Club, Roosevelt and Grinnell were persuaded to assume responsibility for editing and publishing a series of volumes subsequently called the Boone and Crockett Club books. The two editors, working closely together over a period of years, produced three books: *American Big-Game Hunting* (1893), *Hunting in Many Lands* (1895), and *Trail and Camp Fire* (1897).[52] The first appeared while Roosevelt was civil service commissioner, the second during his term with the New York police, and the third after he had gone to Washington to serve as assistant secretary of the Navy. The pages of these books were filled with articles on hunting written by members of the club, including Roosevelt. To the first volume he contributed "Coursing the Prong-buck," to the second "Hunting in the Cattle Country," and to the third "On the Little Missouri." Among other prominent Boone and Crockett Club members contributing to the books were Elliott Roosevelt, Henry L. Stimson, Owen Wister, and Grinnell.

Apart from his brief association with the *Harvard Advocate* and a few perfunctory months with Putnam's, Roosevelt had had no special editorial experience. However, he did have the knack of dashing off a good story, on any familiar topic, in about the time it takes to tell it. Also, he had tireless energy and, when writing about animals, boundless enthusiasm. These qualities tended to offset in good measure his lack of editorial experience, as is evident to one who reads his three Boone and Crockett Club articles.

For much of our knowledge of Roosevelt's editorial ventures with the Boone and Crockett Club books we are indebted to a succession of letters he wrote to Grinnell, Wister, and Grant, to mention just a few of his several correspondents. An early one to Wister alluded to the latter's promised article "The White Goat and His Country" before going on to other matters: "To my delight I received your letter today . . . I could give you till the first of May, but I would much prefer to have the manuscript here by the 20th of the month. I have been very anxious to have you write the white goat piece for us. I have so far five first class articles for the Club book, by [Winthrop] Chanler, [Archibald] Rogers, Grinnell, Col. [Roger D.] Williams, and Col. [W. D.] Pickett. I have three or four others with which I am less contented, and I have the promise of four more, which will be very good indeed, if they are written as they ought to be. In any event I think I can say the success of the [first] volume is assured."[53] (Incidentally, Roosevelt eagerly read all of Wister's stories; in his opinion they ranked with Bret Harte's and Rudyard Kipling's. It was in one of his earlier stories, "Hank's Woman," that Wister had described the pronghorn's "twinkling white tailless rear," thereby eliciting from Roosevelt a "bully for you." The latter soon took great relish in passing along his "tailless rear" bit to Frederic Remington, who, when producing illustrations for one of Roosevelt's articles, had made the monstrous error of drawing a pronghorn complete with tail.[54])

As coeditor of the Boone and Crockett Club books, Roosevelt now and then voiced vigorous personal opinions. For example, he wrote Grinnell that all naturalists worthy of the name should publish their experiences and observations in book form, instead of piecemeal. He then continued: "They would be worth a thousand times as much as dry-as-dust pedantic descriptions by [R. W.] Shufeldt[55] and a lot of other little half-baked scientists. I know these scientists pretty well, and their limitations are extraordinary, especially when they get to talking of science with a capital S. They do good work, but, after all, it is only the best of them who are more than bricklayers, who laboriously get together bricks out of which other men must build houses; when they think they are architects they are simply a nuisance."[56]

Roosevelt could hardly have been exhorting Grinnell to write books instead of articles. The latter, then forty-four—and nine years Roosevelt's senior—had already written two books, *Pawnee Hero Stories and Folk Tales* (1889) and *Blackfoot Lodge Tales* (1892), and would write still others on serious subjects (mainly ethnological) as well as several fictional boys' books. Two of Grinnell's volumes, it is worth noting, are even today regarded highly and still available: *The Fighting Cheyennes* (1915) and *When Buffalo Ran* (1920). Roosevelt's fulmination against the "half-baked scientists" was seemingly the result of experiences with some of his Harvard natural history teachers.

In another letter to Grinnell, Roosevelt stressed that naturalists in their travels should pay more attention to the large game animals. The author of a recent book, he said, would have provided a much more valuable work if he had done so instead of emphasizing insects and working over the geology of the country. "The geology and the beetles will remain unchanged for eons," he declared, "but the big game will vanish, and only the pioneer can tell about it."[57]

In corresponding with fellow members of the club, Roosevelt wrote long and short letters, explosive and cajoling ones. As a rule all were well splashed with interlineations—it was rare, indeed, then and thereafter, when a letter of his did not include some last-minute thought or correction hurriedly scribbled down in his own distinctive handwriting. These letters, too, paraded information on a wide variety of topics, ranging from birds and mammals to club dinners, committee responsibilities, and needed legislation. One included a caustic comment about the sentimentalists who would put an end to hunting: "The more I realize what a quantity of bad people we have around," he contended, "the more I want to see the good people have a little iron in their blood."[58]

The three Boone and Crockett Club books, each edited by Roosevelt and Grinnell, received favorable notices, both at home and abroad. In the preface to the third of these appeared a significant statement: "The two earlier volumes of the Club's publication, though devoted chiefly to accounts of hunting adventure, contain also considerable matter bearing on the natural history of North American game and forest preservation. In the present volume an effort is made to devote somewhat more space to the natural history side of permanent value. . . . The purposes of the Club are serious, and its published papers should be of a lasting character."[59] This volume contained such articles as "The Labrador Peninsula," "Bear Traits," "The Adirondack Deer Law," and "The Origin of the New York Zoological Society," demonstrating rather conclusively that the volume's editors had succeeded in their intention to devote more space to natural history and conservation and less to hunting.

Roosevelt was president of the club for six consecutive years (1888–93) and in that time seems to have been the dominant figure in the club's growth. Writing to Bamie in late October 1892, he said:

"I must have a B and C dinner when I am with you at the end of November, just Rogers, Chanler, Grinnell, etc., to talk it all over. You see I have had to do the whole thing myself so far, in order to get it started at all, and having some other irons in the fire have only been able to see that this one got hot."[60]

Roosevelt was extremely active in club matters until the Spanish-American War. Even before then, however, the club had become a highly prestigious organization, due primarily to the efficient leadership of its cofounders. Grinnell's primary contributions, as already indicated, were his powerfully worded editorials in *Forest and Stream*, which educated readers on the need for increased efforts to protect and preserve forests, wildlife, and other natural resources. Roosevelt's greatest contribution, or so it would appear, was his success in persuading men of prominence to join the club: high-ranking congressmen, cabinet officers, military officers, and noted authors and scientists, all of whom could be counted on to support projects promoted by the club. Because of his years as a student at Harvard, as an assemblyman in Albany, and as civil service commissioner in Washington, Roosevelt had a wider circle of distinguished acquaintances than Grinnell—and among them many close friends. Most important, he had by now plainly demonstrated his outstanding qualities of charisma and leadership. The members Roosevelt succeeded in bringing into the club include such government men as Henry Cabot Lodge, Elihu Root, John F. Lacey, Francis G. Newlands, George Shiras, Charles D. Walcott, Carl Schurtz, G. G. Vest, Redfield Proctor, Thomas B. Reed, Boies Penrose, and Robert Bacon; such army officers as Lieutenant General John C. Bates, Major General A. W. Greely, Major General William D. Whipple, and Colonel Richard Irving Dodge; such noted authors as Francis Parkman[61] and Owen Wister; and such leading scientists as J. A. Allen, C. Hart Merriam, Daniel Giraud Elliot, Gifford Pinchot, William T. Hornaday, Henry W. Henshaw, and Dr. Alexander Lambert.

In Grinnell's history of the Boone and Crockett Club published in 1913—the date of the club's twenty-fifth anniversary—Grinnell named ninety-eight regular members, fifty-three associate members, and four honorary.[62] He listed also fifty-four deceased members. Obviously, it is impossible to name all of them here, and even more impossible to state, either separately or collectively, their contributions, if any, to the conservation of natural resources. Needless to say, however, the sum of their combined contributions had a profound impact on the future of the conservation movement.

After Roosevelt's death, Charles Scribner's Sons published a multivolume memorial edition of Roosevelt's works, and Grinnell, at Mrs. Roosevelt's request, wrote the introduction to the first volume. Grinnell wrote at some length, though one sentence stands out above others: "Perhaps no single thing that Roosevelt did for conservation had so far-reaching an effect as the establishment of the Boone and Crockett Club."[63] Rereading Grinnell's introduction, we found one paragraph that can serve as a fitting conclusion to this chapter. "Only a short time before his death Roosevelt wrote me a letter which referred to the passing of the years and which again expressed his faith. He said: 'You and I and the rest of our generation are now getting within range of the rifle-pits. We all of us have to face the same fate a few years earlier or a few years later, and I think that what really matters is that according to our lights we shall have borne ourselves well and rendered what service we were able to, as long as we could do so.'"[64]

Notes

1. Roosevelt later sold twenty-eight of these acres to Bamie and thirty-two to his Aunt Annie.

2. Roosevelt, *Autobiography*, 318.

3. Ibid., 318–19.

4. Putnam, *Theodore Roosevelt*, 532.

5. In 1980 I revisited Sagamore Hill and was extended the privilege, through the courtesy of Gary G. Roth, museum curator, of examining and appraising Roosevelt's collection of books. Though my visit was too brief to have a look at all of the books, I came away with the impression that almost every other one dealt, either directly or indirectly, with natural history.

6. Roosevelt, *Works, Mem. Ed.*, 1:xv.

7. Ibid.

8. Ibid., xiv–xv.

9. Ibid., xvi.

10. Ibid., xviii.

11. George Bird Grinnell, ed., *Hunting at High Altitudes*, Book of the Boone and Crockett Club (New York: Harper & Bros., 1913), 435. Elliott Roosevelt and West Roosevelt were Theodore's brother and first cousin. The others were prominent New York City business and professional men, who were also hunters of big game.

12. The men present at this meeting, in addition to those who had at-

tended the first, were: Albert Bierstadt, Heber R. Bishop, Benjamin F. Bristow, Daniel Giraud Elliot, Arnold Hague, James E. Jones, Clarence King, William H. Merrill, Jr., John J. Pierrepont, William Hallett Phillips, John E. Roosevelt, W. A. Wadsworth, Bronson Rumsey, Lawrence Rumsey, and W. D. Pickett. These individuals and the others present at the original meeting were the charter members of the club.

13. John F. Reiger, *American Sportsmen and the Origins of Conservation* (New York: Winchester Press, 1975), 22.

14. Donald Jackson to author, Dec. 17, 1979.

15. Reiger, *American Sportsman*, 162.

16. Robert Barnhill Roosevelt, *Superior Fishing, or, the Striped Bass, Trout, and Black Bass of the Northern States* (New York: Carleton, 1865), 184–85.

17. Reiger, *American Sportsman*, 32.

18. Ibid., 45–46.

19. Grinnell, ed., *Hunting at High Altitudes*, 436–37.

20. Ibid., 437.

21. Ibid., 501. The club soon began electing associate and honorary members, the former being "chosen from those who by their furtherance of the objects of the Club, or general qualifications, shall recommend themselves to the Executive Committee."

22. The brown (or the cinnamon) bear is no longer regarded as a distinct species, but a color variant of the black bear; the brown bear mentioned here is not to be confused with the giant Alaskan brown bear (*Ursus middendorffii*), not technically described until 1896.

23. Ibid. The Columbian black-tailed deer is now a subspecies (*Odocoileus hemionus columbianus*) of the mule or black-tailed deer.

24. George Graham Vest (1830–1904), lawyer, was born in Frankfort, Ky., but later moved to Missouri. He later served as U.S. Senator from Missouri (1879–1903). Roosevelt once said of him that he was "half the brains of the Democratic side of the Senate."

25. Arnold Hague (1840–1917), geologist and graduate (1863) of the Sheffield Scientific School of Yale. In 1866 he was made an assistant geologist with the Geological Survey of the 40th Parallel, and, after foreign travels as a government geologist, he rejoined the U.S. Geologic Survey in 1880, where he stayed until his death.

26. William Hallett Phillips (1852–97), Washington, D.C., lawyer, member of the Boone and Crockett Club, and ardent outdoorsman.

27. Reiger, *American Sportsman*, 124.

28. Redfield Proctor (1831–1908), lawyer and legislator, graduated from Dartmouth in 1857. After serving as governor of Vermont, he was secretary of war in Harrison's cabinet and was U.S. Senator from Vermont from 1891 until his death.

29. Thomas Brackett Reed (1830–1902), lawyer and statesman, was born in Portland, Me. He was elected to the U.S. House of Representatives in 1876 and later served as Speaker of the House.

30. John Willock Noble (1831–1912) was born in Lancaster, Ohio, graduated from Yale in 1851, and in 1888 became Harrison's secretary of the interior. Noble was primarily responsible for the introduction of the Forest Reserve sections in the 1891 revision of the land laws. The act of 1891 remains Noble's most significant achievement.

31. Samuel Pierpont Langley (1834–1906), scientist, was born in Roxbury, Mass. In 1887, following the death of Spencer F. Baird, he became the third secretary of the Smithsonian Institution.

32. Reiger, *American Sportsman*, 125–26.

33. Ibid., 126.

34. Cooke City was a small Montana town just outside the northeastern corner of the park and headquarters of the mining and real-estate speculators who were pushing for the railroad and removal of the acreage from the Park.

35. *Forest and Stream* 39 (Dec. 15, 1892): 514.

36. John Fletcher Lacey (1841–1913), lawyer and legislator, was born in a one-room log cabin near New Martinsville, Va. (now W.Va.). His family moved to Iowa when he was fourteen. Between 1889 and 1907 he represented the sixth district of Iowa in Congress continuously except for 1891–93. Lacey was an ardent conservationist. Roosevelt once said of him that, when there was "a matter . . . of consequence to the nation as a whole," he could be relied upon "to approach it simply from the standpoint of service."

37. Grinnell, ed., *Hunting at High Altitudes*, 451. Lacey would later sponsor another important bill, also known as the Lacey Act, which prohibited plume hunting, among other things.

38. Ibid.

39. Ibid., 476.

40. Reiger, *American Sportsman*, 137.

41. Sequoia National Park, not a forest reserve, was established by an act of Congress, Sept. 25, 1890.

42. Grinnell, ed., *Hunting at High Altitudes*, 458.

43. David Seville Muzzey, *A History of Our Country* (Boston: Ginn and Co., 1936), 579.

44. Grinnell, ed., *Hunting at High Altitudes*, 435–91.

45. See Minute Book of Boone and Crockett Club for 1889, Boone and Crockett Club, Arlington, Va.

46. Madison Grant (1865–1937), lawyer and naturalist, was born in New York City. In addition to his labors in founding the Bronx Zoo, in 1905 he also helped to form the American Bison Society and in 1919 the Save-the-Redwoods League.

47. Elihu Root (1845–1937), lawyer and statesman, was born in Clinton, N.Y., and in 1867 graduated from the New York University Law School. He later served as secretary of war in McKinley's cabinet and secretary of war and of state under Roosevelt.

48. TRCHL.

49. Ibid.

50. Reiger, *American Sportsman*, 122.

51. Brooks, *Speaking for Nature*, 121.

52. Grinnell alone later edited two more Boone and Crockett Club books: *American Big Game in Its Haunts* (1905) and *Hunting at High Altitudes* (1913).

53. Wister, *Roosevelt, the Story of a Friendship*, 35.

54. Ibid., 30–31.

55. Robert Wilson Shufeldt (1850–1934), naturalist and anatomist. He graduated from Cornell in 1874 and later wrote such books as *Anatomy of Birds* (1882) and *The Myology of the Raven* (1890).

56. Morison, *Letters*, 1:663.

57. TRCHL.

58. Cutright, *Roosevelt the Naturalist*, 78.

59. Theodore Roosevelt and George Bird Grinnell, eds., *Trail and Camp Fire*, Book of the Boone and Crockett Club (New York: Forest and Stream Publishing Co., 1897), 10.

60. Cutright, *Roosevelt, the Naturalist*, 78.

61. Francis Parkman was an honorary member of the Boone and Crockett Club, along with General William T. Sherman, General Philip Sheridan, and Judge Jonathan Dean Caton.

62. Honorary members of this date were Doctor Daniel Giraud Elliot, Professor Henry Fairfield Osborn, Colonel William D. Pickett, and the Honorable Theodore Roosevelt.

63. Roosevelt, *Works, Mem. Ed.*, 1:xix.

64. Ibid., xxvii–xxviii.

13

"Field Work Also Is Necessary"

IN 1893, thirteen years after he had received his *magna cum laude* at Harvard, Roosevelt accepted an invitation from the Harvard Board of Overseers to serve on a three-member committee, the duties of which would be to report on the condition of the zoology department and to submit recommendations for its improvement. The inclusion of Roosevelt on the same committee with Walter Faxon, still a member of the zoology staff, and Clarence J. Blake, a well-known ear specialist, was possibly in recognition of the stature he had achieved as a legislator, author, and civil service commissioner since leaving Cambridge. The board knew, of course, that at Harvard he had majored in natural history. It may even have learned that Roosevelt had been critical of the zoology department for not offering field courses as a part of its program.

Roosevelt approached his task with vigor. He revisited Harvard Yard and interviewed faculty of the zoology department and members of the Museum of Comparative Zoology, including ornithologists W. E. D. Scott[1] and William Brewster. It will be recalled that Roosevelt had known Brewster as a member of the Nuttall Ornithological Club.

On this return visit Roosevelt promptly learned—if he did not know already—that the general run of zoology courses offered the Harvard undergraduate was substantially the same as those available during his student years and that three of his former zoology professors, Edward L. Mark, William James, and Faxon, were still on the staff. The only significant change effected since his graduation had been the separation of zoology from the natural history department, making zoology an independent curricular unit. Brewster apparently talked freely with Roosevelt about changes that would benefit the zoology department and the museum. In any event, on April 6, 1893, after Roosevelt had returned to his office in Washington, he wrote Brewster, "You have given me the suggestions I need, and they shall all go in [my report to the Overseers]."

After completing his report, Roosevelt sent a copy to Faxon for his comments. Faxon did not like it—at least parts of it. On June 21, 1893, Roosevelt again wrote to Brewster:

> I found that Mr. Faxon radically disagreed with my report. He is evidently a great believer in the school which puts the biologist and embryologist at the head, and which are substituting for the old term "naturalist" the word "biologist," whereas I think that at present we need to develop the old school naturalist much more than is being done. We will probably therefore have to put in two reports. He objected to my putting in the paragraphs which I did after consulting with yourself and Mr. Scott, on the ground that they were irrelevant. . . . If you see Mr. Faxon, you might jog his mind about returning to me my report. He has had it about a month, and I now want to send it to Charles Francis Adams[2] of the Board of Overseers.

Roosevelt's report to the board was lengthy and occasionally repetitious. It was in two parts, the first setting forth recommendations for the improvement of the zoology department and the second making suggestions for exhibiting to better effect the collections in the Museum of Comparative Zoology. In the first part of the report Roosevelt called the attention of the board to the undue emphasis Harvard zoologists had been, and still were, placing on microscopic work. He thought this overemphasis was misplaced because he felt the microscope played such a small part in zoology. "The place of the microscope in biology by no means answers in importance to the telescope in astronomy," he declared. He admitted that the microscopist had an "honourable function" to perform in science, but, in his opinion, it was not nearly so important as that "of the systematist and the outdoor collector and observer of the stamp of Audubon or Bachman, Baird or Agassiz." This overemphasis on the use of the microscope, Roosevelt contended, was due to the effort made by Harvard zoologists[3] to copy the Germans, who were the acknowledged leaders in its use. He insisted that Harvard was going too far in this respect, accepting not only that which was best in the German methods but also imitating the bad and indifferent as well. Proper biological instruction, he said, should include much more than histology and embryology. "Field work also is necessary," and, if impracticable during the regular school year, it should be provided in the summer. Roosevelt concluded: "The highest type of biologist is the naturalist, who can work both in the laboratory and afield."[4]

In the second part of his report Roosevelt stressed the need for arranging to better advantage the exhibit material in the Museum. He thought it should be organized to show, for instance, the systematic position of different animal groups, the effect of environment on those animals that range over large geographical areas, and the relation of mammals and birds to their breeding, feeding, and general life economics.[5]

The Harvard Board of Overseers did not look favorably upon Roosevelt's report. The members tended to resent his making recommendations concerning the museum when he had been instructed to report only on the zoology department. For another, he had been entirely too outspoken and had ignored a fact, probably known to him, that by 1893 Harvard zoologists had already recommended the addition of field courses to the curriculum but had failed in that effort when the Harvard Corporation had vetoed the proposal for lack of funding. One source has stated that the corporation, sympathetic to the idea, did try to obtain financial support from outside sources, even asking Roosevelt himself to contribute; but Roosevelt "never so much as raised a finger."[6] At a somewhat later date, when back home after having made a speech in Boston, Roosevelt told a friend: "After my speech in Boston, I went to the meeting of the Harvard overseers, and they all kept at the other side of the room from me, except old General Hallowell, who acted like a perfect old trump; he stood up by me through it all. I could not help feeling that we were like a pair of Airedale terriers that had walked in on a convention of tom-cats."[7]

Theodore Roosevelt lived through the academic period that, according to C. Hart Merriam, "took the colleges by storm. In a surprisingly brief period microscopes stood in rows on laboratory tables, and the things seen through their lenses came to be called 'Biology.' The more obvious forms of life were no longer of interest."[8] The general use of the microscope in biological instruction had its inception in European countries, Germany in particular. As the nineteenth century had progressed, German scientists, among them M. J. Schleiden[9] and Julius Sachs,[10] published texts in which much of the material had been gained through microscopic studies. Young American biologists—Marks among them first—flocked to German universities to acquire an increased familiarity with German methods of teaching and research. Sachs's *Textbook of Botany,* translated into English in 1875 (the year before Roosevelt entered Harvard), had a tremendous influence on the teaching of biology in American universities. For the first time many students in the United States were introduced to an infinite number of new and exciting fields of inquiry and were stimulated to give their lives to cellular investigation. The microscope had revealed to them animals, and cells of animals, heretofore invisible to the human eye.

But Roosevelt, as a Harvard student, deplored the lack of field work, was disdainful of the microscope, and he was not alone. There were the students of Louis Agassiz and Spencer F. Baird, these two having been faithful exponents of studies in the out-of-doors. Addison E. Verrill,[11] Edward S. Morse,[12] A. S. Packard,[13] and David Starr Jordan were among those who had learned from Agassiz, and C. Hart Merriam, Elliott Coues, and Henry Henshaw from Baird. It seemed to these men, and to others, Roosevelt included, that the microscopists, in their instant, eager embrace of the microscope, had gone too far. Merriam, for one, later supported Roosevelt's position, saying: "T.R lived during the period of ultramicroscopic specialization in the study of animate nature—the sad period in which the good old term 'natural history' fell into disuse, actually disappearing from text-books and college curricula. Nevertheless he was not misled. The keenness of his observations coupled with his intimate, first-hand knowledge of nature enabled him to recognize the necessity for field work and convinced him of the absolute need of museum specimens for exact studies of animals and plants."[14]

If Roosevelt, in addressing the Harvard Board of Overseers, had softened somewhat his critical remarks, his report might have been better received. For instance, he might at least have acknowledged the ways in which the school's natural history courses had supplemented his own earlier self-training. He said nothing of the benefits derived from lessons in anatomy, physiology, and embryology, subjects that were prerequisite to a broader, clearer understanding and appreciation of animals. Nor did he allude to such other courses as botany, geology, and mineralogy, each having relevance to his study of animals.

2

If Roosevelt admired any man in Washington scientific circles above another, that man was C. Hart Merriam, head of the U.S. Biological Survey. In the fall of 1896, during his term as police commissioner of New York City, Roosevelt came to the defense of Merriam after Henry Cabot Lodge had found fault with a particular Merriam monograph. "Now, I was a little disturbed at what you said to me about Hart Merriam. On most matters I accept your judgement as much better than mine. On this will you for the time being accept mine. The only two men in the country who rank with Merriam are [Alexander] Agassiz and [David Starr] Jordan."[15]

Despite his high regard for Merriam, Roosevelt did not hesitate a few months later to differ with him, this over Merriam's published revision of the coyotes in which he broke them into eleven distinct species.[16] Roosevelt had often encountered these prairie wolves in the Badlands and had watched their furtive shapes disappearing into coulees or clumps of vegetation both day and night. To him they all looked much alike; he definitely did not believe they could be dissected into eleven different species no matter who held the scalpel. So, momentarily thrusting other matters from his mind, he wrote a paper for *Science* magazine entitled "A Layman's View of Specific Nomenclature." The opening paragraph read as follows: "Anything that Dr. Hart Merriam writes is sure to be of great value. He is one of the leading mammalogists and he has laid all men interested in biology under a heavy debt by reviving the best traditions of the old-school faunal naturalists and showing that among the students of the science of life there is room for other men in addition to the section-cutter, the microscopist and the histologist."[17] With this agreeable introduction out of the way—which as seen included yet another criticism of the Harvard natural history curriculum—Roosevelt went to the point. In his judgment the division of coyotes suggested by Merriam was just as logical as would be the arbitrary division of Americans into four groups, namely, New Englanders, Kentuckians, Indians, and Negroes. The important point, he argued, was the "essential likeness of all coyotes one to the other." Exorbitant splitting, he added, can serve no useful purpose and may ultimately have the effect of impairing the good features in the Linnean system of nomenclature. By taking this position Roosevelt had aligned himself with the "species lumpers," that recognized body of taxonomists who deprecates undue cleavage of a species, as opposed to the "species splitters," such as Merriam, who espouse the contrary.

Roosevelt's article appeared in the April 30, 1897, number of *Science.* In the May 14 issue, less than a month later, Merriam replied, beginning with a return compliment: "He [Roosevelt] is a writer of the best accounts we have ever had of the habits of the larger animals." He then continued, saying that the rule in vogue for validating or invalidating a species was a matter of integration. "Forms known to integrate, no matter now different," he declared, "should be treated as subspecies and bear trinomial names, forms not known to integrate, no matter how closely related, must be treated as full species and bear binomial names."[18] It was on this basis, Merriam said, that he had seen fit to fragment the coyote as he had. Merriam's rebuttal failed to change Roosevelt's thinking. He made this abundantly clear in a second paper to *Science,* insisting that he had "certain conservative instincts which are jarred when an old familiar friend is suddenly cut up into eleven brand new acquaintances."[19]

In the midst of these exchanges of divergent taxonomic opinion between Roosevelt and Merriam, the venerable Biological Society of Washington, in planning its 277th meeting, proposed a program that would allow the two opponents to present their respective views. It was so arranged, and the meeting was held on the night of May 8, 1897, in the old Cosmos Club assembly hall. At that date, it should be said, Roosevelt was assistant secretary of the Navy, having been appointed to that post one month earlier. The meeting was opened. Merriam was introduced first and read a carefully prepared paper. Roosevelt, after being presented, spoke extemporaneously. L. O. Howard,[20] the presiding officer, later reported:

He [Roosevelt] made a very forceful argument from his viewpoint and from that obviously of other hunters, and rather staggered some of the really scientific men in the audience by the cogency of his reasoning. He talked at length, as was customary with him, and the hour of adjournment (10 o'clock) came before he had finished, but by unanimous vote he was allowed to proceed until he was satisfied. He sat down after having made a distinct impression on his scientific and rather critical audience. Merriam asked for five minutes in which to reply, in the course of which he completely demolished the Rooseveltian argument, and there was nothing more to be said. It was a memorable meeting, and no one who was there will ever forget it. Most of us saw Roosevelt for the first time then, and were greatly impressed by him. Among the taxonomists present there were, of course, lumpers as well as splitters, and the lumpers got some satisfaction from the future President's arguments.[21]

By characterizing Roosevelt as "a hunter," Howard made it plain that he knew little or nothing of Roosevelt's background in zoology, and he may have felt—as did others present—that the assistant secretary of the Navy was presumptuous in questioning the convictions of the head of the U.S. Biological Survey.

Howard was wrong, too, in saying that Merriam's five-minute rebuttal "completely demolished" Roosevelt's arguments. News of the controversy quickly circulated, and prominent scientists sided with Roosevelt. J. A. Allen, distinguished curator of birds and mammals at the American Museum of Natural History, said it was extremely unwise in revising species "to adopt so elastic and unphilosophic basis [as Merriam's], and withal so open to the influence of the personal equation."[22] The news crossed the Atlantic to England, where the noted British zoologist, Richard Lydekker, voiced his opinion: "Roosevelt probably knows more about the big game of North America than any other man . . .[and] is really a very accomplished field naturalist."[23] In the several current books on mammals, one finds listed just one species of coyote. The tendency is to break the genus into subspecies, one text naming nineteen altogether.[24]

One aspect of the Roosevelt/Merriam confrontation has been overlooked, the former being on his good behavior. He did not, for instance, accuse Merriam, as he had others, of "suffering from a species of moral myopia complicated with intellectual strabismus."[25] He had a high regard for Merriam; indeed, he was fearful that he might have hurt his feelings. Writing to Henry Fairfield Osborn at the American Museum of Natural History, he said: "I almost broke the heart of my beloved friend Merriam. He felt as though he had been betrayed in the house of his friends; but he really goes too far. He has just sent me a pamphlet announcing the discovery of two new species of mountain lion from Nevada. If he is right I will guarantee to produce fifty-seven new species of red fox from Long Island."[26]

Yet Roosevelt did not think Merriam had gone "too far" when the latter soon afterward announced his discovery of a new species of elk. Merriam had found it in the Olympic Mountains of Washington and claimed that it differed in coloration, antler shape, and other respects from the common Rocky Mountain elk (*Cervus canadensis*), so much so, in fact, that he named it *Cervus Roosevelti*. In further explanation, Merriam wrote: "It is fitting that the noblest deer of America should perpetuate the name of one who, in the midst of a busy public career, has found time to study our larger mammals in their native haunts and has written the best accounts we have ever had of their habits and chase."[27] Having so recently taken issue with Merriam about creating supernumerary species of the coyote and mountain lion, Roosevelt should at once have been wary of a new species of elk. However, if at all skeptical, he never at any time admitted it. *Cervus Roosevelti* delighted him and, with no delay, he conveyed that delight, undiluted, to its donor: "I am more pleased than I can say at what you have done. No compliment could be paid me that I would appreciate as much as this—in the first place, because of the fact itself, and in the next place because it comes from you. To have this noblest game animal in America named after me by the foremost of living mammalogists is something that really makes me prouder than I can well say. I deeply appreciate the compliment and I am only sorry that it will never be in my power to do anything except to just merely appreciate it."[28]

Roosevelt soon again expressed his delight with *Cervus Roosevelti*, and this time publicly. After thanking Merriam, he was asked by the editors of a British publication, *The Encyclopedia of Sport*, to contribute a number of articles on American game animals. He agreed to do so and, in one about the elk (wapiti), included the following premeditated remarks: "There are several aberrant forms of wapiti, including one that dwells in the great Tule swamps of California. There is also an entirely distinct species with its centre of abundance in the Olympic Mountains of Washington and on Vancouver Island. This species Dr. Hart Merriam has recently done the present writer the honor of naming after him (*Cervus Roosevelti*)."[29] Almost a century has passed since Merriam thus complimented Roosevelt. There is still a Roosevelt's elk, but it is only a subspecies, one bearing the trinomial *Cervus canadensis roosevelti*.

3

Theodore Roosevelt has not been lacking in biographers, particularly of late, but not one of them, we believe, has accorded space to the articles that he contributed, while assistant secretary of the Navy, to the *Encyclopedia of Sport*, a hefty, two-volume publication edited by the earl of Suffolk and Berkshire, Hedley Peek, and F. G. Aflalo and published in London in 1897–98 by Lawrence and Bullen. This work contained eleven articles by Roosevelt, three in volume I and the remainder in volume II. Those in the first volume were titled "Bison," "Caribou," and "Goat—Rocky Mountain." The others, in the second volume, were: "Opossum and Raccoon Hunting," "Peccary," "Prairie Chicken," "Pronghorn," "Puma," "Turkey," "Wapiti," and "Wolf-Coursing."

The British had earlier recognized Roosevelt as an authority on the War of 1812 and now conceded his prowess as a student of the game animals of the United States. He seems not to have had a free hand, however, in choosing his subjects, for he surely would have preferred to air his observations on the grizzly, mule deer, and bighorn, for example, instead of on the opossum, raccoon, and turkey. Even so, he must have been flattered at the opportunity to join with other celebrated sportsmen, mainly European, in the production of this ambitious work. Furthermore, he had not completely recovered from his cattle-raising reverses and probably welcomed the emolument the British offered.

In at least two or three of his articles for the *Encyclopedia of Sport*, Roosevelt expressed concern for the future of American game animals, thereby displaying another example of the well-oriented conservationist. Writing of the prairie chickens, for example, he said: "[These birds] are steadily diminishing in numbers. The efforts of the game associations and sportsmen's clubs to have the game laws properly enforced have done much to arrest the diminution, and here and there to stop it; but the communities as a whole will have to see more clearly than they now do the effects of wasteful slaughter of game birds and game beasts before these birds and beasts can be effectually preserved."[30] Of the bison, which Roosevelt believed to be so near extinction that he could write in the past tense, he noted: "when the fierce greed of the skin hunter and skin buyer had exterminated the last of these great herds, there passed away what was perhaps the most imposing feature of American wilderness life."[31]

Notes

1. William Earl Dodge Scott (1852–1910), ornithologist, was born in Brooklyn and in 1873 graduated from Harvard's Lawrence Scientific School. In 1876 he was appointed acting curator of the Princeton College Museum of Biology, and in 1885 Princeton named him curator of ornithology, a post he held until his death.

2. Charles Francis Adams, 2d (1835–1915), grandson of John Quincy Adams, was born in Boston. In 1856 he graduated from Harvard and, beginning in 1882, served for twenty-four years on Harvard's Board of Overseers. He is perhaps best known for his biographies of Richard Dana and Charles Francis Adams (his father).

3. One in particular having been Edward Laurens Mark.

4. *Report to the Overseers,* Academical Series II, Vol. 7 (1893–96). Report of the Committee on Zoology.

5. Ibid.

6. George Howard Parker, *The World Expands: Recollections of a Zoologist* (Cambridge, Mass.: Harvard University Press, 1946), 87.

7. Roosevelt, *Works, Mem. Ed.,* 3:xix.

8. C. Hart Merriam, "Roosevelt, the Naturalist," *Science* 75 (Feb. 12, 1932): 182.

9. Matthias Jacob Schleiden (1804–81), noted German botanist, was born in Hamburg. In 1842–43 he published *Grundzüge der Wissenschaftlichen Botanik* (Principles of Scientific Botany), a major work.

10. Julius Sachs (1832–97), German botanist, was born in Breslau. He was the author of *Geschichte der Botanik* (History of Botany).

11. Addison Emory Verrill (1839–1926), American zoologist, was born in Greenwood, Me. In 1884 he became a professor of zoology at Yale.

12. Edward Sylvester Morse (1838–1925), American zoologist, was born in Portland, Me. Morse studied under Louis Agassiz at Harvard and was later appointed professor of zoology at Bowdoin College.

13. Alpheus Spring Packard, Jr. (1839–1905), American naturalist, was born in Brunswick, Me. He graduated from Bowdoin College in 1861 and in 1878 was named professor of zoology and geology at Brown University.

14. Merriam, "Roosevelt, the Naturalist," 183.

15. Henry Cabot Lodge, *Selections from the Correspondence of Theodore Roosevelt and Henry Cabot Lodge, 1884–1918,* 2 vols. (New York: Charles Scribner's Sons, 1924), 1:237.

16. Merriam, "Revision of the Coyotes or Prairie Wolves, with Descriptions of New Forms," *Procs. Biol. Soc. of Wash.* 11 (Mar. 15, 1897): 19–31.

17. Roosevelt, "A Layman's Views on Scientific Nomenclature," *Science* (n.s.) 5 (Apr. 30, 1897): 686–88.

18. Merriam, "Suggestions for a New Method of Discriminating between Species and Subspecies," ibid., 5 (May 14, 1897): 753–58.

19. Roosevelt, "The Discrimination of Species and Subspecies," ibid., 5 (June 4, 1897): 877–80.

20. Leland Ossian Howard (1857–1950), American entomologist, was born in Rockford, Ill. In 1877 he graduated from Cornell and served as chief of the Bureau of Entomology, U.S. Department of Agriculture, 1894–1927.

21. L. O. Howard, *Fighting the Insects* (New York: Macmillan Co., 1933), 236–37.

22. J. A. Allen, *Science* (n.s.) 5 (June 4, 1897).

23. Richard Lydekker, *Nature,* July 15, 1897, 265–68.

24. See Gerrit S. Miller, Jr., and Remington Kellogg, *List of North American Recent Mammals* (Washington, D.C.: Smithsonian Institution, 1955), 670–74.

25. Lodge, *Correspondence between Roosevelt and Lodge,* 1:5.

26. Morison, *Letters,* 1:674–75.

27. Merriam, "*Cervus Roosevelti,* a New Elk from the Olympics," *Procs. Biol. Soc. of Wash.* 11 (Dec. 17, 1897): 271–75.

28. Morison, *Letters,* 1:740.

29. *The Encyclopedia of Sport,* ed. Suffolk, Peek, and Aflalo, 2 vols. (London: Lawrence and Bullen, 1897–98), 2:530–31.

30. Ibid., 1:132.

31. Ibid., 118.

This sketch of a pronghorn is one of some eighty that Frederic
Remington did for Theodore Roosevelt's *Ranch Life and the
Hunting Trail* (1888). (Sagamore Hill National Historic Site)

Theodore Roosevelt's Elkhorn Ranch house, built by Bill Sewall
and Wilmot Dow, beside the Little Missouri about thirty-five
miles down the river from Medora. This wash drawing was
done by R. Swain Gifford for Roosevelt's *Hunting Trips of a
Ranchman.* (Sagamore Hill National Historic Site)

George Bird Grinnell, editor of *Forest and Stream* (1876-1911) and author of *Blackfoot Lodge Tales, The Indians of Today,* and *By Cheyenne Campfires.* (Theodore Roosevelt Collection, Harvard University)

C. Hart Merriam, chief of the U.S. Biological Survey (1885-1910) and author of *The Birds of Connecticut, Indian Population of California,* and *Review of the Grizzly and Big Brown Bears of America.* (Fish and Wildlife Service)

Frank M. Chapman, American ornithologist, curator of the American Museum of Natural History (1908-45), founder and editor of *Bird-Lore,* and author of *Handbook of Birds of Eastern North America, Key to North American Birds, My Tropical Air Castle,* and *Life in an Air Castle.* (American Museum of Natural History)

Henry Fairfield Osborn, professor at Columbia University (1890-1935), curator of vertebrate paleontology at the American Museum of Natural History (1891-1935), and author of *The Age of Mammals* and *Men of the Old Stone Age.* (American Museum of Natural History)

President Theodore Roosevelt and Chief Forester Gifford Pinchot on the river steamer *Mississippi,* during a trip of the Inland Waterways Commission in October 1907. (U.S. Forest Service)

Theodore Roosevelt and John Burroughs at Yellowstone National Park, 1903. (Theodore Roosevelt Collection, Harvard University)

Returning from Brazil on the *S.S. Arden*, 1914. Left to right: George Cherrie, Theodore Roosevelt, and Leo Miller. (American Museum of Natural History)

Theodore Roosevelt with John Muir (at TR's left) in Yosemite at the base of one of the park's many giant "big trees" (*Sequoia gigantea*), 1903. (Theodore Roosevelt Collection, Harvard University)

14

"A Primeval Forest Is a Great Sponge"

FOR THEODORE ROOSEVELT, in 1898, the mills of the gods ground with feverish, almost frenetic rapidity: assistant secretary of the Navy in April, Rough Rider in Texas in May, hero of San Juan Hill in July, triumphant leader mustering out at Montauk Point, Long Island, in mid-August, nominee for governor of New York in September, and governor-elect in November.

Two months later, on January 2, 1899, Roosevelt was sworn in as governor, on a day so cold that the brass instruments of the band escorting him to the State Capitol building froze into silence. Seventeen years had elapsed since he had first arrived in Albany, on a warmer day, to assume the responsibilities of an assemblyman. Now, two days after having been sworn in as governor, Roosevelt delivered to the state legislature his first annual message. It was brief—especially in comparison with his second a year later—and dealt with such diverse matters as taxation, the Erie Canal, commerce, labor, the National Guard, roads, civil service, and the economy. Sandwiched between roads and economy was a section called "The Forests of the State." Tersely worded, it read as follows: "The Forest Reserve will be a monument to the wisdom of its founders. It is very important that on acquiring additional land we should not forget that it is even more necessary to preserve what we have already acquired and to protect it, not only against the depredations of man, but against the most serious of all enemies to the forests—fire. One or two really great forest fires might do damage which could not be repaired for a generation. The laws for the protection of the game and fish of the wilderness seem to be working well, but they should be more rigidly enforced."[1]

The brevity of Roosevelt's comment in this section on forests and wildlife is perhaps understandable. Having been governor-elect less than two months, he had had little time in which to get ready for the tasks ahead. As chief executive of the then most populous state in the nation, his responsibilities would be weighty, indeed weightier than those of any other American elected official except the president of the United States. However, his limited remarks about the state's natural resources by no means reflected a disinterest in them. Certainly George Bird Grinnell entertained no such thought; he was soon editorializing: "The State of New York is fortunate at present in having a Governor who is not only deeply interested in all matters of game, fish and forest preservation, but also has so clear an acquaintance with those subjects that he can always be depended upon to act on them for the public good."[2]

At the time Roosevelt took office, the welfare of the state's natural resources was in the hands of a commission, the Fisheries, Forest and Game Commission. On assuming the governorship, Roosevelt lost little time in beginning an investigation of that body, having earlier gained intelligence that individual members, each a political appointee, were lacking in competence and incentive, and thus guilty of neglecting their expected duties.

In his investigation of the commission, Roosevelt would shortly have the support and counsel of Gifford Pinchot, in addition to that of Grinnell and others. Gifford Pinchot (1865–1946), who would later receive national recognition as a conservationist and political figure, was born in Connecticut, the son of wealthy parents. He traveled widely during his youth, spending much time in France, where he learned to speak French almost as well as English. In 1885 he entered Yale University (and later was fond of boasting that he had played varsity football—as a substitute—under the immortal Walter Camp). Sometime before his graduation from Yale in 1889, Pinchot had decided on a career in forestry. In arriving at this decision, he had had the backing of his father, James M. Pinchot, who, at one time, had served as vice-president of the American Forestry Association (founded in 1875).

Since there was no forestry school in the United States, young Pinchot went to Europe in the fall of 1889 and soon afterward enrolled as a student in the École Nationale Forestière, Nancy, France. His education there, financed by his wealthy father, lasted thirteen months, but in that time, as a result of intensive classroom studies and well-supervised field trips to some of the best managed forests in the world (those of France, Germany, and other mid-European countries), he received the training that would make him America's first native-born professional forester. After completing his European schooling, Pinchot returned to the United States, convinced that "forestry is the art of using a forest without destroying it."[3] Early the next year he had his first opportunity to put that conviction into practice when George W. Vanderbilt engaged him to manage a forest on his estate, Biltmore, near Asheville, North Carolina. Within one year Pinchot's methods proved so successful that, as one scientist put it, his "reputation was made."[4]

Since Pinchot's contract with Vanderbilt did not prohibit his engaging in other activities, in 1893 he opened an office in New York City as a consulting forester. At first, clients were few in number. In time, however, he heard from Hoke Smith,[5] then secretary of the interior, who was interested in making a study of the condition of American forests and suggested that the National Academy of Sciences be empowered to appoint a National Forest Commission to make the study. This proposal soon won congressional approval, along with an appropriation of $25,000. Charles S. Sargent[6] of Harvard was named chairman of the commission and Pinchot its secretary. Beginning in the summer of 1896, the commission surveyed western timberlands from Montana to Arizona. Almost from the start, a rift developed between Sargent and Pinchot, which widened as the tour progressed. To Sargent, the forests should be kept inviolate; Pinchot favored regulated use. A memorable event of the tour occurred at the Grand Canyon, when John Muir[7] joined the commission and met Pinchot again (they had first met in 1893, when Muir had been on a trip to New York City). According to one writer, all members of the touring party "were awed by the elemental strength of Muir's personality."[8] At first, Muir and Pinchot were friends; later they quarreled, at times bitterly. The report of the commission appeared belatedly. Because of the differences between Pinchot and Sargent, the two factions agreed only on the need of new reserves, if the forests were to escape ruin.

The following year (1897), President Grover Cleveland added 21.4 million acres of timberland to the forest reserves. With William McKinley succeeding Cleveland as president almost immediately after this creation, the administration of the newly formed reserves fell largely on McKinley's secretary of the interior, Cornelius W. Bliss.[9]

Recognizing at once his need for help in managing the reserves, Bliss turned to Pinchot, asking him to serve as a "confidential forest agent." As news circulated of Cleveland's proclamation and of Bliss's appointment of Pinchot to a federal post, a storm of protest arose, not only from western farmers, who feared that the forests, through Cleveland's action, had been locked up permanently, but also from such prominent preservationists as Muir, Sargent, Robert U. Johnson,[10] and W. T. Hornaday,[11] each a seasoned advocate of absolute protection for the forests. Battle lines were now clearly drawn between amateurs, represented by Muir, Sargent, and others, and professionals, represented by Pinchot and his colleagues in the Department of the Interior.

Pinchot's new post allowed him to travel to the West again, giving him the opportunity to calm fears of the farmers and to increase his knowledge of the forests. Also, in speeches and writings, both in the West and East, he further promoted his ideas on forest management. Impressed with Pinchot, in 1899 McKinley appointed him chief forester and head of the Division of Forestry in the Department of Agriculture as successor to Bernhard E. Fernow. Apparently Pinchot had just been advanced to this post when Roosevelt asked him to come to Albany.

According to one source, Roosevelt and Pinchot first met while the former was civil service commissioner (which could have been any time in the years 1889–95).[12] The two had much in common and quickly became friends. At later date, seemingly in 1897 right after joining Bliss, Pinchot had become a member of the Boone and Crockett Club, possibly influenced to do so by Roosevelt.

When Roosevelt invited Pinchot to come to Albany, he insisted that he stay at the governor's mansion. On his arrival Pinchot found that the mansion was "under ferocious attack from a band of invisible Indians, and the Governor of the Empire State was helping a houseful of children to escape by lowering them out of a second story window on a rope." Later that evening, after all of the youngsters had been "saved," Roosevelt and Pinchot engaged in a boxing match during which the federal forester knocked the New York governor "off his very solid pins."[13] Not until the next morning did the two men settle down to a discussion of the state's forests and how best to handle them. Before this meeting ended, Pinchot may have told Roosevelt of a plan of the Pinchot family to found a School of Forestry in the near future at Yale University. In 1900 the Pinchots offered Yale (1) an endowment of $150,000 to start the school; (2) the appointment of Henry Graves[14] as the dean of the new school; and (3) the offer of a summer camp facility at the Pinchot estate in Milford, Pennsylvania.

2

Roosevelt's investigation of the Fisheries, Forest and Game Commission quickly unearthed further evidence that from the beginning it had been delinquent in enforcing the state's game laws. Armed with this evidence, which he regarded as unimpeachable, he promptly addressed a letter to the head of the commission, stressing the alleged "inefficiency of the State's game wardens" and requesting a full report on "the wardens' capabilities, distribution and numbers."[15]

Just seven years earlier, in 1892, New York had created Adirondack Park, located roughly between the Mohawk River and Lake Ontario and consisting of "a crazyquilt . . . of 'forever wild' land abutting private tracts owned by logging companies, towns, wilderness clubs, and individuals."[16] Within its boundaries the park contained the vast woodland domain of forest and lakes that Roosevelt had visited as a boy and that had served as an unquestioned influence in furthering his studies of birds and other wilderness creatures. It is understandable, therefore, that Roosevelt as governor centered his conservation efforts on this familiar part of the state more than on any other and urged the commission to do the same, "both from the standpoint of forestry and from the less important but still very important standpoint of fish and game protection."[17]

The term of office of the governor of New York State was then only two years. Consequently, Roosevelt's efforts during his stay in Albany to obtain legislation to improve the protection and preservation of the state's natural resources fell short of anticipation, though not greatly to his surprise. He had learned earlier, while an assemblyman, that legislative machinery as a rule moves slowly. The wording of Roosevelt's second annual message, delivered on January 3, 1900, makes this obvious. His remarks on the Fisheries,

Forest and Game Commission greatly exceeded in length those of his first annual message. He said, in part:

Under this Commission great progress has been made through the fish hatcheries in the propagation of valuable food and sporting fish. The laws for the protection of deer have resulted in their increase. Nevertheless, as railroads tend to encroach on the wilderness, the temptation to illegal hunting becomes greater, and the danger for forest fires increases. There is need of greater improvement, both in our laws and their administration. The game wardens have been too few in number. . . . There should be a thorough reorganization of the work of the Commission. A careful study of the resources and condition of the forest on State lands must be made. It is certainly not too much to expect that the State forests should be managed as efficiently as the forests on private lands. . . .

The subject of forest preservation is of the utmost importance to the State. The Adirondacks and Catskills should be great parks kept in perpetuity for the benefit and enjoyment of our people. Much has been done of late years towards their preservation, but very much remains to be done. The provisions of law in reference to sawmills and wood pulp mills are defective and should be changed so as to prohibit dumping dyestuff, sawdust or tan bark in any amount whatsoever into the streams. Reservoirs should be made; but not where they will tend to destroy large sections of the forest, and only after a careful and scientific study of the water resources of the region. The people of the forest regions are themselves growing more and more to realize the necessity of preserving both the trees and the game. A live deer in the woods will attract to the neighborhood ten times the money that could be obtained for the deer's dead carcass. Timber thefts on the State land is, of course, a grave offense against the whole public. . . .

There is a further, and more immediate and practical, end in view. A primeval forest is a great sponge which absorbs and distills rainwater; and when it is destroyed the result is apt to be an alternation of flood and drought. Forest fires ultimately make the land a desert, and are a detriment to all that portion of the State tributary to the streams through the woods where they occur. Every effort should be made to minimize their destructive influence. We need to have our system of forestry gradually developed and conducted along scientific principles. When this has been done it will be possible to allow marketable timber to be cut everywhere without damage to the forests—indeed with positive advantage to them; but until lumbering is thus conducted, on strictly scientific principles no less than upon principles of the strictest honesty toward the State, we cannot afford to suffer it at all in the State forests. Unrestrained greed means the ruin of the great woods and the drying up of the sources of the rivers. . . .

The State should not permit within its limits factories to make bird skins or bird feathers into articles of ornament or wearing apparel. Ordinary birds, and especially song birds, should be rigidly protected. Game birds should never be shot to a greater extent than will offset the natural rate of increase. All spring shooting should be prohibited and efforts made by correspondence with the neighboring States to secure its prohibition within their borders. . . .

The open season for the different species of game and fish should be made uniform throughout the entire State, save that it should be shorter on Long Island for certain species which are not plentiful, and which are pursued by a greater number of people than in other game portions of the State.[18]

Roosevelt's statements mark the first time in the history of New York that a governor publicly, and in detail, revealed his views on conservation. More than that, for the first time in the history of the nation, a prominent political figure had spelled out his convictions on this same subject. Never before had a governor of New York State or a governor of any state spoken out so fully, and so forthrightly, about the related topics of forest preservation, forest fires, flooding, stream pollution, soil erosion, reservoirs, illegal hunting, wildlife controls, and watersheds.

Some of Roosevelt's views were strictly his own, gained from his earlier experiences in the Adirondacks, in Maine, or in the Badlands. Other views were the result of association with members of the Boone and Crockett Club, notably Grinnell. And still others stemmed from conversations with Pinchot. Pinchot, as the only trained forester in our country, could have been the only source of Roosevelt's remarks about "forest management," "scientific studies," and "cutting of marketable timber without damage to the forests." Before the advent of Pinchot, such practices were alien to the United States.

During Roosevelt's governorship, and for many years before and after, lumbering in the United States was deplorably wasteful. It was a period that saw the destruction of the great virgin forests of the East. On entering a forest, axemen cut all marketable trees, thus exposing the land to erosion and flooding. There was no thought of saving smaller logs, limbs, slabs, cut from logs in the mills, or sawdust, and certainly no tangible thought of reforestation.

How different the forest practices in European countries, to which Pinchot had recently been exposed. Axemen cut only certain trees (those marked in advance by the foresters), and the trees were felled in directions to do as little damage to standing trees as possible. All limbs and slabs were cut into meter lengths, these being saved for fuel, as was the sawdust. Indeed, no part of a tree was wasted, and the forest itself through sustained management continued to flourish.

At no time during his political career was Theodore Roosevelt above seeking and accepting advice from other men whose opinions he respected. Just as Pinchot and Grinnell had had a hand in shaping Roosevelt's remarks on forests outlined in his 1900 annual message, so did Frank M. Chapman, by expressing outrage at the killing of our more beautiful birds for female apparel. Soon after taking office as governor, Roosevelt wrote a letter to Chapman, which the latter prized so highly that he had it framed and hung on the wall of his American Museum office. It reads as follows:

March 22, 1899

My dear Mr. Chapman: I need hardly say how heartily I sympathize with the purposes of the [State] Audubon Society.[19] I would like to see all harmless wild things, but especially all birds, protected in every way. I do not understand how any man or woman who really loves nature can fail to try to exert all influence in support of such objects as those of the Audubon Society.

Spring would not be spring without song birds, any more than it would be spring without birds and flowers, and I only wish that besides protecting the songsters, the birds of the grove, the orchard, the garden and the meadow, we could also protect the birds of the seashore and of the wilderness.

The Loon ought to be, and under wise legislation, could be a feature of every Adirondack lake, and Terns should be as plentiful along our shores as Swallows around our barns.

A Tanager or a Cardinal makes a point of glowing beauty in the green woods, and the Cardinal among the snows.

When the Bluebirds were so nearly destroyed by the severe winter a few seasons ago, the loss was like the loss of an old friend, or at least like the burning down of a familiar and dearly loved home. How immensely it would add to our forests if only the great Logcock [pileated woodpecker] were still found among them.

The destruction of the Wild Pigeon and the Carolina Paroquet [both by then nearing extinction] has meant a loss as severe as if the Catskills and the Palisades were taken away. When I hear of the destruction of a species I feel as if all the works of some great writer had perished, as if we had lost all instead of only part of Polybius or Livy. Very truly yours[20]

This letter continued to hang on Chapman's office wall until his death, almost half a century later. In that time many visitors had the privilege of reading it, and more than a few went away with a heightened appreciation of Roosevelt's devotion to birds.

In his *Autobiography* Roosevelt devoted less than a dozen lines to his accomplishments in conservation while governor: "I was able to do a good deal for forest preservation and the protection of our wild life. All that later I strove for in the Nation in connection with conservation was foreshadowed by what I strove to obtain for New York State when I was Governor; and I was already working with Gifford Pinchot and [Frederick H.] Newell.[21] I secured better administration, and some improvement in the laws themselves. The improvement in administration, and in the character of the game and forest wardens, was secured partly as the result of a conference in the executive chamber which I held with forty of the best guides and woodsmen of the Adirondacks."[22] Roosevelt did achieve one specific objective, that of reconstituting the Fisheries, Forest and Game Commission, and he was delighted with his choice of William A. Wadsworth[23] as president of the commission.

Despite the fact that Roosevelt's term as governor was limited to two years, and that his conservation efforts were often impeded by powerful political opponents, he nevertheless succeeded in educating the public in ways resulting in lasting benefit. In years immediately ahead, the state's forests and wildlife enjoyed improved protection, streams ran cleaner, and New Yorkers increasingly demanded that the guardians of their natural resources be freed of political intervention. In addition, adjoining states began imitating Roosevelt's recommended measures for preserving their own natural resources.

3

With the beginning of his second year as governor, Roosevelt moved into the twentieth century. Before the year ended, he would be projected—by two events—into national, even international, prominence. On July 12, 1900, in ceremonies at Sagamore Hill, he was officially informed of his nomination by Republicans as vice-president, to run with William McKinley. Four months later, on November 6, he and McKinley were chosen by the people to serve as their next vice president and president. In no way could Roosevelt have then foreseen that in ten more months insensate fate would place him in the White House.

Notes

1. Theodore Roosevelt, *Annual Message of the Governor of the State of New York* (New York: Wynkoop Hollenbeck Crawford Co., 1899), 32.

2. *Forest and Stream* 52 (May 6, 1899): 341.

3. M. Nelson McGeary, *Gifford Pinchot, Forester-Politician* (Princeton, N.J.: Princeton University Press, 1960), 23.

4. Frank Graham, Jr., *Man's Dominion, the Story of Conservation in America* (New York: M. Evans and Co., 1971), 95.

5. Hoke Smith (1855–1931) was born in Newton, N.C., and served as secretary of the interior in Grover Cleveland's cabinet from 1893 to 1896.

6. Charles Sprague Sargent (1841–1927), dendrologist, a Harvard graduate and, for many years, director of the Arnold Arboretum, Harvard. He was the author of many books, including *Silva of North America.*

7. John Muir (1838–1914), naturalist and author, was born in Scotland and educated at the University of Wisconsin. He later moved to California, where he fought vigorously for the preservation of the western forests. He was the author of *The Yosemite* (1912) and other books.

8. Graham, *Man's Dominion,* 96.

9. Cornelius Newton Bliss (1833–1911), American merchant and politician, served in McKinley's cabinet as secretary of the interior.

10. Robert Underwood Johnson was, during the 1880s, an editor of *Century* magazine, successor to the old *Scribner's* magazine. He published many of Muir's articles and was, like Muir, opposed to Pinchot's ideas for sustained yield forests.

11. William Temple Hornaday (1854–1937), naturalist, conservationist, and writer. In the years 1896–1926, Hornaday was director of the New York Zoological Park. He initiated the movement leading to the formation of the Montana National Bison Range and Wichita National Bison Range. Among his published books is *Wildlife Conservation in Theory and Practice* (1914).

12. McGeary, *Gifford Pinchot,* 53.

13. Sylvia Jukes Morris, *Edith Kermit Roosevelt* (New York: Coward, McCann & Geoghegan, 1980), 196–97.

14. Henry Solon Graves (1871–1952), forester, was a graduate (1892) of Yale University, director (1900–1910) of the Yale School of Forestry, and (1910–20) chief of the U.S. Forest Service.

15. Reiger, *American Sportsmen,* 143.

16. *Smithsonian* 10 (Feb. 1980): 45.

17. *Forest and Stream* 53 (Dec. 9, 1899): 469.

18. Roosevelt, *Annual Message of the Governor of the State of New York* (New York: James B. Lyon, 1900), 30–32.

19. The State Audubon Society preceded the National, which was not formed until 1905.

20. Chapman, *Autobiography of a Bird-Lover,* 180–81.

21. Frederick Haynes Newell (1862–1952), civil engineer, was born in Bradford, Pa., and in 1888 was named assistant hydraulic engineer in the U.S. Geological Survey. He later figured prominently in the passage of the Reclamation Act of 1902 and, as a consequence, was soon named head of the Reclamation Service.

22. Roosevelt, *Autobiography,* 289–90.

23. William Austin Wadsworth (1847–1918), farmer, was born in Boston and in 1870 graduated from Harvard. In 1900, when Roosevelt named him head of the Fisheries, Forest and Game Commission, he was president of the Boone and Crockett Club.

15

"For Our People Unborn"

THEODORE ROOSEVELT was inaugurated as vice-president of the United States on March 4, 1901. The Senate convened on the following day and was in session until March 9, on which date Roosevelt had his last opportunity to preside over that body. When Congress reconvened in the fall, he was president, having been elevated to that position by the simple pressure of an index finger, the finger of the anarchist, Leon Czolgosz.

William McKinley died on September 14, 1901, and Roosevelt was sworn in as the nation's chief executive later that same day. He was the youngest man to assume that office, just six weeks short of his forty-third birthday—and the first conservationist to take up residence in the White House.

If the people of the nation were still unaware that Theodore Roosevelt loved the woods and the fields and the creatures living in them, and that he was perhaps the strongest advocate then alive of their protection and preservation, he did not leave them long in doubt. In his first annual message to Congress, delivered on December 3, 1901, he said in part:

Public opinion throughout the United States has moved steadily toward a just appreciation of the value of forests. . . . The great part played by them in the creation and maintenance of the national wealth is now more fully realized than ever before. . . . The fundamental idea of forestry is the perpetuation of forests by use. . . . The preservation of our forests is an imperative business necessity. . . . The [present] forest reserves will inevitably be of still greater use in the future than in the past. . . . The forests are natural reservoirs. By restraining the streams in flood and replenishing them in drought they make possible the use of waters otherwise wasted. They prevent the soil from wasting, and so protect the storage reservoirs from

210

filling up with silt. Forest conservation is therefore an essential condition of water conservation. . . . Some at least of the forest reserves should afford perpetual protection to the native fauna and flora, safe havens of refuge to our rapidly diminishing wild animals of the larger kinds, and free camping grounds for the ever-increasing numbers of men and women who have learned to find rest, health and recreation in the splendid forests and flower-clad meadows of the mountains. . . . The reclamation of the unsettled arid public lands presents a different problem. Here it is not enough to regulate the flow of streams. The object of the Government is to dispose of the land to settlers who will build homes upon it. To accomplish this object water must be brought within their reach. . . . The reclamation and settlement of the arid lands will enrich every portion of our country, just as the settlement of the Ohio and Mississippi valleys brought prosperity to the Atlantic States.

In this same message Roosevelt further said: The forest reserves should be enlarged and "set apart forever, for the use and benefit of our people as a whole and not sacrificed to the shortsighted greed of a few."[1]

2

The story is told of a congressman who, when pressed to aid in the conservation of his country's natural resources for posterity's sake, retorted, "What has posterity ever done for me?"

This was the prevailing attitude of most people toward conservation at the advent of the twentieth century. Ever since John Smith in 1607 had felled the first trees in Jamestown, America's steadily growing population had regarded its trees, game animals, topsoil, water, and minerals as inexhaustible; each generation had thought only in terms of the present, rarely of the future, and public welfare yielded to private interests. Not until 1873, when the American Association for the Advancement of Science petitioned Congress to enact conservation legislation, was there actually any concerted action taken to preserve our natural resources, and it was not until 1891, after the AAAS had repeated its petition, that the federal government took its first steps: establishing a Bureau of Forestry and giving the president of the United States the authority to set aside forest reserves from the public domain.

In 1901, when Theodore Roosevelt took office as president, the nation's natural resources had been shockingly depleted. Roughly one-half of the timber in the United States had been cut, an incalculable amount of precious topsoil had been washed into the seas, minerals (all nonrenewable, of course) had been wasted, and many species of animals—the passenger pigeon, Carolina paroquet, and heath hen among them—were threatened with extinction.

In light of these foreboding facts, the currently existing population of the United States should be forever grateful that in 1901 a man came to Washington as chief executive who, by instinct, training, and practical knowledge, was a conservationist. No other president—before or since—has been so well prepared for the task of inaugurating and implementing a comprehensive, aggressive, nationwide conservation program. His preparation, comprising some thirty-five years, had begun, as we have learned, in the fields of the Hudson River valley, in the wood lots of Long Island, in the forests of the Adirondacks, and in the arid lands of Egypt and Syria. It had been continued in the classrooms and laboratories of Harvard, in the northern woodlands of Maine, in the broken Badlands of Dakota Territory, and in the wilderness areas of the Rocky Mountains. And this extravagant and varied background had given certain meaning and direction to his previous actions as member of the Boone and Crockett Club and governor of the State of New York.

Some earlier increments to Roosevelt's knowledge previously mentioned will bear repeating—perhaps here need repeating. His active outdoor life, as boy and man, had made him thoroughly alive to the value of timberland and its essential relation to soil, flood control, and water conservation. His years in the West had provided abundant opportunities to observe firsthand the rapid destruction of the buffalo, elk, and other large game animals, and in the more arid lands—including the barren, exposed walls of the Badlands' canyons—he had become more deeply aware of the effects of perennial, unchecked erosion and of the urgent need of reclamation through irrigation. His association with the Boone and Crockett Club had brought him in to close association with men who, like him, were becoming more and more concerned about the appalling decrease in our natural resources. Furthermore, his period as governor of New York State had taught him much about the preliminary infighting necessary to the passage of constructive legislation. Without this background, both generous and conspicuously germane, Roosevelt's accomplishments as president in the several areas of conservation could not have been as far-reaching nor as certain of eventual and enduring acceptance.

By and large, Roosevelt's conservation program was threefold: (1) reclaiming arid lands through irrigation; (2) setting aside additional timberlands as forest reserves; and (3) creating wildlife refuges.

3

Roosevelt tackled reclamation first. Even before he had moved his family and belongings into the White House, he had met with men who would prove vital in months ahead to the success of the reclamation program, including Major John Wesley Powell,[2] founder of the U.S. Geological Survey; Senator Francis G. Newlands,[3] sponsor of the Reclamation Act of 1902; Frederick H. Newell, founder of the U.S. Reclamation Service; Charles D. Walcott,[4] director (1884–1907) of the U.S. Geological Survey; and, of course, Gifford Pinchot, chief forester.

Theodore Roosevelt was not alone in formulating, implementing, and executing his wide-ranging conservation program. Admittedly many of the ideas he espoused did originate in the minds of Pinchot and others, but, as one historian has well said: "Originality in a statesman is rarely the discovery of an idea, but the power to secure its application. The public man has to persuade the vast and indifferent aggregates who compose a modern democracy to adopt the opinions of a few till they believe these to be the expression of their own wishes."[5] It was only after Roosevelt put the full force of his power as president behind the conservation program that it got off the ground.

In his first message to Congress Roosevelt had said: "The western half of the United States would sustain a population greater than that of our whole country today if the waters that now run to waste were saved and used for irrigation. Great storage works are necessary to equalize the flow of streams and to save the flood waters. Their construction has been conclusively shown to be an undertaking too vast for private enterprise."[6]

The artificial watering of arid terrain in the United States had its inception centuries ago among the cliff-dwelling Indians of the Southwest (remains of ancient canals still exist there) and was con-

tinued at much later dates by Spanish missionaries. The earliest An-
glo-Saxon attempts to irrigate were made in 1847 by Mormons, in
the Salt Lake valley, and somewhat later by the Union Colony (early
experimenters in socialism) at Greeley, Colorado. It naturally follows that these attempts were on a small scale, so that as late as
1870 no more than 20,000 acres in the United States had been
irrigated.[7]

Newlands, after graduating in law at Georgetown University,
went West, where, in Nevada, he quickly saw "the necessity for
water projects if the West was to grow as he believed it should."
Once in Congress, first as a representative and later as senator, he
found in Roosevelt the support he sought, for Roosevelt had also
"seen the West's need for irrigation."[8] As a result, Newlands drafted
a reclamation bill and introduced it into Congress. Such was the
vigor with which Roosevelt, Newlands, and others pushed this bill
that it soon won congressional approval and became law on June 17,
1902. This measure, the Reclamation Act, made it possible for the
federal government to begin at once the construction of dams at spe-
cially chosen western sites, whose impounded water would irrigate
lands heretofore arid and incapable of growing crops.

Within twenty-four hours after Roosevelt had put his signature
to the Reclamation Act, his secretary of the interior, Ethan A. Hitch-
cock, began putting it to work. Red tape was disregarded unflinch-
ingly, and the measure expedited in a manner previously unknown
in the nation's capital. By 1904 at least sixteen reclamation projects,
all in western states, were underway, and Roosevelt was able to report to Congress: "During the two and a half years that have elapsed
since the passage of the Reclamation Act rapid progress has been
made. . . . Construction has already begun on the largest and most
important of the irrigation works [namely, the Roosevelt Dam]."[9]

Some of these works were of startling magnitude, at least for
that day. There was, for example, the engineering feat of leading the
water of Colorado's Gunnison River to the Uncompahgre valley, requiring the construction of a tunnel ten feet high, ten feet wide, and
five miles long through an intervening mountain. There was, too,
the Roosevelt Dam, 280 feet high, which impounded the water of
Arizona's Salt River. When this dam was completed (in 1911), it created one of the largest artificial bodies of water then existing anywhere in the world and was responsible for the irrigation of more

than a million acres of land thereafter given over largely to the growing of alfalfa, sugar beets, and semitropical fruits.

Roosevelt's 1907 annual message to Congress provided evidence that his outlook on irrigation since taking office had broadened: "Irrigation should be far more extensively developed than at present, not only in the States of the Great Plains and the Rocky Mountains, but in many others, as, for instance, in large portions of the South Atlantic and Gulf States, where it should go hand in hand with the reclamation of swamp land." [10]

When Theodore Roosevelt left office in 1909, the program of reclaiming western arid lands had succeeded beyond his most sanguine expectations. Thousands upon thousands of acres, so recently agriculturally unproductive, were now abundantly green with vegetation, as water with the aid of sunlight gave them life, while numerous small towns, peopled with enthusiastic homeowners, had subsequently sprung into being. The earlier Roosevelt-Newlands' vision of millions of desert acres in bloom was well on its way to reality. Two years later Roosevelt dedicated the Roosevelt Dam. At that especially memorable moment Roosevelt, according to one commentator, "was looking upon what was largely a product of his idealism." [11]

4

The great hardwood and softwood forests, which originally covered so much of the United States, had no actual counterpart in any other country on this planet. They overlaid an estimated billion acres, roughly one-half of the entire land's surface. They were particularly valuable because of the immense stands of pine, spruce, fir, redwood, and other conifers that have always been in much demand for building purposes and more recently for pulp. By the end of the nineteenth century, approximately half of this magnificent original stand of timber had been cut, with four-fifths of what remained being in private hands. No longer ago than the closing year of the Civil War—to illustrate how rapidly the federal government had been disposing of the public domain—only one-fourth of the primeval forest had been privately owned.

The single significant move that Congress had made toward saving the forests previous to Roosevelt's presidency had been the passage in 1891 of the Forest Reserve Act which authorized the chief executive to create forest reserves. By virtue of this power, Presidents Benjamin Harrison, Grover Cleveland, and William McKinley had established forest reserves encompassing some 50 million acres. This step had been accomplished, of course, through the authorized expedient of withdrawing timbered land from the public domain. Although a promising beginning—an insurance that these woodlands would henceforth be free of exploitation—it was no more than that, as lumbermen and others, unmindful of the future, continued to cut the trees far more rapidly than they planted them. Conditions in this respect had changed but little since pioneer days. As Roosevelt would soon be forcefully asserting, "The American had but one thought about a tree, and that was to cut it down."[12]

At quite an early date, Roosevelt had embraced Pinchot's European-inspired idea of managing our nation's forest reserves on a sustained-yield basis. It seems likely that he knew at least the broad outlines of the plan even before he invited Pinchot to Albany in 1900; otherwise he would not have extended his invitation. As previously noted, Roosevelt's annual message that year to the New York State Assembly, with its references to "forest management" and "scientific studies," strongly indicated the hand of Pinchot in the preparation of that message. Roosevelt's message a year later to Congress, containing the sentence "The fundamental idea of forestry is the perpetuation of forests by use" surely reflected the Pinchot persuasion. The portion of the message about forests may have been written by Pinchot, as some writers have said, though Roosevelt by that date could easily have assimilated the major tenets of Pinchot's thinking and thus have written it himself.

Roosevelt may have experienced moments of indecisiveness before he embraced the Pinchot forest program with its insistence on perpetual human use. He knew full well the strength of opposing forces, led by such influential stalwarts as John Muir, Charles S. Sprague, Robert U. Johnson, and William T. Hornaday, each a rational, unrelenting convert to the inviolability of the forests. He was aware, too, of their aloof disdain of Pinchot and all that he contemplated.

However, Roosevelt did come to a decision, and, once made, there was no turning back. The nation's forest reserves, throughout his years as president of the United States were managed in conformity with Gifford Pinchot's dictates of sustained yield and, in the main, have been ever since. Manifestly, Roosevelt's decision was a triumph for Pinchot. Almost overnight, he was accorded special recognition as an up-and-coming leader in federal circles, due, in part at least, to the special relationship he enjoyed with the president.

"For a country returning to nature on many levels," one historian has said, "TR was the right President at the right time. He knew everyone, read everything, and leaped into nature controversies with the aplomb of a man who had killed a grizzly at close range." [13]

A controversy, one that both Roosevelt and Pinchot leaped into immediately, had to do with the administration of the forest reserves, which, in 1901, involved three federal agencies: (1) the General Land Office that protected the reserves; (2) the U.S. Geological Survey that supervised the mapping and general description of timber in the reserves; and (3) the Bureau of Forestry that was charged with "the preparation for their conservative use." Roosevelt, after discussion with Pinchot, was soon on record urging that the functions of these three agencies be united in the Bureau of Forestry, Department of Agriculture, since "the present diffusion of responsibility is bad from every standpoint." [14]

Pending this recommended union (unrealized until three years later), the Bureau of Forestry, with Roosevelt's vigorous support and Pinchot's trained supervision, accelerated its program. It enlarged its corps of foresters; it made a careful survey of the western timberlands to determine their condition and needs, thereby laying the groundwork for possible future expansion; it began experimental planting on the existing reserves; and, perhaps most important, it initiated plans for the creation of eastern forest reserves. Of even greater significance, the bureau initiated a program of education. In this it was aided tremendously by the press, which gratuitously accorded space to every page of copy it received. This educational program progressed at such a rate that, by the time Roosevelt left the White House, information about forests was being given space in some 15 million copies of newspapers. Also, as new and significant forest facts came to light, the bureau substantially increased the number of printed bulletins, from three in 1901 to sixty-one in 1907. In these and other ways the public was informed, as never before, of the needs and purposes of practical forestry. "Without this publicity," Roosevelt declared, "the Forest Service could not have survived the attacks made upon it by the representatives of the great special interests in Congress, nor could forestry in America have made the rapid progress that it has."[15]

Sensing from the beginning that the fate of the forests and other natural resources depended upon education, Roosevelt himself, by bringing the conservation message into homes of farmers and merchants, factory workers and professionals, proved to be a most decisive factor. Over and over again, he said: "Every lover of nature, every man who appreciates the majesty and beauty of the wilderness, should strike hands with the far-sighted men who wish to preserve our forests."[16] In an address to the Society of American Foresters (in March 1903), he told its members that they must play a major role in educating the people, in convincing them that the future welfare of the homeowners depended upon the wisdom with which the nation took care of its forests.[17] To the residents of Sacramento, California, after a visit to Yosemite in the company of John Muir, Roosevelt vigorously and eloquently declared:

> Lying out at night under those giant Sequoias was like lying in a temple built by no hand of man, a temple grander than any human architect could by any possibility build, and I hope for the preservation of the groves of giant trees simply because it would be a shame to our civilization to let them disappear. They are monuments in themselves. . . . In California I am impressed by how great your state is, but I am even more impressed by the immensely greater greatness that lies in the future, and I ask that your marvelous natural resources be handed on unimpaired to your posterity. We are not building this country of ours for a day. It is to last through the ages.[18]

If Roosevelt hammered home one thought more than any other, it was that the forests are not alone for the present generation. The words, "for the people," he insisted, "must always include the people unborn as well as the people now alive, or the democratic ideal is not realized."[19]

In his speeches and published writings, Roosevelt stressed increasingly the importance of the forests in soil and water conservation, saying that the wholesale cutting of trees, particularly on the watersheds, multiplied the likelihood of erosion and floods. He gave space to these matters in all of his annual messages to Congress, including his last, in 1908. In this message—unique in that it was illustrated—he treated the members of both houses of Congress to an elaborate disquisition on the havoc caused in the Wu Tain Shan

Mountains of northern China, and, as evidence of the devastation there, he attached to his message enlarged photographs showing denuded mountain sides and other treeless expanses, where in the days of Marco Polo had flourished one of the most productive and heavily forested regions in all of China. These photographs showed bottom lands devoid of mulberry trees that once had been centers of a flourishing silkworm industry; they showed hillsides, once abundantly cultivated, now barren and gullied; and they showed streams, at one time wide and deep, now shallow currents between shrunken banks.

After completing this illustrated portion of his message, Roosevelt then went on to explain: "The lesson of deforestation in China is a lesson which mankind should have learned many times already from what has occurred in other places. Denudation leaves naked soil; then gullying cuts down to the bare rock; and meanwhile the rock-waste buries the bottom-lands. When the soil is gone, men must go, and the process does not take long. . . . What has thus happened in northern China, what has happened in central Asia, in Palestine, in north Africa, in parts of the Mediterranean countries of Europe, will surely happen in our country if we do not exercise that wise foresight which should be one of the chief marks of any people calling itself civilized."[20] Roosevelt's use of photographs to point up his message impressed David Fairchild,[21] then one of the younger members of the Bureau of Plant Industry: "I have always felt that this incident," he wrote, "showed an alertness in matters of a biological character which it would be hard to duplicate in the careers of other Presidents. He was a great biologist and those of us who were believers in the world as a biological one, not only of merely men and women, were deeply affected."[22]

Roosevelt, when delivering this 1908 message to Congress, had no intimation of what would soon happen to the grasslands of mid-America. Those of us whose memories go back to the 1930s will recall the dust storms that in those years reduced portions of the south-central states to semiaridity after the land had been stripped of its cover (in this case grass, not forest). Someone quickly, and aptly, coined the term "Dust Bowl" for this ravished part of our nation. As more and more people invaded the grasslands, they brought with them more and more plows, to grow more and more corn and wheat, and thus destroyed more and more of the land's pristine cover

219

of grass. Inevitably and unfortunately, the land has further deteriorated since the 1930s, especially in years of drought, so that what happened in ages past in the countries of Asia and Africa may in the future happen here in the Midwest.

During his presidency Roosevelt went far beyond exhorting the public to preserve the forests. While the Forest Service was being shaped into a highly efficient branch of the federal government, and the people were being taught to use their natural resources wisely, he was taking advantage of the authority earlier given to the presidents to set aside forest reserves from the public domain. In the seven years of his administration, Roosevelt added almost 150 million acres of timberland to the reserves, thereby more than trebling the acreage set aside by preceding presidents. This acreage equaled in area all of the states touching the Atlantic from Maine to Virginia, with the addition of Vermont, Pennsylvania, and West Virginia, and exceeded that of France, Belgium, and the Netherlands combined.

A substantial slice of this acreage was added by Roosevelt in 1907 after a group of congressmen, swayed by lumber lobbyists, had tried to prevent it. In a clever move they attached an amendment to an Agricultural Appropriations Bill, which, if the bill passed, would have effectively quashed the president's power to create additional forest reserves. They did this secure in the knowledge that Roosevelt could not afford to veto the bill, for to do so would have seriously crippled the work of the Agriculture Department and that of the Forest Service, as well.

What Roosevelt did to evade the rider is told in most of his biographies and in many American history textbooks. Aware that Pinchot had made a careful study of the western timberlands eligible to be set aside as reserves, Roosevelt was in a position to act immediately. He asked Pinchot to give him a plan for incorporating the forests in mind into the forest reserve system, this to be in his hands before the deadline for his signature on the Agricultural Appropriation Bill. Without hesitation, and with clear conscience, he approved the plan and signed the requisite papers, beating the deadline by two days. It was a *tour de force* of which he was justly proud, for, when the congressmen who had inserted the rider realized what the president had done, they were helpless to do anything about it. Pinchot was proud, too, for by this prompt and expedient move Roosevelt

had succeeded in placing 16 million more acres of timberland beyond the reach of covetous lumbermen.

The nationalization of the western forests had been accomplished in the face of bitter opposition. The term forest reserve—
later changed to national forest—was responsible for much of the
opposition, many individuals interpreting the word reserve to mean
that the reserves, like the national parks, were to be maintained as
virgin playgrounds where no timber could be cut and no game shot.
By and large the special interests knew this to be untrue but, nevertheless, took advantage of the misinterpretation. It took considerable time to reverse the public thinking, to assure men and women
that the forest reserves (national forests) were not sanctuaries, but
were areas where trees could be cut, game hunted, and, indeed, most
every natural advantage, within limits, could be used. Imposed re-
strictions were to safeguard against future damage and waste.

As Roosevelt neared the end of his presidency, he knew that the
battle for the trees had barely begun, that major fights lay ahead. For
one thing, no national forests had as yet been created in the East. In
an address to Congress as early as 1905, he deplored this exclusion:
"The forests of the White Mountains and Southern Appalachian regions should also be preserved, and they can not be unless the people
of the States in which they lie, thru their Representatives in the
Congress, secure vigorous action by the National Government."[23]

In an impassioned speech to an Arbor Day audience in 1907, he
expressed concern, both deep and disquieting, about the future of
our nation's trees: "It is well that you should celebrate your Arbor
Day thoughtfully, for within your lifetime the nation's need of trees
will become serious. We of the older generation can get along with
what we have, though with growing hardship, but in your full manhood and womanhood you will want what nature once so bounti-
fully supplied and man so thoughtlessly destroyed; and because of
that want you will reproach us, not for what we have used, but for
what we have wasted. . . . So any nation which in its youth lives only
for the day, reaps without sowing, and consumes without husband-
ing, must expect the penalty of the prodigal whose labor could with
difficulty find him the bare means of life."[24]

By the date of this Arbor Day talk, Roosevelt had seen far more
of our country's sylva than most Americans. He was well acquainted
with the prodigious stands of virgin timber in the Adirondacks, in

the State of Maine, and in the heights of the Rockies, all visited during the years of his young manhood. In 1903 he had spent time in Yosemite National Park, where, in the company of John Muir, he had been awe-struck at the sight of the most magnificent trees on earth, the California big trees (*Sequoia gigantea*). Yet, though having seen the extent of the nation's forests, Roosevelt did not regard them as permanent or imperishable. Instead he envisioned them as being so rapidly depleted that within the lifetime of his Arbor Day audience "the nation's need of trees will become serious." Is it necessary to add that Roosevelt's warning came true?

5

In 1894 Congress had made it illegal to kill the birds, mammals, and other animals in Yellowstone National Park, thus establishing our country's first federal wildlife sanctuary—not to be confused with the wildlife refuges, of which more hereafter. The creation of the Yellowstone sanctuary made it possible for ousel and nutcracker, as well as bison, bighorn, and elk, to live out their lives relatively free from the dangers of rifle and shotgun.

The idea developed slowly that wildlife throughout the United States needed protection similar to that accorded the species in Yellowstone. Already many important forms of life had been radically reduced in number, and some were threatened with extinction. Just as most Americans regarded trees as something to cut down, so did they think of birds and other animals as something to be shot down. They might have continued such thinking if the sorry plight of the buffalo and passenger pigeon had not claimed their attention. These two animals, among the most valuable and distinctive of all American species, were so close to extinction that it was doubtful if either would survive. Through flagrant, unremitting slaughter, man had reduced the original number of buffalo from millions to less than one thousand; similarly, the passenger pigeon, once present in the billions (sufficient at times to blot out the mid-day sun, thus causing chickens to take to their roosts), had suffered diminution to the point where any report of seeing one alive, even by such a creditable observer as Theodore Roosevelt,[25] was viewed with skepticism. Providentially, the buffalo survived; the passenger pigeon, lamentably, did not.

By the time Roosevelt had taken up residence in the White House, still other animals were approaching a similar vanishing point. Earlier, as we know, he had spoken out against those who had killed game animals wantonly, and this criticism, more recently, had been leveled at plume hunters, who annually slaughtered countless beautifully plumaged birds to satisfy the demands of costume designers. As governor of New York, it will be recalled, he had urged that the state make it illegal for factories to make bird feathers into articles of apparel. Birds in the trees and on the beaches were far lovelier, he insisted, than on women's hats. As president of the United States, he was obviously in a much better position to do even more for the protection of the nation's wildlife. He took his first significant step on March 14, 1903, a date to be held in memory.

For some time ornithologists had been making a determined effort to obtain protection for the birds of Pelican Island, a pinpoint of land in Florida's Indian River, where the plume hunters had been making such inroads on the numbers of egrets, ibises, roseate spoonbills, and other birds of lively color that it was feared they would soon be exterminated, at least on the island and contiguous terrain. When all other efforts failed, the ornithologists—spearheaded by Frank M. Chapman, who from past visits knew conditions on Pelican Island—appealed directly to Roosevelt. In the course of pondering this plea, Roosevelt asked: "Is there any law that will prevent me from declaring Pelican Island a Federal Bird Reservation?" When assured there was none, the island being federal property, he replied, "Very well, then I so declare it."[26] In this manner, promptly and without public stir, Theodore Roosevelt established our country's first federal wildlife refuge. Though Pelican Island was only a speck of land on Florida's east coast, less than four acres in extent, from that day its birds and other animals were free to mate, raise their young, and live their allotted years without undue fear of human molestation.

This modest though auspicious start in bringing protection to the nation's fauna (and flora) stimulated Roosevelt to further action. Between March 14, 1903, and March 4, 1909, he created fifty additional wildlife refuges (for a total of fifty-one).[27] They were scattered from the Gulf of Mexico to North Dakota, Oregon, and California, even to Puerto Rico, Alaska, and Hawaii. In so doing he gave protection to the colonies of laughing gulls, black skimmers, and brown pelicans on Breton Island Wildlife Refuge, Louisiana; he provided safe nesting sites for the migratory waterfowl on Klamath Lake and Malheur Lake Refuges of Oregon; he gave sanctuary to the sooty and noddy terns on the Dry Tortugas Refuge in the Gulf of Mexico; he supplied safety for the homes of petrels, cormorants, puffins, and murres on the Three Arch Rocks Wildlife Refuge off the coast of Oregon. And so it went—on forty-seven other refuges established by the twenty-sixth president of the United States.

Of course others, in addition to Roosevelt, deserve credit for roles played in the wildlife refuge movement: individual crusaders like George Bird Grinnell, Chapman, and T. Gilbert Pearson,[28] and such powerful organizations as the American Ornithologists' Union, the National Audubon Society, and the U.S. Biological Survey. But the question may be asked: "What would have been the result if someone else had been president of the United States when these friends of wildlife visited the White House to intercede on behalf of the birds on Pelican Island?"

The mere recapitulation of measures Roosevelt promoted to protect "all the delicate beauty of the lesser and all the burly majesty of the mightier forms"[29] does not begin to tell the full story. He gave the refuge movement such momentum that today—some eighty years after Pelican Island—the birds and other animals are protected on almost 400 federal wildlife refuges. Even this is far from the complete story, for most if not all of the states have created state wildlife refuges, as have numerous counties, municipalities, and even individuals. The simple truths advocated by Roosevelt have by now sunk deep into the national consciousness, even to the extent that a swelling host of conservation-minded Americans are convinced, with Roosevelt, that "wild flowers should be enjoyed unplucked where they grow, and that it is barbarism to ravage the woods and fields, rooting out the mayflower and breaking branches of dogwood as ornaments for automobiles filled with jovial but ignorant picnickers from cities."[30]

As of 1983 forty men have served as president of the United States. Two of them demonstrated clearly a love of natural history, Thomas Jefferson and Theodore Roosevelt. The latter, however, accomplished more in the way of protection for the nation's wildlife than all of the others combined.

6

At the date of Theodore Roosevelt's elevation to the presidency, there were five national parks in the United States: Yellowstone, Yosemite, Sequoia, General Grant, and Mt. Rainier. With occasional prodding from Roosevelt, Congress added five more during Roosevelt's term of office: (1) Oregon's Crater Lake, a six-mile wide lake of exceptional beauty, situated in the crater of an extinct volcano; (2) Oklahoma's Platt National Park, the scene of unusual mineral springs; (3) South Dakota's Wind Cave Park, noted for its limestone caverns; (4) North Dakota's Sully Hill Park, a wooded, hilly tract encircling Devil's Lake; and (5) Colorado's Mesa Verde National Park, renowned as the site of the best-preserved prehistoric Indian cliff dwellings in the United States. (Oklahoma's Platt National Park has been renamed and is now the Chickasaw National Recreation Area, though it is still administered by the National Park Service. North Dakota's Sully Hill National Park is today a wildlife refuge.)

Roosevelt had deeply entrenched feelings about our country's national parks. He expressed some of them at Gardiner, Montana, on April 24, 1903, when he laid the cornerstone of the gateway to Yellowstone Park: "The Yellowstone Park is something absolutely unique in the world, so far as I know. Nowhere else in any civilized country is there to be found such a tract of veritable wonderland made accessible to all visitors, where at the same time not only the scenery of the wilderness, but the wild creatures of the Park are scrupulously preserved; the only change being that these same wild creatures have been so carefully protected as to show a literally astounding tameness. The creation and preservation of such a great natural playground in the interest of our people as a whole is a credit to the nation."[31] Today the United States has some two score national parks. If Roosevelt had had the power to create national parks—a power vested in Congress—he would definitely have brought at least one other into being, namely, the Grand Canyon.

Congress, on June 8, 1906, passed a most significant measure, the Antiquities (or National Monuments) Act. This measure authorized the president of the United States, at his discretion, "to declare by public proclamation historic landmarks, historic and prehistoric structures, and other objects of historic and scientific interest that are situated upon lands owned or controlled by the Government of the United States to be National Monuments."[32] In the period left to him as president, less than three years, Roosevelt established eighteen national monuments, the first of close to 100 that presently (1984) exist. The names of those created by Roosevelt, with dates of formation, are:

Devil's Tower, Wyoming, September 24, 1906
El Morro, New Mexico, December 8, 1906
Montezuma Castle, Arizona, December 8, 1906
Petrified Forest, Arizona, December 8, 1906 (now part of a national park)
Chaco Canyon, New Mexico, March 11, 1907
Lassen Peak, California, May 6, 1907 (now part of a national park)
Cinder Cone, California, May 6, 1907 (now part of a national park)
Gila Cliff Dwellings, New Mexico, November 16, 1907
Tonto, Arizona, December 19, 1907
Muir Woods, California, January 9, 1908
Grand Canyon, Arizona, January 11, 1908 (now part of a national park)
Pinnacles, California, January 16, 1908
Jewel Cave, South Dakota, February 7, 1908
Natural Bridges, Utah, April 16, 1908
Lewis & Clark, Montana, May 11, 1908 (later given to the state of Montana; now abolished as a national monument)
Tomacacori, Arizona, September 15, 1908
Wheeler, Colorado, December 7, 1908 (given to the Forest Service in 1950; now abolished as a national monument)
Mount Olympus, Washington, March 2, 1909 (now part of a national park)

A few of the above national monuments are today celebrated, among them Wyoming's Devil's Tower, an 865-foot pillar of volcanic rock, perhaps the plug of an ancient volcano; California's Muir Woods, an impressive stand of redwood (*Sequoia sempervirens*); New Mexico's Petrified Forest, known for its exceptional aggregation of fossilized conifers; and Arizona's Grand Canyon, one of the world's preeminent natural wonders, with its mile-deep gorge containing, at its bottom, the Colorado River.[33]

While on a western tour in 1903, Roosevelt addressed an audience at the Grand Canyon, saying: "In the Grand Canyon, Arizona has a natural wonder which . . . is in kind absolutely unparalleled throughout the rest of the world. I want to ask you to do one thing in connection with it in your own interest and in the interest of the country—to keep this great wonder of nature as it is. I hope you will not have a building of any kind, not a summer cottage, a hotel, or anything else to mar the wonderful grandeur, the sublimity, the great loneliness and beauty of the canyon. You can not improve it. The ages have been at work on it, and man can only mar it."[34]

Figures indicate all too plainly the popularity of our national parks. In 1910 some 200,000 visited them, and by 1916 approximately 350,000. As the twentieth century nears an end, visitors to the national parks number in the millions. Indeed, so many are the visitors that the task of maintaining the "grandeur, the sublimity, the great loneliness and beauty" becomes increasingly difficult and, in some parks, an impossibility. However, no one is likely to quarrel with a later statement by Roosevelt, that the national parks and monuments represent "one of the best bits of National achievement which our people have to their credit in recent years."[35]

7

The natural resources of a nation include not only forests, soil, water, and wildlife but also minerals. Roosevelt early learned a most significant fact about minerals: "The mineral wealth of the country, the coal, iron, oil, gas and the like, does not reproduce itself [is nonrenewable], and therefore is certain to be exhausted ultimately."[36] Only recently, as the United States has become more and more dependent on other countries for oil and other minerals, has the full impact of that statement been recognized by our citizenry.

Overall conservation, that is, attention to each and every natural resource, was advocated as early as 1873, but little or nothing was actually accomplished as a consequence until near the end of Roosevelt's second term as president. In 1907, while the Inland Waterways Commission (established by Roosevelt that same year) was investigating the question of water development on the Lower

Mississippi, the commission suggested to Roosevelt—who was traveling with the commission—that a conference be held to consider all aspects of conservation. Roosevelt was so taken with the proposal that he agreed to call the conference himself. He made public his decision in Memphis, Tennessee, in October 1907: "As I have said elsewhere, the conservation of natural resources is the fundamental problem. To solve it the whole nation must undertake the task through the men whom they have made specifically responsible for the welfare of the several states, and finally through the Congress and the Chief Executive. As a preliminary step, the Inland Waterways Commission has asked me to call a conference on the conservation of natural resources, including, of course, the streams, to meet in Washington the coming winter. I shall accordingly call such a conference. It ought to be among the most important in our history."[37]

The conference was held May 13–15, 1908, in the East Room of the White House. Preparations had been elaborate, and in the hands of a committee headed by Pinchot. According to one source, "Almost every morning, from October to May, they [the committee] met at the Cosmos Club in Washington to plan and handle the innumerable details connected with the staging of such a conference."[38] The selection of persons to attend the conference was a primary item on the agenda. With Roosevelt's concurrence, the list, as finally established, included: governors of all the forty-six states, Supreme Court justices, congressmen, foreign dignitaries, representatives of learned societies, and leading authorities on the natural resources of the nation. Among the authorities were a number of prominent American scientists, the first time that they had met on an equal footing with statesmen.

Roosevelt opened the conference and spoke for fifty minutes. According to one observer, he "pointed the way to a more extended use of government powers, not only for the national government but [also] for municipal and state governments. Yet there was universal assent to every proposition that was presented. Those present felt they were witnessing an important historical event. In its earnestness and restraint and suggestiveness it was perhaps the best speech Roosevelt ever made."[39]

An incident reflecting the goodwill and unadulterated rapport between Roosevelt and his fellow scientists occurred at the conclusion of the first session, as the guests filed by him to be greeted individually. L. O. Howard (who had presided, it will be recalled, at the meeting when Roosevelt and C. Hart Merriam had argued over the revision of the coyote genus) later described the president's greeting on this occasion:

I found myself in line immediately behind Dr. C. Hart Merriam, the animal and bird man. Immediately in front of him was William J[ennings] Bryan. As we reached the President, Mr. Bryan, in a pompous and somewhat condescending way (at least it seemed so to me), said, "Mr. President, I congratulate you, sir, on having started this conservation movement, which, in my opinion, has tremendous possibilities of good for the future of the country. I assure you, sir, that it meets my approval and will receive my hearty support." The President, with a trace of a humorous gleam in his eye, as he looked over Mr. Bryan's shoulder and saw Merriam and myself, said simply, "Mr. Bryan, I am pleased. Praise from Sir Hubert is praise indeed." Then, turning instantly to Merriam, he said, "How are you, Hart? What do you suppose John [Burroughs] and I saw on the twenty-fifth of March at Pine Knot? A Yellow Warbler, by George!" And then, turning to me, he said, "Hello, Doctor! How are the bugs?"[40]

The results of the conference were immediate and far reaching. The state governors drew up a unanimous declaration in support of conservation, thirty-six state conservation commissions at once sprang into being, scientific bodies appointed numerous conservation committees, and a National Conservation Commission was organized. In short, the sum of these several events gave the conservation movement a prestige and momentum previously unknown and raised it to a plane that enabled it to survive the various reversals it later suffered as a consequence of periodic shifts in the political climate. One historian described the conference as the "great showpiece of Roosevelt's last year as President,"[41] and another as "one of the landmarks in conservation history."[42]

Because of Roosevelt's opening address and other contributions to the success of the conference, Roosevelt himself came in for a share of the praise. Wrote one observer: "He has never appeared more statesmanlike than in looking to the physical future of the country; and in so easily and naturally obtaining the assistance of the Governors."[43] Another commented: "President Roosevelt does new things, and usually good things, with an audacity that commends and only occasionally condemns him; and one of the most remarkable, even unparalleled, is that by which he invited the Governors of all the states and territories in the Union to come to Washington to consult as to the preservation of the natural resources of the country."[44]

Pinchot was exuberant about the success of the conference, writing a friend that he was as pleased "as a hen that has laid an egg."[45] Even though Pinchot played a major role in planning (and paying for) the conference, he, the perennial publicist, made decisions that afterward brought censure. In his eagerness to insure that the sessions would run smoothly, if possible with never a dissenting word, he actually helped to write the speeches later given by several of the governors and other attending dignitaries.[46] More than that, when extending invitations, he ignored John Muir, Charles S. Sargent, and other preservationists, who, if given the floor at any time during the conference, would surely have introduced comment contrary to the sentiment hoped for by Pinchot. Reflecting his personal resentment at thus having been so pointedly snubbed, Muir later confided to Robert Johnson: "P[inchot] is ambitious, and never hesitates to sacrifice anything or anybody in his way."[47]

With the Governors' Conference concluded and adjourned, the National Conservation Commission promptly began the near herculean task of inventorying the nation's natural resources. Headed by Pinchot, the commission completed its work in less than a year.[48] It was the first time any country had ever attempted such a project.

Roosevelt was so favorably impressed by the commission's report that he, without delay, sent it to Congress along with an accompanying letter. Portions of the letter, dated January 22, 1909, follow: "With the statements and conclusions of this report I heartily concur, and I commend it to the thoughtful consideration both of the Congress and of our people generally. It is one of the most fundamentally important documents ever laid before the American people. . . . As it stands it is an irrefutable proof that the conservation of our resources is the fundamental question before this nation, and that our first and greatest task is to set our house in order and begin to live within our means."[49]

As an almost immediate consequence of the enthusiasm generated by the highly successful Governors' Conference, Roosevelt was soon entertaining thoughts of holding a North American Conservation Conference, which would bring together representatives from Canada and Mexico as well as from the United States. Roosevelt promptly sent invitations to Lord Grey, governor general of Canada; to Sir Wilfred Laufier; and to President Jose Diaz of Mexico, saying, in part: "It is evident that natural resources are not limited by the boundary lines which separate nations, and that the need for conserving them upon this continent is as wide as the area upon which they exist."[50]

The North American Conservation Conference convened in Washington, D.C., at the White House, on February 18, 1909, approximately two weeks before Roosevelt's term as president expired. This conference, like its predecessor of the year before, also met with success. The delegates agreed upon a declaration of principles and then, persuaded by the worthiness and exigency of the conservation effort, urged "that all nations should be invited to join together in conference on the subject of world resources, and their inventory, conservation and wise utilization."[51]

Roosevelt was delighted with this proposal of an international conference, so much so that he forthwith instructed his secretary of state to extend invitations to forty-five nations to attend such a global conference, one that would be held, by preference in The Hague, at a date to be determined. Since, within a matter of days, Roosevelt would again become a private citizen and, as such, bereft of power to further this plan, the proposed International Conservation Conference died aborning. His successor, William Howard Taft, was more absorbed in antitrust legislation, tariff revision, and jurisprudence than in conservation.

More than half a century would pass before truly international, widely publicized conferences on conservation were held. However, in the United States, the conservation movement made steady progress. Many of the state commissions formed in 1908 continued to function, and the National Commission lived on until 1923. By that date, there were hundreds of enthusiastic converts to the wise use of our natural resources for every one when Roosevelt succeeded McKinley as president twenty-two years earlier.

9

Modern historians may disagree as to Theodore Roosevelt's most important achievement during his years as president of the United States. He himself, in a letter to a London publicist shortly before he left the White House, enumerated four that then stood out most prominently in his mind: (1) his actions in more than doubling the size of the U.S. Navy; (2) his role in building the Panama Canal; (3) his success in terminating the war between Russia and Japan (which resulted in his being awarded the 1906 Nobel Peace Prize); and (4) his contributions to conservation, these including reclamation of arid lands, reorganization of the forest service (placing it under the Department of Agriculture), trebling the size of the forest reserves, and, "as a small incident, creating a number of reservations for preserving the wild things of nature, the beasts and the birds as well as the trees."[52] If Roosevelt, in enumerating the above, listed them in the order of their importance to him—as may have been the case— he obviously placed last his contributions to conservation.

Many of the individuals most familiar with Roosevelt's accomplishments as president have thought that his achievements in conservation should have headed his list. As early as 1911, Robert La Follette, U.S. senator from Wisconsin, predicted: "When the historian of the future shall speak of Theodore Roosevelt, he is likely to say that he did many notable things, but that his greatest work was inspiring and actually beginning a world movement for staying territorial waste and saving for the human race the things on which alone a peaceful, progressive, and happy life can be founded."[53]

During the years since Senator La Follette's prophetic utterance, the majority of American historians have tended to agree with him. One of them, writing in 1937, said that conservation was decidedly Roosevelt's "greatest service to the nation."[54] Another (in 1952) declared: "Roosevelt's pioneering work in the conservation of natural resources was his most enduring contribution. . . . Even his most vehement detractors have found little to criticize in his work as a conservationist."[55] In 1955 yet another historian wrote: "Probably Roosevelt's most important contribution to the national welfare was his encouragement of conservation. He was the first President to realize the vital importance of this question."[56]

At about this same time, and writing to the point even more convincingly, was the well-schooled team of historians, Samuel Eliot Morison and Henry Steele Commager. "Unquestionably," they stated, "the most important achievement of the [Theodore] Roosevelt administration was in the conservation of the natural resources of the nation. Roosevelt's love of nature and knowledge of the West gave him a sentimental yet highly intelligent interest in the preservation of soil, water, and forest. . . . Alone of our Presidents up to his time, Theodore Roosevelt had grasped the problem of conservation as a unit and comprehended the basic relationship to national affairs."[57] Another pair of historians, equally convincing and explicit, noted: "It was under Theodore Roosevelt, however, that the movement for conservation really got under way on a large scale and was brought home to the people. . . . His knowledge and love of the West and his passionate devotion to an out-door life, in addition to his general crusade for the betterment of social and business conditions, were probably powerful influences in making him the first real leader in the conservation movement."[58]

Not surprisingly, it was the conservationists themselves who most vigorously endorsed Roosevelt's conservation policies. One of them insisted that these policies "will place him not only as one of the greatest statesmen of this nation but one of the greatest statesmen of any nation of any time."[59] And Pinchot (though hardly a disinterested bystander) forthrightly declared: "The greatest work that Theodore Roosevelt did for the United States, the great fact which will give his influence vitality and power long after we shall all have gone to our reward, is . . . that he changed the attitude of the American people toward conserving the natural resources."[60]

To the contrary—and commendably—Roosevelt credited Pinchot, Newell, Powell, and other federal employees with being primarily responsible for the successes of the conservation program. "I saw them work," he said, ". . . and I can speak with the fullest knowledge of what they did. They took the policy of conservation when it was still nebulous and they applied it and made it work. They actually did the job that I and others talked about."[61]

Beyond question, Roosevelt held Pinchot in high, even affectionate, esteem. Just two days before his administration ended, he wrote to him: "I have written you about many public matters; now just a line about yourself. As long as I live I shall feel for you a mixture of respect and admiration and of affectionate regard. I am a better man for having known you . . . and I cannot think of a man in the country whose loss would be a real misfortune to the nation more than yours would be. For seven and a half years we have worked together, and now and then played together—and have been altogether better able to work because we have played; and I owe to you a peculiar debt of obligation for a very large part of the achievements of this administration."[62]

The Roosevelt-Pinchot relationship, according to one writer, was "without question, one of the most significant in the history of the Forest Service."[63] Manifestly, their common interest in conservation drew the two men close together, though other more personal matters, such as their mutual enjoyment of horseback riding, boxing, and tennis, were possibly more important in this respect.

Pinchot's main strengths as chief forester were his powers of persistence, persuasion, untiring energy, and competency as an innovator. He was particularly successful in convincing Americans that the nation's natural resources should be developed for the people, that they should not be wasted, and that the forests should be managed according to positive scientific methods.

For a time, especially during the period coinciding with Roosevelt's presidency, historians enthusiastically applauded Pinchot's actions. Some went so far as to declare that Roosevelt had caught his enthusiasm for conservation from Pinchot,[64] thereby revealing—or so it would seem—a complete ignorance of Roosevelt's earlier background as a naturalist, as well as a prejudiced approach to his broadgauged, enduring achievements as a conservationist.

Time is an acknowledged factor in attaining the objectivity usually regarded as significant in appraising the debits and credits of men's lives. With the passage of three score and more years, Pinchot's popularity has ebbed. In 1965 a director of the American Forestry Association said: "Nobody has a higher regard for Gifford Pinchot than I, but I think it is time we realized that something was deficient in the man."[65] Another scientist was soon listing a number of impulsive, ill-considered actions that had marred Pinchot's tenure as chief forester, two in particular: (1) his lack of historical perspective in respect to the growth of sentiment for conservation and (2) his failure to give credit to individuals who were important in furthering conservation.[66] (We have already alluded to Pinchot's deliberate and inexcusable snub of Muir, Sargent, and other preservationists in failing to invite them to the 1908 Governors' Conference.)

With the passage of the same number of years, the standing of Roosevelt as a conservationist has steadily mounted. No later than 1965, for instance, the National Wildlife Federation, through a poll of its members, established its Conservation Hall of Fame. Not surprisingly, Theodore Roosevelt was first, John Muir was second, and Gifford Pinchot eighth.[67]

Notes

1. Theodore Roosevelt, *A Compilation of the Messages and Papers of the Presidents*. Prepared under the Direction of the Joint Committee on Printing of the House and Senate. XIV, 6655–58. Hereafter cited as Roosevelt, *Annual Messages*."

2. John Wesley Powell (1834–1902), distinguished American geologist and ethnologist, was born in Mt. Morris, N.Y. In 1875 he published *Explorations of the Colorado River of the West and Its Tributaries*, which brought him immediate fame. Beginning in 1875 he was, first, director of the U.S. Geological and Geographical Survey and then in 1879, following consolidation, director of the U.S. Geological Survey.

3. Francis Griffith Newlands (1848–1917), American statesman, was born in Natchez, Miss. He attended Columbian College Law School, Washington, D.C., and afterward moved to Nevada. In 1892 he was elected to the U.S. House of Representatives from that state and in 1903 to the U.S. Senate. He vigorously supported the Reclamation Act of 1902.

4. Charles Doolittle Walcott (1850–1927), American paleontologist, was born in New York Mills, N.Y. In 1894 he became head of the U.S. Geological Survey, a post he held until 1907.

5. Einstein, *Roosevelt, His Mind in Action*, 91.

6. Roosevelt, *Annual Messages*, 14:6657.

7. Roosevelt, *Works, Mem. Ed.*, 18:135.

8. Graham, *Man's Dominion*, 111.

9. Roosevelt, *Annual Messages*, 14:6908.

10. Ibid., 7095. It is now generally agreed that the "swamplands" to which Roosevelt referred should be preserved intact, if at all possible.

11. *Outlook* 97, 708–9.

12. Roosevelt, *Works, Mem. Ed.*, 18:135.

13. Stephen Fox, *John Muir and His Legacy* (Boston: Little, Brown, 1981), 124.

14. Roosevelt, *Annual Messages*, 14:6655–56.

15. Roosevelt, *Autobiography*, 401.

16. Roosevelt, *Works, Mem. Ed.*, 17:119.

17. Ibid., 18:128–29.

18. Roosevelt, *California Addresses* (San Francisco: The Promotion Committee, 1903), 40. In speaking of the "giant trees," Roosevelt meant both the redwoods (*Sequoia sempervirens*) and the big trees (*Sequoia gigantea*).

19. Roosevelt, *Works, Mem. Ed.*, 4:229.

20. Roosevelt, *Annual Messages*, 15:7218–22.

21. David Fairchild (1869–1954), botanical explorer, was born in Lansing, Mich. In search of plants to introduce into the United States, he made trips to many parts of the world; he also wrote such books as *Exploring for Plants* and *The World Was My Garden*.

22. David Fairchild to author, July 17, 1944.

23. Roosevelt, *Annual Messages*, 14:7047.

24. Roosevelt, *Works, Mem. Ed.*, 18:166–67.

25. In May 1907 Roosevelt, while at Pine Knot, his summer place in Albemarle County, Va., reported seeing a small flock of passenger pigeons. Ornithologists at the American Museum of Natural History believed the report, though others elsewhere were skeptical.

26. Chapman, *Autobiography of a Bird-Lover*, 181–82.

27. For a full listing of the wildlife refuges created by Roosevelt, see Roosevelt, *Works, Mem. Ed.*, 4:609–12.

28. Thomas Gilbert Pearson (1873–1943), ornithologist, was born in Illinois and in 1899 graduated from the University of North Carolina. He was a longtime director of the National Audubon Society and editor-in-chief of *Birds of America* (1917).

29. Roosevelt, *Works, Mem. Ed.*, 14:567.

30. Ibid.

31. "Presidential Addresses," *Review of Reviews* 1 (1910): 328.

32. *Congressional Record* 40:7888.

33. Not to be overlooked are the four national game preserves created by Roosevelt during his presidency: Wichita Forest, Oklahoma, June 2, 1905; Grand Canyon, Arizona, June 23, 1908; Fire Island, Alaska, February 27, 1909; and National Bison Range, Montana, March 4, 1909. For the information on national monuments and national game preserves, see *Theodore Roosevelt Association Journal* 10 (Fall 1984): 8–9.

34. "Presidential Addresses," *Review of Reviews* 1:370. The Grand Canyon did not achieve national park status until 1919.

35. Roosevelt, *Works, Mem. Ed.*, 14:569.

36. Ibid., 17:526.

37. *World's Work* 16 (1909): 10419.

38. McGeary, *Gifford Pinchot*, 96.

39. *Chautauqua* 55 (1909): 44–47.

40. Howard, *Fighting the Insects*, 239–40.

41. Fox, *John Muir*, 130.

42. Wayne Hanley, *Natural History in America, from Mark Catesby to Rachel Carson* (New York: Quadrangle/The New York Times Book Co., 1977), 284.

43. *Nation* 86:460.

44. *Independent* 64:1151–52.

45. McGeary, *Gifford Pinchot*, 99.

46. Graham, *Man's Dominion*, 133.

47. Fox, *John Muir*, 130.

48. Roosevelt, *Autobiography*, 409.

49. Roosevelt, *Annual Messages,* 15:7258–60.

50. Roosevelt, *Autobiography,* 410.

51. Ibid., 410.

52. To Sydney Brooks, Dec. 28, 1908; Morison, *Letters,* 6:1444–45.

53. Robert M. La Follette, *Autobiography* (Madison, Wis.: Robert M. La Follette Publishing Co., 1913).

54. David Seville Muzzey, *A History of Our Country* (New York: Ginn and Co., 1937), 578.

55. Harry J. Carman and Harold C. Syrett, *A History of the American People,* 2 vols. (New York: Alfred A. Knopf, 1952), 2:369.

56. Henry B. Parkes, *The United States of America* (New York: Alfred A. Knopf, 1955), 554.

57. S. E. Morison and Henry S. Commager, *The Growth of the American Republic,* 2 vols. (New York: Oxford University Press, 1952), 2:399–400.

58. James Truslow Adams and Charles Garrett Vannest, *The Record of America* (New York: Charles Scribner's Sons, 1955), 621–22.

59. Charles E. Van Hise, *The Conservation of Natural Resources in the United States* (New York: Macmillan Co., 1910), 10.

60. Gifford Pinchot, *The Fight for Conservation* (Washington, D.C.: Government Printing Office, 1908), 94–95.

61. Roosevelt, *Works, Mem. Ed.,* 15:558.

62. Morison, *Letters,* 6:1541.

63. Harold K. Steen, *The United States Forest Service, a History* (Seattle: University of Washington Press, 1976), 70.

64. Charles A. and Mary Beard, *A Basic History of the United States* (Philadelphia: Blakiston Co., 1944), 408.

65. Fox, *John Muir,* 289.

66. Gerald D. Nash, in his introduction to Pinchot, *Fight for Conservation,* xxiv–xxv.

67. Fox, *John Muir,* 289–90. Others elected to the Conservation Hall of Fame were: Aldo Leopold (3d), J. N. Darling (4th), John James Audubon (5th), Henry David Thoreau (6th), and Hugh Bennett (7th).

16

"I Fairly Fell in Love with Him"

"THE WORD 'conservation' in its present sense," a current writer reminds us, "did not come into official use until the Theodore Roosevelt administration."[1] During the years after 1909, Theodore Roosevelt saw to it that the word did not languish. In speeches and published writings—perhaps more often in talks with individuals—he continued to preach conservation; indeed, he said so much on the subject that only a few excerpts can be presented here:

1910—To a group of Kansas farmers: "Conservation means development as much as it does protection. I recognize the right and duty of this generation to develop and use the natural resources of our land; but I do not recognize the right to waste them."[2]

1912—At the Progressive National Convention, Chicago: "There can be no greater issue than that of conservation in this country. Just as we must conserve our men, women, and children, so we must conserve the resources of the land on which they live."[3]

1913—In *Outlook* magazine: "Here in the United States we turn our rivers and streams into sewers and dumping-grounds; we pollute the air; we destroy forests; and exterminate fishes, birds, and mammals—not to speak of vulgarizing charming landscapes with hideous advertisements."[4]

1915—In *Outlook* magazine: "We are fast learning that trees must not be cut down more rapidly than they are replanted."[5]

1916—From *A Book-Lover's Holidays in the Open:* "Birds should be saved. . . . The extermination of the passenger pigeon means that mankind was just so much poorer; exactly as in the case of the destruction of the cathedral at Rheims. And the chance to see frigate-birds soaring in circles above the storm, or a file of pelicans winging their way homeward across the crimson afterglow of the sunset, or a myriad of terns flashing in the bright light of midday as they hover in a shifting maze above the beach—why the loss is like a gallery of the masterpieces of the artists of old times."[6]

As this last passage surely demonstrates, Theodore Roosevelt, when reflecting on the extinction of the passenger pigeon, or the loss of any other cherished avian species, was capable of distinguished prose, of stirring his readers with language apt, colorful, and vigorous.

2

During his tenure as president Theodore Roosevelt entertained more naturalists at the White House than any president before or since; but the naturalists he enjoyed most, and therefore entertained oftener, were also writers and conservationists. Like Roosevelt himself, they had spent much of their lives in the open, had used their eyes to good effect, and had consistently detailed their observations in books. Thus, when entertained at the White House, they were never embarrassed for lack of conversational gambits. Roosevelt usually started the conversation, perhaps with mention of a rare bird he had just seen on the White House lawn, after which his guests possibly shifted the talk to one or another aspect of conservation, such as the latest wildlife refuge the president had created, for instance, the Breton Island Reservation in Louisiana that gave protection to large colonies of laughing gulls, black skimmers, and other birds. These naturalists/writers/conservationists had followed eagerly and enthusiastically, and had applauded, each of Roosevelt's determined moves in gaining increased protection for the nation's natural resources, and Roosevelt was far happier talking nature with them than politics with any group of congressmen, mayors, or governors.

Roosevelt's interest in the naturalists/writers/conservationists went beyond having them at luncheons in the White House or at Sagamore Hill, the summer White House. If he learned that one of them had a manuscript in preparation, he often agreed to read it critically. If another asked him to write a foreword, he agreed; if still another produced a book he liked, he wrote a favorable review of it for *Outlook* or the *New York Times*. These men were delighted, and understandably so; they had been recognized by the president of the United States.

When Frank T. Bullen, prominent writer and authority on whales, wrote Roosevelt asking him if he could dedicate his next book to him, Roosevelt replied that he would be more than pleased, for he thought Bullen's *The Cruise of the Cachalot* better than anything of the kind since Herman Melville's *Moby-Dick*.[7]

After Roosevelt had read Ernest Ingersoll's[8] *The Life of Animals*, he wrote the author: "I have long admired your writings, and it would be a great pleasure if some time I could have the chance of meeting you, by preference at the White House, if not there, out here [at Sagamore Hill] at lunch some day this summer. By the way, in your 'Life of Animals,' which I gave to my son Archie, your quotation from [Elliott] Coues[9] at the outset embodies just what I think is the goal which the best scientists and the best nature writers should always have before them. There is no use in having a book scientific in its accuracy if no one will read it, and it is worse than no use to have a book that is readable and at the same time false."[10] Apropos of the remark to Ingersoll about the best nature writers, Roosevelt often relished telling of the scientist who, instead of writing "Pigeons walk, and don't hop," had written: "The terrestrial progression of the *Columbidae* is gradient, but never saltatorial."[11]

Roosevelt lauded Frank Chapman's initial literary ventures: "I wonder how I ever got on without your 'Birds of the Eastern United States' and your book on warblers," he told him. And again, on Chapman's publication of *Camps and Cruises of an Ornithologist:* "Not only shall I enjoy the book, but what is more important, I feel the keenest pride in your having written it. . . . I like to have an American do a piece of work really worth doing."[12]

Following the publication of *The Reptile Book* (1907) by Raymond C. Ditmars,[13] Roosevelt endeared himself to the author by writing that he had found his reptile book "genuinely refreshing," that he wished he had written more fully about the many exciting experiences he must have had, and that "it would be a great pleasure if I could see you some time."[14]

In years ahead Ditmars wrote more books, but whether any of them were in response to Roosevelt's complimentary letter cannot be said. However, Roosevelt was definitely responsible for a book by Frederick Courtenay Selous, British-born African explorer and sportsman. During his several years in Africa Selous had amassed a sizable body of notes on the behavior of African animals, but, regarding them of little value or interest to anyone except himself, he had stowed them away in a desk drawer. There they would have probably remained if Roosevelt, while Selous was a visitor at the White House in 1903, had not learned of them and insisted that they be put into a book. Having previously read some of Selous's writings, Roosevelt was in a position to say to him: "You have the most extraordinary power of seeing things with minute accuracy of detail, and the equally necessary power to describe vividly and accurately what you have seen."[15]

Thus motivated, Selous produced *African Nature Notes*, which appeared in 1908. It was dedicated to Roosevelt, "not only because it was entirely owing to his inspiration and kindly encouragement that it was ever written but also because both in private and public life he has always won the sincere admiration and esteem of the author." *African Nature Notes* possessed an uncommon feature. Previous to its publication, Selous had asked Roosevelt if he would write a foreword for it, and Roosevelt had graciously consented to do so. Thus, this book is the only one with a foreword by, and a dedication to, Theodore Roosevelt.

It was during Roosevelt's presidency that pioneers in the photography of wildlife first gained the attention of the public. As books appeared, some of them copiously illustrated with excellent black-and-white pictures of wilderness animals, Roosevelt commended some of the authors. Shooting birds and other animals with a camera instead of with a gun was a good conservation practice. He said as much to Richard Kearton, British photographer-naturalist, who spent time at the White House at Roosevelt's invitation. Kearton soon afterward published a volume of his photographs, *Wild Life Across the World*, and, reasonably enough, it contained a flattering introduction by Roosevelt.

On obtaining a copy of *With Flashlight and Rifle*, a picture study of the wild, nocturnal life of equatorial Africa by the German photographer, G. C. Shilling, Roosevelt wrote to him saying: "I congratulate myself continually on what you have done, and I confess that I envy you your experiences. I wish that I could have the good fortune of meeting you some time in America."[16]

Roosevelt took particular notice of *Wild Wings*, a volume illustrated with pictures done by an American photographer, Herbert K. Job.[17] In a 1906 letter to Job, Roosevelt said in part: "As a fellow Harvard man I must thank you for your exceedingly interesting book. I have been delighted with it. . . . If we can only get the camera in place of the gun and have the sportsman sunk somewhat in the naturalist and lover of wild things, the next generation will see an immense change for the better in the life of our woods and waters."[18]

Roosevelt was early impressed with the flashlight photographs of animals by George Shiras,[19] a Pennsylvanian who mixed politics with nature photography, being a Republican congressman and also a grand prize winner in photography at the 1904 St. Louis World Fair. When Shiras showed Roosevelt some of his pictures, the latter insisted that Shiras would be remiss if he did not produce a book to give permanence to them. Shiras eventually published *Hunting Wild Life with Camera and Flashlight*, but not until 1935. Even though Roosevelt had died earlier, Shiras's work may be regarded as yet another tribute to the friendly, purposeful encouragement of Roosevelt.

As early as 1901, Roosevelt was telling C. Hart Merriam how "lamentable" it was that he had not written a detailed history of the mammals of North America. Five years later, with Merriam meanwhile having done nothing toward the history, Roosevelt again told him: "Oh Heavens! how I wish I could make you really appreciate what I said the other day, and sit down in good faith and all solemnity and write the great formal natural history of the mammals of North America, life histories and all, which you alone can write."[20] In this specific instance, Roosevelt's encouragement produced no result.

To one naturalist, William J. Long,[21] Roosevelt extended no encouragement whatsoever. In several books Long had written animal stories that Roosevelt as well as men like John Burroughs and Frank Chapman thought were products of an ailing, unconfinable imagination. In 1907 Roosevelt, while still president, spoke out against Long's stories and thus was born the "Nature Faker Controversy," which received much attention, then and since, in editorial and biography.[22]

3

During his years as president Roosevelt manifested a greater interest for the company of John Burroughs than for that of any other naturalist/writer. Beyond a mutual interest in wildlife, in the out-of-doors, and nature writing, the two men had little in common, Burroughs being a product of the hardscrabble country of the Catskills and Roosevelt of the cobblestoned streets of Manhattan. Except for a ten-year period in Washington, D.C., where he worked as a clerk in the Treasury Department and subsequent timeouts for travel in such countries as England, France, Japan, and Hawaii, Burroughs rarely left the Catskills. It was here that he gained fame nationally as a superlative essayist, writing principally about birds, flowering plants, and rural scenes. These essays graced his many books, among them *Wake-Robin* (1871), *Birds and Poets* (1877), and *Locusts and Wild Honey* (1879).

On his return to the Catskills from the nation's capital, Burroughs bought a farm and on it built a home he called Riverby, situated on the west side of the Hudson River some eighty miles north of New York City. In 1895, in the hills back of Riverby, he built a rustic, bark-covered home he named Slabsides, where he sought to find quiet and to escape from the public. As his popularity grew— Henry James and others comparing him to Henry David Thoreau— he became known affectionately as "The Sage of Slabsides," and all manner of people, including such notables as Henry Ford, Thomas A. Edison, and Roosevelt, made visits to Slabsides.

Roosevelt and Burroughs apparently first met about 1890, when the former was civil service commissioner. It was at an early meeting that Roosevelt told him how homesick his books had made him on one of his boyhood trips to Europe. In 1903, soon after Roosevelt became president, he extended a special invitation to Burroughs: "I would like to visit the Yellowstone Park for a fortnight this spring. I want to see the elk, deer, sheep, and antelope there, for the Superintendent of the Park, Major [John] Pitcher, tells me that they are just as tame as the domesticated animals. I wonder whether you could not come along? I would see that you endured neither fatigue nor hardship."[23] Burroughs, at that date an alert sixty-six, was delighted. "I knew," he later wrote, "that there was no man in the country with whom I should so like to see it as Roosevelt."[24]

The two weeks in Yellowstone passed rapidly, with Roosevelt, who knew the park from earlier visits, eagerly showing his companion Old Faithful, Mammoth Hot Springs, Yellowstone Falls, and other celebrated sights. Both men enjoyed the animals, though, to Burroughs, Roosevelt was the most fascinating animal of all. He later wrote:

I cannot now recall that I have ever met a man with a keener interest and a more comprehensive interest in the wild life about us—an interest that is at once scientific and thoroughly human. And by human I do not mean anything akin to the sentimentalism that sicklies o'er so much of our more recent natural history writing, and that inspires the founding of hospitals for sick cats; but I mean his robust, manly love for all open-air life, and his sympathetic insight into it. When I first read his "Wilderness Hunter," many years ago, I was impressed by his rare combination of the sportsman and the naturalist. When I accompanied him on his trip to the Yellowstone Park in April, 1903, I got a fresh impression of the extent of his natural history knowledge and of his trained powers of observation. Nothing escaped him, from bears to mice, from wild geese to chickadees, from elk to red squirrels; he took it all in, and he took it in as only an alert, vigorous mind can take it in. On that occasion I was able to help him identify only one new bird . . . all the other birds he recognized as quickly as I did.[25]

Before the Yellowstone trip ended, Roosevelt exhibited a mounting regard and affection for Burroughs by addressing him familiarly as "Oom John," "Oom" being the Dutch word for uncle. In 1906 he showed his affection in a more felicitous way, by dedicating to him his latest book, *Outdoor Pastimes of an American Hunter*. His dedicatory remarks read, in part, as follows: *"Dear Oom John:* Every lover of outdoor life must feel a sense of affectionate obligation to you. Your writings appeal to all who care for the life of the woods and fields, whether their tastes keep them in the homely, pleasant farm country or lead them into the wilderness. It is a good thing for our people that you should have lived, and surely no man can wish to have more said of him."

Oom John, eminently pleased, soon returned the compliment, writing a tribute he entitled "Theodore Roosevelt as a Nature-lover and Observer."[26] The piece was essentially Burroughs's description of a day that he and a fellow naturalist, John Lewis Childs, spent with Roosevelt stirring up warblers, sparrows, purple finches, red-winged blackbirds, "highholes" (flickers), yellow-billed cuckoos, and other birds in the woods and fields surrounding Sagamore Hill. The description also included a running commentary on various aspects of the president's capabilities as a naturalist. One incident of the day remained in Burroughs's memory. As he and the two others neared the end of their ramblings, Roosevelt recalled that his sons had recently found a bird's nest in the grass close by the house, and, since they had reported seeing grasshopper sparrows in the vicinity, Roosevelt surmised that the nest in question had been built by that species. They soon located the nest and found that it contained eggs. After little more than a glance, the president exclaimed: "That is not the nest of the grasshopper sparrow, after all; those are the eggs of the song sparrow . . . the eggs of the grasshopper sparrow are much lighter in color—almost white, with brown spots." In reporting this incident, Burroughs disclosed his astonishment: "For my part," he admitted, "I had quite forgotten for the moment how the eggs of the little sparrow looked . . . but the President has so little to remember that he forgets none of these minor things; his bird-lore and wood-lore seem as fresh as if just learned."[27]

Burroughs also was invited to luncheons at the White House. Of one visit he reported: "I sat between Mrs. Roosevelt and Secretary [Elihu] Root. The President sat opposite and talked over to me, and was very jolly—called me 'Oom John,' and 'beloved Oom John' when he greeted me first." Following another White House luncheon, Roosevelt took the Sage of Slabsides for a walk along Rock Creek. "It was a lively walk," Burroughs reported. "We went at a four-mile gait. . . . We saw no birds—they couldn't keep up with us."[28]

Theodore Roosevelt was the first president to have a "Camp David." It was located in Albemarle County, Virginia, and consisted of five acres of land and a small frame house; it was bought in 1905 for $195.[29] To this place, named Pine Knot by Mrs. Roosevelt, the president from time to time repaired with members of his family and occasional guests, to escape executive demands and to have the birds around him. This frame house, as Roosevelt described it, consisted "of one long room, with a broad piazza below, and three small bedrooms above . . . [and] with big outside chimneys at each end."[30]

In the spring of 1908 Roosevelt invited Burroughs to spend a weekend at Pine Knot with him and Mrs. Roosevelt. As a special inducement, he said: "We would show you many birds, some of them new, and we *might* see passenger pigeons."[31] Roosevelt's mention of passenger pigeons puzzled Burroughs not at all. A year earlier, while at Pine Knot, the president had seen a flock of birds that he took to be passenger pigeons and was so excited with his observation that he immediately wrote nearly identical letters to both C. Hart Merriam and Burroughs. To Merriam he had said: "On May 18th [1907] near Keene, Albemarle County, Virginia, I saw a flock of a dozen passenger pigeons. I have not seen any for twenty-five years and never dreamed I should see any again, but I could not have been mistaken (tho I did not kill any for I did not have a gun, and in any event nothing could have persuaded me to shoot them). I saw them flying to and fro a couple of times and then they all lit in a tall dead pine by an old field. There were doves in the field for me to compare them with, and I do not see how I could have been mistaken."[32] Both Merriam and Burroughs, however, did think that Roosevelt had been mistaken, and, when replying to him, pointed out that the last unquestioned instances of passenger pigeons having been seen in the wild had been in 1898, nine years earlier. Consequently, for some time most ornithologists had been of the opinion that the bird was extinct—except for a few still alive in zoological parks.

However, ornithologists at the American Museum of Natural History sided with Roosevelt. One of them advised this writer that Roosevelt, from his earlier years, knew the passenger pigeon well, and his statement that "mourning doves were present for comparison seemed to take his observation out of the realm of the dubious."[33] It seems likely, therefore, that Roosevelt, twenty-sixth president of the United States, was the last reputable naturalist to see *and report* live passenger pigeons in the wild.

When, a year later, Burroughs joined Mr. and Mrs. Roosevelt in Washington to go to Pine Knot, they took an early train for North Garden, then a small Virginia town distant some 100 miles from Washington. From there they traveled in a horse-drawn vehicle (Burroughs called it a buggy) over a bumpy road the remaining miles, about fifteen, to Pine Knot. During the weekend, in cross-country ramblings, the two naturalists encountered and identified some seventy-five species of birds. Burroughs knew all but two, and Roosevelt all but two. Burroughs later wrote: "He taught me Bewick's wren and the prairie warbler, and I taught him the swamp sparrow and one of the rarer warblers, I think it was a pine warbler. If he had found the Lincoln sparrow [that he had earlier found at Pine Knot] he would have been ahead of me."[34] A disappointment to Roosevelt was the failure of the passenger pigeons to reappear.

Before Burroughs left for his Catskill home, Roosevelt gave him a list of the birds they had identified at Pine Knot and, at the same time, expressed the hope to him that he would soon write an account of their visit together in Virginia. After a lapse of years, Burroughs, having meanwhile failed to write the account, Roosevelt repeated the request: "I do hope that you will include in your coming volume of sketches a little account of the time you visited me at Pine Knot, our little Virginia camp, while I was President. I am very proud of you, Oom John, and I want the fact that you were my guest when I was President, and that you and I looked at birds together, recorded there."[35] By the time Burroughs wrote the account, Roosevelt had died; however, he did not forget to include the fact that the president had introduced him to the Bewick's wren and the swamp sparrow.

4

At the end of their fortnight in Yellowstone National Park, Roosevelt and Burroughs separated, Burroughs returning home and Roosevelt going to California to spend time with John Muir. While planning this 1903 invasion of the West, Roosevelt had written Muir: "I write to you personally to express the hope that you will be able to take me through Yosemite National Park. I do not want anyone with me but you, and I want to drop politics absolutely for four days and just be out in the open with you."[36]

John Muir, senior to Roosevelt by twenty years, had long since achieved prominence as a naturalist, conservationist, explorer, and writer. Born in Scotland, he came to the United States at an early age and, soon afterward, entered the University of Wisconsin, where he exhibited a particular interest in botany, geology, and chemistry (though he left the school before graduating).

In September 1867, he began an indefinite journey on foot to the South, which he later described in *A Thousand-Mile Walk to the Gulf*. After a brief visit to Cuba, he went to New York City, and, finding that metropolis uncongenial, he took passage for the Isthmus of Panama and California—and for a fateful rendezvous with Yosemite. There, among the mountains and the giant Sequoias, he felt at home for the first time in his life.

In years ahead, impelled by an eagerness to learn more about the forested western wilderness, he traveled, always on foot, through the mountains of Nevada, Utah, Oregon, Washington, and Alaska. It was while on his first trip to Alaska that Muir met the celebrated Alaskan missionary, S. Hall Young, and Young's dog Stickeen, a canine of uncertain lineage. Young became a lifelong friend and Stickeen became famous, when Muir later wrote a biography entitled *Stickeen*, perhaps the most popular of all his books. And Young, exhibiting genuine affection, wrote *Alaskan Days with John Muir.* In the Sierras it was the trees, more than any other object of nature, that engaged and held Muir's attention. In Alaska it was the glaciers. Often, with Stickeen as a companion, he climbed, explored, even discovered, the Alaskan glaciers (with the result that one of them is today the Muir Glacier).

Muir soon bought California land, adopted horticulture as a profession, and by 1891 had been so successful that he retired and, inspired by his love of trees, traveled throughout Australia, Africa, and South America. On all of his travels, both as boy and man, Muir kept journals. This practice made possible the posthumous publication of two of his books, *Travels in Alaska* (1915) and *A Thousand-Mile Walk to the Gulf* (1916).

Celebrities, on visits to Yosemite, made the acquaintance of Muir. In 1871 it was Ralph Waldo Emerson, whom Muir described as "the most serene, majestic, sequoia-like soul I ever met."[37] The following year it was two of Harvard's most distinguished botanists, John Torrey and Asa Gray. Thereafter, it was a succession of figures, among them Charles S. Sargent, Robert U. Johnson, and Gifford Pinchot. To each of his visitors, whatever their calling, Muir unburdened himself; he wanted the forests to remain forever wild and those of certain areas, such as Yosemite, to be given national park status. And it was largely through the efforts of Muir that in 1890 Congress created Yosemite National Park. Also, just two years later (1892), Muir was largely responsible for the formation of the Sierra Club, and became its first president, an office he held until his death. This club, with Muir at the helm, grew rapidly and was soon well launched on its long and distinguished course.

As mentioned, there is today Muir Glacier, but there is also, and much better known, Muir Woods, the stand of redwoods on the Marin peninsula some twenty miles north of San Francisco. Undoubtedly Muir was deeply moved, when, on January 9, 1908, Theodore Roosevelt designated Muir Woods a national monument.

John Muir and Theodore Roosevelt first met on May 15, 1903, when the train carrying the latter arrived in Raymond, California, a small town located a few miles south of Yosemite. Detaching themselves at once from a crowd at the railroad station, the two men headed for the park. Report has it that Roosevelt's first question to Muir was, "How do you tell the Hammond from the Wright flycatcher?"[38]

Regretfully, neither Roosevelt nor Muir later wrote an account of their days together in Yosemite, in certain respects the most impressive and beautiful of all of the national parks. As a result, to gain particulars about the trip, one has to depend on scattered bits of information from different sources, such as a letter of May 19 from Roosevelt to Muir: "I trust I need not tell you, my dear sir, how happy were the days in Yosemite I owed to you, and how greatly I appreciated them. I shall never forget the three camps, the first in the solemn temple of the great Sequoias [*Sequoia gigantea*], the next in the snow storm among the silver firs near the brink of the cliff, and the third on the floor of the Yosemite, in the open valley fronting the stupendous rocky mass of El Capitan with the falls thundering in the distance on either hand."[39]

Writing to Burroughs on about this same date, the president supplied additional news about the Yosemite visit—and also about Muir: "I have just come from a four day trip into the Yosemite with John Muir. Both the Yosemite and the big trees were all that any human could desire. John Muir is a delightful man, and with the exception of yourself, the pleasantest possible companion on a trip of this kind. I was a little surprised that he knew nothing about any of the birds save a few of the most conspicuous, but he knows so much about rocks, trees, glaciers, flowers, etc., that it is simply captious to complain."[40]

We know of two letters that Muir wrote about the days with Roosevelt. To his wife he confided: "I had a perfectly glorious time with the President and the mountains. I never before had a more interesting, hearty, and manly companion."[41] And to C. Hart Merriam: "Camping with the President was a remarkable experience. I fairly fell in love with him."[42]

We learn, too, from Muir's biographer, William Frederick Badè, that the main topic of conversation between the two men was conservation, with Muir dwelling at length on the need of urgent action to save the big sequoias and other unrivaled attractions of the western wilderness areas. He spoke so forcefully that Roosevelt came away "with a greatly quickened conviction that vigorous action must be taken, ere it would be too late."[43]

It later was revealed that Roosevelt felt more at home with Burroughs than with Muir. "I think I could see where the rub was," Burroughs afterward explained, "both are great talkers, and the talkers, you know, seldom get on well together. Now he finds me an appreciative listener, and that suits him better."[44]

When John Muir died—on Christmas Eve, 1914—Roosevelt's tribute was spontaneously warm and generous: "Ordinarily, the man who loves the woods and the mountains, the trees, the flowers, and the wild things, has in him some indefinable quality of charm which appeals even to those sons of civilization who care for little outside of paved streets and brick walls. John Muir was a fine illustration of this rule. He was by birth a Scotchman, a tall and spare man, with the poise and ease natural to him who has lived much alone under conditions of labor and hazard. His was a dauntless soul, and also one brimming over with friendliness and kindness."[45]

5

David Starr Jordan once wrote that during Theodore Roosevelt's presidency it had been his good fortune "to visit Washington on fur seal or fishery business once every year," and he had been "each time a guest at luncheon in the White House."[46] He further said: "As naturalists we always met on common ground, for Natural History was Roosevelt's first love as well as his last. . . . and it may fairly be stated that under his government science reached its high-water mark."[47]

When and where Roosevelt and Jordan first met we cannot say, though the event for the former must have been a memorable one, since he at last had the pleasure and satisfaction of meeting the author of *Manual of the Vertebrates of the Northern United States*, a volume that he had acquired in 1876 (the year of its publication) and afterward had found of tremendous value to him in identifying birds, mammals, reptiles, and other vertebrate animals. After initial greetings, Roosevelt doubtless told Jordan how much the *Manual* had aided his boyhood studies.

Jordan achieved eminence both as a scientist and as an educator. Born in Gainesville, New York, he obtained his education at Cornell University (A.B., 1872), Indiana Medical College (M.D., 1875), and Butler University (Ph.D., 1878). He served as professor of biology at Butler 1875–79, went to Indiana University in 1879 as professor of biology, and served as president of Indiana University from 1885 to 1891. Earlier Jordan had studied for a summer at Harvard under Louis Agassiz, who had persuaded him to undertake a study of the fishes of the Boston area. Thereafter Jordan's interest in fishes developed rapidly, and this led to his appointment as a member of the U.S. Fish Commission (1879–1908) and as head of the Fur Seal Commission (1896–98). As an ichthyologist, Jordan published extensively, including (jointly with B. W. Evermann)[48] the popular *Fishes of North and Middle America.* Jordan's successes as president of Indiana University attracted the attention of Leland Stanford, who in 1901 offered him the presidency of Stanford University. Jordan accepted the position and held it with distinction until 1913.

Jordan thought highly of Roosevelt's performance as president. He even provided specific proof of his regard, though he did so in an uncommon way. In 1901, while exploring Pacific waters surrounding Hawaii, he and his companion (Evermann) discovered "a very beautiful fish, the *kali kali,* golden yellow with broad crossbands of deep crimson. It then bore the name of *Serranus brighami* . . . but this species was no *Serranus* . . . was plainly the type of a new genus." Accordingly, and with deep satisfaction, Jordan and Evermann agreed on a new generic name: *Rooseveltia,* in honor of "Theodore Roosevelt, naturalist, and in recognition of his services in the promotion of zoological research." On being informed of this honor, Roosevelt, according to Jordan, "was delighted."[49]

Jordan complimented Theodore Roosevelt again—perhaps even more handsomely—when after Roosevelt's death, he said: "In the various natural history explorations undertaken by me—and by others—during his administration, one could always count on intelligent and effective sympathy; and in so far as scientific appointments rested with him, he always gave them full and intelligent consideration. In 1905 I was preparing with much enthusiasm to take charge of an exploration on the Albatross of the deep seas around Japan. Talking it over with me and pounding the table with his fist for emphasis, he said: 'It was to help along things like this, Dr. Jordan, that I TOOK THIS JOB!'"[50]

On another occasion, as a White House guest, Jordan turned to the president and said: "They spoiled a good naturalist in making you a statesman."[51] Only Jordan and a few others, then and since, have had sufficient knowledge of Roosevelt's natural history background to make that statement, confident that it was the truth and that the words could not be successfully challenged or refuted.

6

Writing to Frederick Selous on March 20, 1908, Theodore Roosevelt said: "A year hence I shall stop being President, and while I can not be certain of what I shall do, it may be that I can afford to devote a year to a trip to Africa."[52] At this state of his thinking, Roosevelt had in mind a hunting trip to be made solely by himself and his son Kermit. But by June, three months after writing the above to Selous, he had conceived a more ambitious plan: possible sponsorship by the Smithsonian Institution. Accordingly, to find out if the idea appealed to that body, he forthwith addressed a carefully worded letter to its secretary, Charles D. Walcott. After first giving Walcott a rough outline of his plan, Roosevelt continued: "Now it seems to me that this opens up the best chance for the National Museum [Smithsonian] to get a fine collection, not only of the big game beasts, but of the smaller animals and birds of Africa; and looking at it dispassionately, it seems to me that the chance ought not to be neglected. I shall make arrangements in connection with publishing a book which will enable me to pay the expenses of myself and son. But what I would like to do would be to get one or two professional field taxonomists, field naturalists, to go with me, who should prepare and send back the specimens we collect. The collection which would thus go to the National Museum would be of unique value."[53] The response to this letter delighted Roosevelt. Walcott promised not only Smithsonian sponsorship but also agreed to provide three professional field naturalists, each a multitalented, experienced taxonomist. Because of the importance of these three to the success of the expedition, they need appropriate introductions.

One, the oldest, was Edgar Alexander Mearns (1858–1916). Walcott chose Mearns for two reasons: he was a seasoned field naturalist and was also a physician (a graduate of Columbia's Medical School). In 1861 Mearns had joined the U.S. Army, ultimately attaining the rank of colonel. After the war he became one of the founders of the American Ornithologists' Union, as well as an industrious field collector, mainly in the Southwest. His findings there resulted in the publication of *Mammals of the Mexican Boundary of the United States* (1907), a highly acclaimed treatise. In respect to Mearns's value as a physician on the African trip, we have Roosevelt's word that he treated disorders of Nasai and other African natives as well as those of the expedition's personnel. Of his manifold contributions as a naturalist, Roosevelt wrote: "Dr. Mearns, in addition to birds and plants, never let pass the opportunity to collect anything from reptiles and fishes to land shells."[54]

A second naturalist was Edmund Heller (1875–1939). Illinois-born and educated at Stanford University, Heller had traveled and collected in many parts of the world, including China, Alaska, and the Galapagos Islands. Either by chance or design, Heller became Roosevelt's taxidermist extraordinaire, always at hand to take care of bodies of pachyderms, such as the rhinoceros, hippopotamus, and elephant.

The third naturalist was John Alden Loring (1871–1945), an Ohio-born man with vast natural history experience, having served (1892–97) as naturalist with the U.S. Biological Survey and (1897–1901) as curator of animals in the New York Zoological Park. Roosevelt praised him as "a remarkably successful trapper of small mammals."[55]

Mearns, Heller, and Loring were closely associated with Roosevelt in Africa—mainly in British East Africa and the Sudan—for the better part of a year, from April 21, 1909, when the party arrived in Mombasa, until March 14, 1910, when at Khartoum they separated. The three had heard in advance that Roosevelt would be a hard man to get along with, but they quickly found the opposite to be true. Roosevelt at once favorably impressed them by eating at the same mess and by occupying the same kind of tent. Long before the expedition ended, they had come to admire his unflinching courage, his cordial companionship, his lively and unfailing humor, and his ever-present concern about their day-to-day well-being. "His chief thought," Loring afterward wrote, "was for the welfare of the party."[56]

Heller admired Roosevelt the man and also Roosevelt the naturalist. As Heller put it: "He demonstrated in his African expedition what a marvellous faunal naturalist he was by acquiring a great mass of new observations on the life histories of the animals with which we met."[57] And Heller's admiration increased on learning that his leader had written Walcott, insisting that the naturalists with him, on their return from Africa, be allowed to publish their observations on the African fauna[58] (on a previous trip to Africa, Heller had been denied that privilege). This stand, when it became generally known, drew from a prominent scientist the comment: "In natural history circles his influence in this direction marked a new era."[59]

But, however much Mearns, Heller, and Loring may have admired Theodore Roosevelt, he seems to have admired them just as much: "I do not believe," he said, "that three better men . . . could be found anywhere."[60]

Leaving Mombasa on April 21, the Roosevelt-Smithsonian Expedition traveled inland by way of Nairobi and Lake Victoria to Lake Albert. Here, in early January 1910, the party took boats and began the descent of the White Nile. Some forty-eight hours later, they stopped in the Lado country, home of the square-mouthed rhinoceros—a rare beast which Roosevelt here hunted—as well as the habitat of the tsetse fly, swarms of mosquitoes, and crashes of crocodiles.

It was here in this pest-ridden part of Africa that Roosevelt, on January 17, 1910, wrote a letter to Gifford Pinchot, saying: "We have just heard by special runner that you have been removed. I cannot believe it. I do not know any man in public life who has rendered quite the service you have rendered; and it seems to me absolutely impossible that there can be any truth in the statement."[61] Roosevelt soon received confirmation. A political feud over the withdrawal of coal lands had developed between Pinchot and R. A. Ballinger, William Howard Taft's secretary of the interior, and Taft had felt obliged to fire Pinchot. Thus, in distant Africa while far from home, Roosevelt had received intelligence that would ultimately lead to events of national import. An unmendable, ever-widening rift developed between Roosevelt and Taft—who had been hand-picked by Roosevelt to succeed him as president; Roosevelt would become a Bull Mooser, and Pinchot, in time, governor of Pennsylvania.

7

After completing his descent of the Nile, Roosevelt went directly to England, where, as prearranged, he met Sir Edward Grey,[62] then Britain's foreign secretary. Before leaving the United States for Africa, Roosevelt had let it be known that while in England he would like to spend a day in the country with someone capable of identifying the English birds and their songs. Sir Edward, one of Britain's more knowledgeable amateur ornithologists, had been chosen to accompany Roosevelt. On June 9, 1910, the two men traveled by train from London to Basingstoke and from there by car to the lovely, placid valley of the Itchen, Hampshire, some fifty miles southwest of London. It was a part of the British countryside earlier made celebrated by other naturalists, among them Gilbert White and W. H. Hudson.

Looked at from most any point of view, this meeting of the former president of the United States, brilliant and versatile, with the British foreign secretary, also intellectual and many-sided, was extraordinary. For one thing, never before had two important political figures met to enjoy birds. For another, each was quite unfamiliar with the other's ornithological capabilities. Grey, from the start, was surprised to learn that Roosevelt knew more about British birds than he knew about those of the United States. Because of extensive boyhood reading, Roosevelt could declare: "I knew the lark of Shakespeare and Shelley and the Etrick Shepherd [James Hogg, Scottish poet]; I knew the nightingale of Milton and Keats; I knew Wordsworth's cuckoo; I knew mavis and merle singing in the merry wood of the old ballads; I knew Jenny Wren and Cock Robin of the nursery books."[63]

Though initially somewhat apprehensive as to how the day with Roosevelt would go, Sir Edward later wrote: "I found out not only that he had a remarkable and abiding interest in birds, but a wonderful knowledge of them."[64] He soon discovered, too, as Burroughs had earlier, that Roosevelt had an inherent and well-trained ear for bird music. As Sir Edward explained: "He had one of the most perfectly trained ears for bird songs that I have ever known, so that if three or four birds were singing together he would pick out their songs, distinguish each, and ask to be told each separate name, and when, further on, we heard any bird for a second time, he would remember the song from the first telling and be able to name the bird itself."[65]

The foreign secretary was intrigued by yet another fact: Roosevelt had a discriminating ear and was quick to express preferences between bird songs. Of all the songs he heard that day, he definitely liked best that of the blackbird (the merle) and was almost indignant that its mellow, leisurely voice had received such a modicum of praise. The song of another British bird, the golden-crested wren (*Regulus cristatus*) drew from Roosevelt the comment: "I think that is exactly the same song as that of a bird we have in America." Sir Edward, unable to do more than name the bird, later relayed Roosevelt's comment to a professional ornithologist in London's National Museum, who told him that the song of this British bird was probably the only one that the two countries had in common.[66] The American bird Roosevelt had had in mind was the golden-crowned kinglet (*Regulus satraps*), sometimes regarded as a subspecies of the golden-crested wren (which, of course, is no wren at all).

This exhibition of Roosevelt's remarkable auditory acuity and his alertness to the similarity of the two songs so impressed Sir Edward that he was soon writing: "It was the business of the bird expert in London to know about birds, [but] Colonel Roosevelt's knowledge was a mere incident acquired, not as a part of the work of his life, but entirely outside it."[67] Not entirely true, of course, since Sir Edward knew little or nothing about Roosevelt's active boyhood years among the avifauna of Long Island, the Hudson River valley, the Adirondacks, and other places.

After enjoying for a few hours the avian lyrics and choruses common to the valley of the Itchen, Roosevelt and Grey took a car to the New Forest, a nearby uninhabited area of woodland and heath in which grew many gnarled and ancient oaks. Here they heard only a few more bird songs, but among them was that of the English robin or redbreast, which is of the thrush family, as is the American robin, though the two are generically different. Roosevelt had no idea that it sang so well; he took delight in its gushing, careless strain. He heard here, too, and for the first time, the fine, clear notes and trills of the English wren, and found himself comparing its beautiful and finished performance with that of America's winter wren. To his trained ear, the two were much alike though, in his opinion, that of the British species was less musical.

At the end of the day, Sir Edward made a list of the birds he and Roosevelt had encountered, starring those they had heard singing. They had seen a total of forty-two species, twenty-three of which they had heard. But, as Sir Edward later revealed, there was not one of the forty-three whose character and classification his celebrated companion did not know. Before the day ended, the learned British foreign secretary had learned other facts about Roosevelt. One of them, perhaps the most meaningful, he subsequently put into words: "I saw enough of him to know that to be with him was to be stimulated in the very best sense of the word for the work of life."[68]

8

In mid-1913, the Bull Moose having been shorn of its antlers, Theodore Roosevelt made an extraordinary decision: he would explore the wilds of South America. His itinerary showed that he would begin his trip by an ascent of the Paraguay River and then, after crossing the divide, go down one of the larger southern Amazonian tributaries, most likely the Tapajós. Having reached the Amazon, Roosevelt proposed to follow one of two routes, either continue north by way of the Rio Negro, Casiquiare, and the Orinoco to the Caribbean, or take the simpler eastern route down the Amazon to Pará and the Amazon. To Roosevelt, at this point in his planning, the Rio Negro-Casiquiare-Orinoco road seemed to entail greater risk and derring-do and was thus preferable.

Roosevelt could not have chosen a more perilous route. It included some of the most forbidding parts of the continent, yet Roosevelt, despite his fifty-five years, deteriorating reflexes, and expanded waistline, was determined. Not until later did he, from added experience, advise: "The man should have youth and strength who seeks adventure in the wide, waste spaces of the earth."[69]

Early in his planning, Roosevelt conferred with Henry Fairfield Osborn and Frank M. Chapman of the American Museum of Natural History. He sought sponsorship by the museum for the trip and also at least two trained naturalists. Osborn and Chapman agreed to both requests, recommending two naturalists, George K. Cherrie and Leo E. Miller.

George Kruck Cherrie (1865–1948), naturalist and explorer, was Iowa-born. After graduating from the State Agricultural College at Ames, Iowa, he shortly began a museum career, serving such institutions as the U.S. National Museum, Museo National (San Jose, Costa Rica) Field Museum, and the Museum of Natural History. While with these various museums, Cherrie had spent more than twenty years collecting in countries of both Central and South America. He was a member of the American Ornithologists' Union and the Boone and Crockett Club. Chapman described him as "a prince of tropical American bird collectors,"[70] and Roosevelt later complimented him by saying, "Like most of the field-naturalists I have met, he was an unusually efficient and fearless man."[71]

Leo Edward Miller (1887–1952), naturalist, was a native of Indiana, who, though much younger than Cherrie, had already demonstrated his talents as a collector in the hinterlands of Colombia, Venezuela, and British Guiana. Roosevelt described him as "an enthusiastic naturalist with good literary as well as scientific training."[72]

Roosevelt and Cherrie sailed from New York to South America on October 4, 1913. After a brief stop in the Barbados to take aboard Miller (who had been collecting in British Guiana) and in Bahia to pick up Kermit Roosevelt (who had been bridge-building in Brazil), Roosevelt arrived in Rio de Janeiro on October 21. Here, by chance, he met a Brazilian official who provided him with intelligence that significantly altered original plans. The official informed Roosevelt of a recent discovery on the Brazilian Plan Alto by Colonel Candido Mariano da Silva Rondon of the Brazilian Telegraphic Commission. Colonel Rondon had found the headwaters of a large, previously unknown and unmapped stream flowing northward toward the Amazon. Would Colonel Roosevelt, the Brazilian official asked, like to meet Colonel Rondon to discuss the possibility of exploring this uncharted river? Unhesitatingly, Roosevelt replied, "We will go down that unknown river."[73] First known to the world as the Rio da Duvida (the River of Doubt), this stream today appears on maps as the Roosevelt.

Relatives and close friends of the former president had expressed some concern as to his safety on this expedition from the beginning; but, when news got back to them about his proposed descent of an unknown river, they vigorously protested. Osborn, for one, stated that he "would never consent to his going to this particular region under the American Museum flag," and that he "would not assume even part of the responsibility for what might happen in case he did not return."[74] Undaunted, Roosevelt replied: "I have already lived and enjoyed as much of life as any other nine men I know . . . and if it is necessary for me to leave my remains in South America, I am quite ready to do so."[75]

Roosevelt retained his original intention of first ascending the Paraguay, but, because of speaking engagements to which he had earlier committed himself, it was December 9 before the Expedicão Scientifica Roosevelt–Rondon actually got underway. Three days later it reached the Brazilian border, where Colonel Rondon and associates awaited Roosevelt's arrival. From this point, it was a near endless trek to the headwaters of the River of Doubt, one consuming sixty-seven days (from December 9 to February 14). Here, or nearby, two contingents left Roosevelt, one to descend the Tapajós and the other, including Miller, to go down the Gy-Paraná and the Madeira.

It was February 17, 1914, when Theodore Roosevelt, taking with him Cherrie, Colonel Rondon, a physician and an army lieutenant (both Brazilian), and sixteen boatmen, began the descent of the River of Doubt. They traveled in seven dugout canoes. No member of the party knew where the river would take them nor how long they would be on it. When they ultimately found out, they had endured some eight weeks of continuous hardship, danger, privation, and near tragedy. Not until mid-April did they discover that the waters of the River of Doubt emptied into the Madeira, the largest of the southern tributaries of the Amazon. From this confluence, two more weeks expired before Roosevelt and the others reached the Amazon and the nearby city of Manaos and rejoined Miller.

Geographically and zoologically, Roosevelt's exploration through a remote sector of the Brazilian wilderness was a tremendous, even triumphant, success. He had placed on South American maps, where heretofore had been only a large blank space, a river near 1,000 miles in length, and Cherrie and Miller had collected for the American Museum approximately 2,500 birds and 500 mammals, these exclusive of numerous reptiles, amphibia, fishes, and insects, many of which proved to be new to science.

In another way, the exploration, specifically the day-to-day harrowing conflict with the river, had been nearly tragic. Roosevelt, as a result of malaria, dysentery, and a severely infected leg, would rarely again display the ebullience of spirit the American people had come to expect of him; his health had suffered permanent impairment. At one point on the river he had despaired of living and had urged the others of the party to go on without him.

Roosevelt's account of his South American adventures, *Through the Brazilian Wilderness*, revealed again and again his admiration for Cherrie and Miller. He said of them, as he had said of Mearns, Heller, and Loring, that no better men could have been found. He was particularly generous in his praise of Cherrie, who had endured the ordeals of the River of Doubt: "He had more than withstood every test, and in him Kermit and I had come to recognize a friend with whom our friendship would never falter or grow less."[76]

As additional evidence of Roosevelt's high regard for Cherrie and Miller, before leaving Brazil, he arranged with Chapman for a sum of $1,000 to be given to each of them as "a nest egg" toward "meeting the costs of their further work in South America for the Museum."[77] More than that, when later he addressed the National Geographic Society, he complimented them again by insisting that they occupy the platform with him and by relating to his audience the parts each had played "in an undertaking that narrowly escaped a tragic end."[78]

And how did Cherrie and Miller regard Roosevelt? Later Cherrie published an autobiography, and in it appeared an arresting sentence, one reflecting Miller's sentiments as well as Cherrie's: "As I look back over my life's winding trails I realize that the journey down the River of Doubt overshadows all the rest and when I recall the companions I have had, good, bad, and indifferent, Theodore Roosevelt stands apart."[79]

9

After a leisurely boat trip down the Amazon from Manaos, Roosevelt left Pará, on May 7, for New York. He did not—could not if he had wished—make the Rio Negro-Casiquiare-Orinoco transit he had earlier envisioned. At Sagamore Hill, once he had returned, he was soon writing Surgeon-General F. M. Rixey, his personal physician: "As for me, my dear doctor, I am personally through. I am not a man like you who keeps his youth almost to the end, and I'm now pretty nearly done out."[80] Though physically impaired, Roosevelt had lost little, if any, of his mental vigor and agility. The years remaining to him, few in number, were filled with activity, but, since they were largely war years, they brought concern (for his sons in uniform), anger (at being disallowed to command troops), and despair (on receiving news of Quentin's death).

Yet, during these same years, despite failing health and intermittent grief, Roosevelt experienced moments of unclouded happiness and keen satisfaction, and such moments, more often than not, coincided with hours or days in the company of naturalists, particularly William Beebe, with whom during this period he spent more time than with any other naturalist.

William Beebe (1877–1962), a Brooklyn-born naturalist, author, and explorer, received his education at Columbia University. Beginning in 1899, when just twenty-two, he was continuously associated with the New York Zoological Society, first as curator of birds, and later as director of the society's Department of Tropical Research. He led several scientific expeditions and published many books. At least two of his books, *Jungle Peace* (1918) and *Monograph of the Pheasants* (1918), came from the press before Roosevelt died.

The friendship between Roosevelt and Beebe, once begun, seems to have developed rapidly, and in 1916 Beebe succeeded in persuading Roosevelt and Mrs. Roosevelt to visit British Guiana, where the former had recently founded a tropical laboratory. To make a trip of such length, and at a time when he was still suffering the ill effects of his River of Doubt venture, suggests a powerful incentive, such as close friendship often provides.

Roosevelt was impressed with his host's research, so much so that he agreed to write an introduction to *Tropical Wildlife in British Guiana*, a book co-authored by Beebe. A portion of his introduction, each line flattering to Beebe, reads as follows: "The establishment of the Tropical Research station . . . marks the beginning of a wholly new type of biological work, capable of literally illimitable expansion. It provides for intensive study, in the open field, of the teeming animal life of the tropics."[81]

On invitation of Roosevelt, Beebe often spent time at Sagamore Hill. The latter subsequently described a whimsical incident there:

After an evening of talk, we would go out on the lawn, where we took turns at an amusing little astronomical rite. We searched until we found, with or without glasses, the faint, heavenly light-mist beyond the lower left-hand corner of the Great Square of Pegasus, when one or the other of us would then recite:

> That is the Spiral Galaxy in Andromeda.
> It is as large as the Milky Way.
> It is one of a hundred million galaxies.
> It is 750,000 light years away.
> It consists of one hundred billion suns,
> each larger than our sun.

After an interval Colonel Roosevelt would grin at me and say: "Now I think we are small enough! Let's go to bed."[82]

Further evidence of the close friendship between the two men is that the Roosevelts had planned a voyage to the Pacific that was to include Beebe. Details of this projected trip are in a letter Roosevelt wrote Henry Osborn in early December 1916: "Dear Osborn: I have spoken to [Frank] Chapman . . . about a Polynesian trip which I would greatly like to take next year. Mrs. Roosevelt will go with me. We would like to take a steamer for a six or eight month's trip, to visit the various Polynesian islands. I have asked Beebe to go along. I would like to take the trip under the auspices of the American Museum of Natural History, substantially as I took the Brazilian trip."[83] With the intervention of World War I Roosevelt abandoned plans for this ambitious trip. Beebe may have been more disappointed than anyone else. To have sailed the southern Pacific for months on end with the ex-president and his lady would surely have been an extraordinary and unforgettable experience.

10

Before anyone quite really realized it, 1918, the last full year of existence for Theodore Roosevelt, began. As though sensible of the fact, he sought increasingly to recapture a measure of his boyhood joys in the out-of-doors. Again and again, during his final months, he reaffirmed his love of the animate world. As January and February gave way to March, and then to April, he rediscovered the miracle of spring. To his three sons, by then all overseas with the American Expeditionary Force, he transmitted his euphoria: "Spring has fairly begun. The frogs are noisy in the ponds, the robins and song sparrows and redwing blackbirds are in song, the maple buds are red and the willow tips green; the first mayflowers and bloodroot have appeared."[84] In a letter to Quentin, he was more communicative: "Here, spring is now well underway, although the weather is cold and gray. The woods are showing a green foam, the gay yellow of forsythia has appeared; the bloodroot spangles with brilliant white the brown dead leaves of the hillside across the wet hollow by the frog spring."[85] Later, as summer displaced spring, he wrote again to the boys: "The country is beautiful beyond description. It is the high time of the year, with tree and flower and bird."[86]

In his *Autobiography*, published in 1913, Roosevelt gave scant space to his activities as a boy naturalist. In the May 1918 number of the *American Museum Journal* appeared an article by him entitled "My Life as a Naturalist" (which might better have been titled "My Boyhood as a Naturalist," since the contained information was limited to the years of his youth). The article is brief, containing less than 3,000 words, and is a first-rate illustration of self-deprecation. It alludes to his "wooden methods of mounting birds," to his "clumsy industry in skinning specimens," and to his collection exhibiting "nothing but enthusiasm" on his part. It concludes with a meaningful and arresting statement: "while my interest in natural history has added very little to my sum of achievement, it has added immeasurably to my sum of enjoyment."[87] The article is yet another instance of aging minds turning to thoughts of a youthful past.

Roosevelt retained to the very end an intense concern for the welfare of the large game animals. As the summer of 1918 approached, he read an article by George Bird Grinnell, stating that the elk in Yellowstone Park, because of the protection given them, had multiplied far beyond the limits of their natural food supply, and consequently were dying in ever larger numbers. Roosevelt responded: "It is a mere question of mathematics," he wrote Grinnell, "to show that if they [the elk] are protected as they have been in the Park, they would, inside of a century, fill the whole United States, so that they would die of starvation."[88]

In mid-July news was brought to Sagamore Hill of Quentin's death: he had been shot down over enemy lines. Roosevelt bore his grief with fortitude, but, as one observer reported, "The old side of him was gone . . . the boy in him had died."[89] Several years earlier, on learning of the death of Muir's wife, Roosevelt had written Muir: "Get out among the mountains and trees, friend, they will do more for you than either man or woman could."[90] It was impossible on hearing of Quentin's death for Roosevelt to visit the mountains. He did, however, more often than before, it was noted, leave his study to stroll alone through the countryside bordering the Sound, thereby gaining at least a degree of comfort in his sorrow.

The summer days gave way to those of autumn. Birds began their annual pilgrimages to warmer climes. Asters and goldenrod colored roadsides. The trees turned red and yellow and gold. Armistice Day came, and Roosevelt was hospitalized with crippling inflamatory rheumatism and other related disorders, sequalae of Brazilian jungle fevers and abscesses. Though bedridden, he surrendered no time to inactivity. He reviewed for the *American Museum Journal* Leo E. Miller's *In the Wilds of South America*, page proofs having been given to him by Miller's publisher. The editor of the museum journal, aware of Roosevelt's pains, was so impressed that, in introducing the review to readers, he felt moved to comment: "Colonel Roosevelt prepared this article during his recent stay at a New York hospital, showing his vast interest in natural history, his great energy under trying conditions of ill health, and his loyalty to the men [like Leo Miller] whose work he had come to know personally on his [South American] expedition."[91]

Earlier in the year, Roosevelt had reviewed Beebe's *Jungle Peace*, having first been moved by its dedication: "To Colonel and Mrs. Roosevelt I offer this volume with deepest friendship." Roosevelt's review of *Jungle Peace* appeared first in the *New York Times* and then, at later date, as a foreword to a paperback edition of *Jungle Peace*. The opening paragraph of the review/foreword, intended as a glowing tribute to his friend, reads: "Mr. Beebe's volume is one of the rare books which represents a positive addition to the sum total of genuine literature. It is not merely a 'book of the season' or 'book of the year'; it will stand on the shelves of cultivated people, of people whose taste in reading is both wide and good as long as men and women appreciate charm of form in the writings of men who also combine love of daring adventure with the power to observe and vividly record the things of strange interest they have seen."

Roosevelt returned to Sagamore Hill from the hospital on the morning of Christmas Day. It was an extremely happy homecoming for him, not only because, after a hospitalization which had lasted six weeks, he could rejoin his family on this significant holiday, but also because his doctors had encouraged him to believe that he would again enjoy at least a measure of good health. He certainly entertained no thought that his days were "dwindling down to a precious few." To the contrary, on New Year's Day, he wrote to a deep-sea fisherman, Russell Coles: "My doctors tell me that in all probability I shall be able to go with you on March 1st. . . . I hope you understand how deeply I appreciate your taking [my son] Archie along. My great desire is that he shall get a devil fish."[92]

At almost this same time Roosevelt received a copy of William Beebe's latest published book, *Monograph of the Pheasants*. He read it at once and was so pleased with its content—which displayed more of Beebe's literary artistry—that he determined to review it without delay. On the morning of January 5, 1919, before proceeding with the review, he wrote to Beebe, first expressing his enthusiasm for the overall excellence of the monograph, and then asking for explanation of a few points he thought needed clarification. This was Theodore Roosevelt's last letter—the last of an estimated 150,000. We herewith reproduce it:

I have read through your really wonderful volume and I am writing Colonel Knox about it. I cannot speak too highly of the work. Now one question: on page xxiii, final paragraph, there is an obviously incorrect sentence about which I formerly spoke to you. Ought you not to call attention to it and correct it in the second volume? In it you say, by inference, that the grouse of the Old World and the grouse of the New World are in separate families, although I believe that three of the genera and one of the species are identical. Moreover, you say that the family of pheasants includes not only the pheasants but the partridges and quails of the old and the grouse of the new world, and furthermore red-legged partridges and francolins, which of course you have already included in the term of partridges and quail of the old world. Obviously someone has made a mistake and I cannot even form a guess of what was originally intended. Do you mind telling me and I can say in my review that this slip of the printer will be corrected in some subsequent edition?[93]

At four o'clock the next morning Theodore Roosevelt died in his sleep, a victim of a thrombus in the artery feeding blood to the heart. Within a few hours the entire listening world knew that the twenty-sixth president of the United States had joined "the innumerable caravan."

Leo Miller, on a flight from Camp Jackson, South Carolina, to Langley Field, Virginia, had set down his plane at Fayetteville. He was walking along a street when newsboys began shouting "Roosevelt is dead." "For a long time," Miller later said, "it seemed that it could not be possible that a man like that could ever die. The shock was very great and lasted for days."[94] The news reached Frank Chapman in Valparaiso, Chile, where he had gone in the interests of the Red Cross. "He had been my inspiration for nearly twenty years," he lamented. "Suddenly life seemed to lose its flavor."[95] John Burroughs, still relishing the poetry of life at eighty-two, was by his fireside in the Catskills when the news was brought to him. "The old man's tears come easily, and I can hardly speak his name without tears in my voice," he confessed. "I have known him since his ranch days in Montana, and to know him was to love him. . . . The world seems more bleak and cold since he is no longer in it."[96]

But in one particular John Burroughs was wrong. Theodore Roosevelt is still very much in the world. He is alive, innumerable times, and in countless places. He is seen, through his writings, in all the vigor of his youth, as he watched the prairie fowl or the Missouri skylark or the pronghorn of the Badlands, or, as a grown man, seeking to separate the arcane threads surrounding the lives of leopard, koodoo, dikdik, and rhinoceros in that land "where the wayfarer sees the awful glory of sunshine and sunset in the wide waste spaces of the earth."[97] He is seen in the books of others—Chapman, Selous, Shiras, Ditmars—that were written because he believed in them, and they in him. Travelers to out-of-the-way places have seen him on the Farallon Islands and on any one of the scores of other wildlife refuges, where birds today, in the thousands, raise their families rarely molested by people or other enemies. Others see him almost daily in verdant lands once arid, in rivers that run cleaner, in great forests standing virginal, in covered watersheds, in tree farms, in trout-filled streams, in bird sanctuaries, and in huge reservoirs. Millions of Americans see him each year in the national forests that he established for them, and for their children, and for their children's children.[98]

Notes

1. Brooks, *Speaking for Nature*, 21n.
2. Roosevelt, *Works, Mem. Ed.*, 19:22.
3. Ibid., 404.
4. *Outlook*, Jan. 25, 1913. See also Roosevelt, *Works, Mem. Ed.*, 14: 561–62.
5. *Outlook*, Jan. 20, 1915. See also Roosevelt, *Works, Mem. Ed.*, 14: 567.
6. Roosevelt, *A Book-Lover's Holidays in the Open* (New York: Charles Scribner's Sons, 1916), 316–17.
7. Morison, *Letters*, 3:231–32.
8. Ernest Ingersoll (1852–1946), American naturalist, studied at Oberlin College and Harvard. For a time he was with the Hayden Survey and then with the U.S. Fish Commission.
9. Eliott Coues's statement reads: "An article [about birds] may be made a contribution to literature as well as to science." See Coues, *Bulletin, Nuttall Ornithological Club* 4 (Apr. 1897): 112–13.
10. TRCHL.
11. *Bulletin of the University of the State of New York*, Mar. 1, 1917, 39–44.
12. TRCHL.
13. Raymond Lee Ditmars (1876–1942), herpetologist, was born in Newark, N.J. In 1899 he was made curator of reptiles at the New York Zoological Park and in 1910 was placed in charge of mammals also. Among his several published books are *Reptiles of the World* (1909) and *Confessions of a Scientist* (1931).
14. TRCHL.
15. Ibid.
16. Ibid.
17. Herbert Keightley Job (1864–1933), nature photographer and author, was born in Boston and in 1888 graduated from Harvard. He was the author of *Water Fowl* (1902), *Wild Wings* (1905), and other works.
18. Herbert K. Job, *Wild Wings* (Boston: Houghton Mifflin Co., 1905), xiii. Job, with Roosevelt's permission, used this letter as a foreword to the book.
19. George Shiras, 3d (1859–1942), naturalist, photographer, and politician, was born in Allegheny, Pa., and in 1881 graduated from Cornell University. As a Republican, he served in the 58th Congress (1902–5). He early distinguished himself as a pioneer in flashlight photography, winning gold medals for his pictures both at home and abroad. In 1935 he published *Hunting Wild Life with Camera and Flashlight.*
20. Morison, *Letters*, 6:1023.
21. William Joseph Long (1867–1952), naturalist, author, and clergyman. Long was a graduate of Harvard (1892), of Andover Theological Seminary, and held M.A. and Ph.D. degrees from Heidelberg University. At the

height of the nature faker controversy, and afterward, Long was pastor of the First Congregational Church, Stamford, Conn.

22. At later date Roosevelt became involved in yet another controversy, this with Abbott H. Thayer, New Hampshire artist, on the topic of concealing coloration.

23. TRCHL.

24. John Burroughs, *Camping and Tramping with Roosevelt* (Boston: Houghton Mifflin, 1906), 6.

25. Ibid., 79–81.

26. This tribute appeared in a final chapter of Burroughs's *Camping and Tramping with Roosevelt*, 79–111.

27. Ibid., 92–93.

28. Clara Barrus, *The Life and Letters of John Burroughs*, 2 vols. (Boston: Houghton Mifflin, 1925), 1:90–91.

29. Morris, *Edith Kermit Roosevelt*, 290.

30. Roosevelt, *Works, Mem. Ed.*, 3:366.

31. TRCHL.

32. Ibid.

33. Robert Cushman Murphy, American Museum of Natural History ornithologist, to author, Jan. 14, 1943.

34. John Burroughs, *The Complete Nature Writings of John Burroughs*, 8 vols. (New York: William H. Wise & Co., 1904), 6:103–4.

35. Ibid., 107–8.

36. TRCHL.

37. Fox, *John Muir*, 7.

38. Donald Culross Peattie, *A Gathering of Birds* (New York: Dodd, Mead & Co., 1939), 4.

39. Morison, *Letters*, 3:476.

40. TRCHL.

41. William Frederick Badè, *The Life and Letters of John Muir*, 2 vols. (Boston: Houghton Mifflin, 1924), 2:412.

42. Ibid.

43. Ibid., 411.

44. Barrus, *Letters of Burroughs*, 2:69.

45. Roosevelt, *Works, Mem. Ed.*, 3:566.

46. David Starr Jordan, *The Days of a Man*, 2 vols. (Yonkers-on-Hudson, N.Y.: World Book Co., 1922), 1:310.

47. Ibid., 307, 309.

48. Barton Warren Evermann (1853–1932), naturalist, was born in Iowa and educated at Indiana University.

49. Jordan, *Days of a Man*, 1:308.

50. Ibid., 308–9.

51. Ibid., 307–8.

52. TRCHL.

53. Roosevelt, *Works, Mem. Ed.*, 12:566.

54. Roosevelt, *African Game Trails*, 139.

55. Ibid.

56. Wood, *Roosevelt as We Knew Him*, 219.

57. *Roosevelt Wild Life Bulletin* 1 (Dec. 1921): 50.

58. Morison, *Letters*, 7:56.

59. Roosevelt, *Works, Mem. Ed.*, 5:xvi.

60. Roosevelt, *African Game Trails*, 140.

61. Morison, *Letters*, 7:47.

62. Sir Edward Grey (1862–1933), prominent British statesman, writer, and amateur naturalist, was born in London, though his early years were largely spent at the family seat, Falladon, Northumberland. There he acquired his love of fishing and bird-watching, which remained avocations throughout life.

63. Roosevelt, *Autobiography*, 322.

64. Edward Grey (Viscount Grey of Falladon), *Falladon Papers* (Boston: Houghton Mifflin, 1926), 68.

65. Ibid., 69.

66. Ibid., 71.

67. Ibid.

68. Ibid., 74.

69. Roosevelt, *Works, Mem. Ed.*, 4:xxi.

70. T. S. Palmer, ed., *Biographies of Members of the American Ornithologist's Union* (Washington, 1954), 125.

71. Theodore Roosevelt, *Through the Brazilian Wilderness* (New York: Charles Scribner's Sons, 1914), 3.

72. Ibid.

73. George Cherrie, *Dark Trails: Adventures of a Naturalist* (New York: G. P. Putnam's Sons, 1930), 260.

74. *Natural History* 19:9–10.

75. Cutright, *Roosevelt the Naturalist*, 240

76. Roosevelt, *Through the Brazilian Wilderness*, 332–33.

77. Chapman, *Autobiography of a Bird-Lover*, 218.

78. Ibid.

79. Cherrie, *Dark Trails*, 322.

80. TRCHL.

81. William Beebe, G. Inness Hartley, and Paul G. Howes, *Tropical Wild Life in British Guiana* (New York: New York Zoological Society, 1917), ix.

82. Roosevelt, *Works, Mem. Ed.*, 4:ix.

83. Morison, *Letters*, 8:1133.

84. Hermann Hagedorn, *The Roosevelt Family of Sagamore Hill* (New York: Macmillan Co., 1954), 398.

85. Ibid., 400.

86. Ibid., 408.

87. Roosevelt, *Works, Mem. Ed.*, 4:596–602.

88. TRCHL.

89. Pringle, *Roosevelt*, 601.

90. Badè, *Letters of Muir*, 2:353.
91. *American Museum Journal*, Dec. 1918.
92. Cutright, *Roosevelt the Naturalist*, 269.
93. Ibid., 269–70.
94. Leo Miller to author, July 8, 1945.
95. Chapman, *Autobiography of a Bird-Lover*, 289.
96. Barrus, *Letters of Burroughs*, 2:364.
97. Roosevelt, *African Game Trails*, ix.
98. Cutright, *Roosevelt the Naturalist*, 270–71.

Bibliography

Unpublished Manuscripts of Theodore Roosevelt at Harvard University

Juvenile Natural History Essays

"About Insects and Fishes, Natural History"
"A Jackal Hunt"
"*Ardea russata* (Buff-fronted cow heron)"
"*Blarina talpoides* (Short-tailed shrew)"
"Ornithology of Egypt Between Cairo and Assouan"
"Coloration of Birds"
"Sou-sou-southerly [Old squaw, *Clangula hyemalis*]"
"The Egyptian Plover"

Boyhood Natural History Notebooks

"Record of the Roosevelt Museum"—[1867–74]
"Notes on Natural History"—[Undated, ca. 1869–71]
"Remarks on Birds (of Egypt and Syria)"—[1872–73]
"Ornithological Records Made in Europe, Syria and Egypt"—[1872–73]
"Ornithological Observations Made in Europe, Syria and Egypt"—[1872–73]
"Catalogue of Birds Collected in Europe, Syria and Egypt"—[1872–73]
"Zoological Record"—[1872–73]
"Journal of Natural History"—[1874–75]
"Remarks on the Zoology of Oyster Bay"—[1874–76]
"Notes on the Fauna of the Adirondack Mts."—[1871, 1874, 1875, 1876]
"Journal of a Trip to the Adirondacks, 1874"
"Journal of a Trip in Adirondack Mts., August 1875"
"St. Regis Lake, Adirondack Mts., 1875"
"Field Book of Zoology"—[1876–79]

Published Works of Theodore Roosevelt

Roosevelt, Theodore, Jr., and H. D. Minot. *The Summer Birds of the Adirondacks in Franklin County, N.Y.* Salem, Mass.: Naturalists' Agency, 1877.

271

———. *Notes on Some of the Birds of Oyster Bay, Long Island.* Privately printed, March 1879.

———. *Hunting Trips of a Ranchman.* New York: G. P. Putnam's Sons, 1886.

———. *Ranch Life and the Hunting Trail.* New York: The Century Co., 1888.

———. *The Wilderness Hunter.* New York: G. P. Putnam's Sons, 1893.

———. "A Layman's Views on Scientific Nomenclature." *Science* (n.s.) 5 (Apr. 30, 1897).

———. "The Discrimination of Species and Subspecies." *Science* (n.s.), 5 (June 4, 1897).

———. T. S. Van Dyke, D. G. Elliot, and A. J. Stone. *The Deer Family.* New York: Macmillan Co., 1902.

———. *Outdoor Pastimes of an American Hunter.* New York: Charles Scribner's Sons, 1905.

———. *African Game Trails.* New York: Charles Scribner's Sons, 1910.

———. *An Autobiography.* New York: Charles Scribner's Sons, 1913.

———. *Through the Brazilian Wilderness.* New York: Charles Scribner's Sons, 1914.

———. *A Book-Lover's Holidays in the Open.* New York: Charles Scribner's Sons, 1916.

———. *Diaries of Boyhood and Youth.* New York: Charles Scribner's Sons, 1928.

———. *Works, Memorial Edition.* 24 vols. Edited by Hermann Hagedorn. New York: Charles Scribner's Sons, 1923.

———, and George Bird Grinnell. *American Big-Game Hunting.* Book of the Boone and Crockett Club. New York: Forest and Stream Publishing Co., 1893.

———, and George Bird Grinnell. *Hunting in Many Lands.* Book of the Boone and Crockett Club. New York: Forest and Stream Publishing Co., 1895.

———, and George Bird Grinnell. *Trail and Camp Fire.* Book of the Boone and Crockett Club. New York: Forest and Stream Publishing Co., 1897.

———, and Edmund Heller. *Life Histories of African Game Animals.* New York: Charles Scribner's Sons, 1914.

GENERAL LITERATURE

Badè, William Frederic. *The Life and Letters of John Muir.* 2 vols. Boston: Houghton Mifflin Co., 1924.

Barrus, Clara. *The Life and Letters of John Burroughs.* 2 vols. Boston: Houghton Mifflin Co., 1925.

Batchelder, Charles F. *An Account of the Nuttall Ornithological Club.* Cambridge, Mass.: Nuttall Ornithological Club, 1937.

Beebe, William. *The Book of Naturalists.* New York: Alfred A. Knopf, 1945.

———. *Jungle Peace.* New York: Henry Holt & Co., 1918.

————, G. Inness Hartley, and Paul G. Howes. *Tropical Wildlife in British Guiana*. New York: New York Zoological Society, 1917.

Bishop, Joseph Bucklin. *Theodore Roosevelt and His Time*. 2 vols. New York: Charles Scribner's Sons, 1919.

————, ed. *Theodore Roosevelt's Letters to His Children*. New York: Charles Scribner's Sons, 1919.

Blackorby, E. C. "Theodore Roosevelt's Conservation Policies and Their Impact upon America and the American West." *North Dakota History* 25 (Oct. 1958).

Bridges, William. *Gathering of Animals*. New York: Harper & Row, 1974.

Brooks, Paul. *Speaking for Nature*. Boston: Houghton Mifflin Co., 1980.

Burroughs, John. *Camping and Tramping with Roosevelt*. Boston: Houghton Mifflin Co., 1906.

Chapman, Frank M. *Autobiography of a Bird-Lover*. New York: D. Appleton-Century Co., 1933.

————. *Handbook of Birds of Eastern North America*. 7th ed. New York: D. Appleton and Co., 1906.

————. *Life in an Air Castle*. New York: D. Appleton-Century Co., 1938.

————. *My Tropical Air Castle*. New York: D. Appleton and Co., 1927.

Cherrie, George K. *Dark Trails: Adventures of a Naturalist*. New York: G.P. Putnam's Sons, 1930.

Churchill, Winston Spencer. *My African Journal*. London: Hodder and Stoughton, 1908.

Coues, Elliott. *Birds of the Northwest*. Washington, D.C.: Government Printing Office, 1874.

————. *Field and General Ornithology*. London: Macmillan Co., 1890.

————. *Key to North American Birds*. Salem: Naturalists' Agency, 1872.

Cowles, Anna Roosevelt, ed. *Letters from Theodore Roosevelt to Anna Roosevelt Cowles, 1870–1918*. New York: Charles Scribner's Sons, 1924.

Cutright, Paul Russell. *Theodore Roosevelt, the Naturalist*. New York: Harper & Brothers, 1956.

Einstein, Lewis. *Roosevelt, His Mind in Action*. Boston: Houghton Mifflin Co., 1930.

Fox, Stephen. *John Muir and His Legacy*. Boston: Little, Brown and Co., 1981.

Graham, Frank, Jr. *Man's Dominion, the Story of Conservation in America*. New York: M. Evans and Co., 1971.

Grey, Edward (Viscount Grey of Falladon). *Falladon Papers*. Boston: Houghton Mifflin Co., 1926.

Grinnell, George Bird. *American Big Game in Its Haunts*. Book of the Boone and Crockett Club. New York: Forest and Stream Publishing Co., 1904.

————, ed. *Hunting at High Altitudes*. Book of the Boone and Crockett Club. New York: Harper & Brothers, 1913.

Hagedorn, Hermann. *The Boys' Life of Theodore Roosevelt*. New York: Harper & Brothers, 1918.

———. *The Roosevelt Family of Sagamore Hill.* New York: Macmillan Co., 1954.

———. *Roosevelt in the Bad Lands.* Boston: Houghton Mifflin Co., 1921.

Hanley, Wayne. *Natural History in America, from Mark Catesby to Rachel Carson.* New York: Quadrangle/The New York Times Book Co., 1977.

Hart, Albert Bushnell, and Herbert Ronald Perleger, eds. *Theodore Roosevelt Encyclopedia.* New York: Theodore Roosevelt Association, 1941.

Howard, L. O. *Fighting the Insects.* New York: Macmillan Co., 1933.

Jordan, David Starr. *The Days of a Man.* 2 vols. Yonkers-on-Hudson, N.Y.: World Book Co., 1922.

———. *Manual of the Vertebrates of the Northern United States.* Chicago: Jansen, McClurg & Co., 1876.

Lang, Lincoln A. *Ranching with Roosevelt.* Philadelphia: J. B. Lippincott Co., 1926.

Laughlin, J. Laurence. "Roosevelt at Harvard." *Review of Reviews,* Oct. 1924.

Lewis, William Draper. *The Life of Theodore Roosevelt.* Philadelphia: John C. Winston Co., 1919.

Lindsey, Alton A. "Was Theodore Roosevelt the Last to See Passenger Pigeons?" *Proceedings of the Indiana Academy of Science for 1976* 86 (1977).

Lodge, Henry Cabot. *Selections from the Correspondence of Theodore Roosevelt and Henry Cabot Lodge, 1884–1918.* 2 vols. New York: Charles Scribner's Sons, 1924.

Longstreet, T. Morris. *The Adirondacks.* New York: The Century Co., 1920.

Loring, J. Alden. *African Adventure Stories.* New York: Charles Scribner's Sons, 1914.

McCullough, David. *Mornings on Horseback.* New York: Simon and Schuster, 1981.

McDermott, John Francis, ed. *Up the Missouri with Audubon, the Journal of Edward Harris.* Norman: University of Oklahoma Press, 1951.

McGeary, M. Nelson. *Gifford Pinchot, Forester-Politician.* Princeton: Princeton University Press, 1960.

Merriam, C. Hart. *Cervus Roosevelti,* a New Elk from the Olympics." *Proceedings of the Biological Society of Washington* 11 (Dec. 17, 1897).

———. "Revision of the Coyotes or Prairie Wolves, with Descriptions of New Forms." *Proceedings of the Biological Society of Washington* 11 (Mar. 15, 1897).

———. "Roosevelt, the Naturalist." *Science* 75 (Feb. 12, 1932).

———. "Suggestions for a New Method of Discriminating between Species and Subspecies." *Science* (n.s.) 5 (May 14, 1897).

Miller, Leo E. *In the Wilds of South America.* New York: Charles Scribner's Sons, 1919.

Minot, H. D. *The Land and Game Birds of New England.* Boston: Estes & Lauriat, 1877.

Morison, Elting E., John M. Blum, and John J. Buckley, eds. *The Letters of*

Theodore Roosevelt. 8 vols. Cambridge, Mass.: Harvard University Press, 1951–54.

Morris, Edmund. *The Rise of Theodore Roosevelt.* New York: Coward, McCann & Geoghegan, 1980.

Morris, Sylvia Jukes. *Edith Kermit Roosevelt.* New York: Coward, McCann & Geoghegan, 1980.

Muir, John. *The Mountains of California.* New York: The Century Co., 1894.

Osborn, Henry Fairfield. *Impressions of Great Naturalists.* New York: Charles Scribner's Sons, 1924.

Parker, George Howard. *The World Expands: Recollections of a Zoologist.* Cambridge, Mass.: Harvard University Press, 1946.

Parsons, Frances Theodora. *Perchance Some Day.* Privately printed, 1951.

Pearson, T. Gilbert, ed. *Birds of America.* 3 vols. Garden City, N.Y.: Garden City Publishing Co., 1944.

Peattie, Donald Culross. *A Gathering of Birds.* New York: Dodd, Mead & Co., 1939.

Pinchot, Gifford. *The Fight for Conservation.* Washington, D.C.: Government Printing Office, 1908.

Pinkett, Harold T. *Gifford Pinchot: Private and Public Forester.* Urbana: University of Illinois Press, 1970.

Pringle, Henry F. *Theodore Roosevelt, A Biography.* New York: Harcourt, Brace and Co., 1931.

Putnam, Carleton. *Theodore Roosevelt, the Formative Years, 1858–1886.* New York: Charles Scribner's Sons, 1958.

Reiger, John F. *American Sportsmen and the Origins of Conservation.* New York: Winchester Press, 1975.

Riley, Laura, and William Riley. *Guide to the National Wildlife Refuges.* Garden City, N.Y.: Anchor Press/Doubleday, 1979.

Robinson, Corinne Roosevelt. *My Brother, Theodore Roosevelt.* New York: Charles Scribner's Sons, 1921.

Roosevelt, Robert Barnhill. *Superior Fishing, or, the Striped Bass, Trout, and Black Bass of the Northern States.* New York: Carleton, 1865.

Roosevelt, Nicholas. *Theodore Roosevelt, the Man as I Knew Him.* New York: Dodd, Mead & Co., 1967.

Schullery, Paul. *American Beast: Selections from the Writings of Theodore Roosevelt.* Boulder: Colorado Associated University Press, 1983.

———. "A Partnership in Conservation: Theodore Roosevelt and Yellowstone." *Montana, the Magazine of Western History,* July 1978.

Seton, Ernest Thompson. *Trail of an Artist-Naturalist.* New York: Charles Scribner's Sons, 1940.

Sewall, William Wingate. *Bill Sewall's Story of T.R.* New York: Harper & Brothers, 1919.

Smith, Alfred Charles. *The Attractions of the Nile and Its Banks, a Journal of Travel in Egypt and Nubia.* 2 vols. London: John Murray, 1868.

Smith, Guy-Harold. *Conservation of Natural Resources.* New York: John Wiley & Sons, 1958.

Steen, Harold K. *The U.S. Forest Service, a History.* Seattle: University of Washington Press, 1976.

Sterling, Keir B. *Last of the Naturalists: The Career of C. Hart Merriam.* New York: Arno Press, 1974.

Suffolk, earl of, Berkeley Hadley Peek, and F. G. Aflalo, eds. *The Encyclopedia of Sport.* 2 vols. London: Lawrence and Bullen, 1897–98.

Thayer, William Roscoe. *Theodore Roosevelt.* Boston: Houghton Mifflin Co., 1919.

Trefethin, James. *An American Crusade for Wildlife.* New York: Winchester Press, 1975.

Vail, R. W. G. "Your Loving Friend, T. R." [Letters of Theodore Roosevelt to H. D. Minot]. *Collier's,* Dec. 20, 1924.

White, G. Edward. *The Eastern Establishment and the Western Experience.* New Haven, Conn.: Yale University Press, 1968.

Wilhelm, Donald. *Theodore Roosevelt as an Undergraduate.* Boston: John W. Luce and Co., 1910.

Wister, Owen. *Roosevelt, the Story of a Friendship.* New York: Macmillan Co., 1930.

Wood, Frederick G. *Roosevelt as We Knew Him.* Philadelphia: John C. Winston Co., 1927.

Index

Seiurus aurocapillus. See Warbler,
ovenbird
Selkirk Mountains, 158, 159
Selous, Frederick Courtenay, 240, 252
Sequoia gigantea, 222
Sequoia National Park, 225
Seton, Ernest Thompson, 172; *re*
Coues's *Key*, 79
Sewall, William Wingate, 119, 122, 125;
re TR, 110–11; TR takes thirty-mile
walk with, 112; to Badlands, 151
Shaler, Nathaniel S., 104, 105, 109
Sharpe, Richard B.: recipient of TR du-
plicates, 138
Shilling, G. C., 241
Shiras, George, 183, 242
Shoveler, northern, 154
Shrew, short-tailed, 142
Siskin, pine, 89
Skimmer, black, 223
Skunk, striped (common), 29, 155
Smith, Reverend Alfred Charles, author
of book on Egyptian birds, 44, 48
Smith, Frances ("Fanny") Theodora, 75,
94
Smith, Hoke, 201
Smithsonian Institution: TR gives boy-
hood natural history specimens to,
136; accession records of TR collec-
tions, 137
Snake, hog-nosed: behavior observed by
TR, 27
"Sou'-sou'-southerly": TR essay about
the oldsquaw, 141
Sparrow:
—Chipping, 77, 82
—Fox, 82, 89
—Grasshopper, 80
—House (English), 33, 108
—Ipswich, 121–22
—Lincoln, 246
—Sharp-tailed, 80, 81
—Song, 77, 80, 82, 139
—Swamp, 246
—Tree, 92
—White-throated, 82, 91, 138
Spizella passerina. See Sparrow,
chipping
Sprague, Charles S., 216
Spuyten Duyvil: TR visits, 26

Squirrel:
—Gray, 78; TR raises three young ones,
28–29
—Red, at Tarrytown, 28
Starling, 140
Stilt, black-necked, 154
Stimson, Henry L., 180
Stone, Witmer: *re* TR's interest in bird
habits, 81
Stuyvesant, Rutherford, 169
Suez Canal, 54
Sully Hill Park, 225
*Summer Birds of the Adirondacks in
Franklin County, N.Y., The*, 102
Swallow, barn, 78; migration of observed
by TR, 28
Syria, 212

Taft, William Howard, 231, 254
Tarrytown, N.Y., 28
Teal, blue-winged, 154
Tetrao canadensis. See Grouse, spruce
Thebes, 49
Thoreau, Henry David, 243
Thrasher, brown, 77, 80
Three Arch Rocks Wildlife Refuge, 224
Thrush:
—Hermit, 92; song of, 101–2
—Robin, 77, 137
—Swainson's, 80, 89, 100
—Veery, 139
—Wood, 77, 80, 82, 93, 101
Toad, horned, 156
Towhee, eastern, 93
Toxostoma refum. See Thrasher
Trail and Camp Fire, 180
Tranquillity, summer home of Roose-
velts, 75, 93
Troglodytes aedon. See Wren, house
Troglodytes troglodytes. See Wren,
winter
Turdus migratorius. See Thrush, robin
Turner, Frederick Jackson, 172
Tyrannus carolinensis. See Kingbird
Two-Ocean Pass Mountains, 158

Uncompahgre valley, 214
U.S. Biological Survey, 224, 253
U.S. Geological Survey, 213, 217

Note on the Author

Paul Russell Cutright was educated at Davis and Elkins College, West Virginia University, from which he took A.B. and A.M. degrees, and the University of Pittsburgh, from which he obtained his Ph.D. in zoology. He has served on the faculties of the University of Pittsburgh; Geneva College, Beaver Falls, Pennsylvania; and Beaver College, Glenside, Pennsylvania. He is presently professor emeritus of the biology department of Beaver College. His books include *The Great Naturalists Explore South America; Theodore Roosevelt, the Naturalist; Lewis and Clark: Pioneering Naturalists; Meriwether Lewis: Naturalist; A History of the Lewis and Clark Journals;* and, with Michael J. Brodhead, *Elliott Coues: Naturalist and Frontier Historian.*